Classical Subjects Creatively Taught™

Well-Ordered Language

TEACHER'S EDITION

Level 1B

The Curious Child's Guide to Grammar

Tammy Peters and Daniel Coupland, PhD

Well-Ordered Language:
The Curious Child's Guide to Grammar
Level 1B Teacher's Edition

Version 1.0

ISBN: 978-1-60051-292-6

Classical Academic Press
515 S. 32nd St.
Camp Hill, PA 17011

www.ClassicalAcademicPress.com

Content editor: Marie Kramb Campbell, PhD
Illustrator: Katharina Drees
Series editor and book designer: Lauraine Gustafson

BB.04.21

Acknowledgments

Tammy Peters

I am deeply indebted to Mars Hill Academy in Cincinnati, Ohio. I give a sincere thanks to the students, families, and teachers who have supported me and contributed to this work over the last fifteen years. A special thanks to Sharon Peterson, Ellen Liebing, and Traci DeBra for their constant encouragement and insights, as well as to Alicia Weber, Natalie Walls, and Molly Milligan.

With a grateful heart, I thank Dr. Dan Coupland for his insights and love of language. It has been a privilege to coauthor Well-Ordered Language with him. I also thank Dr. Marie Campbell, our content editor, for her expertise and precision in the English language. She is a joy and a friend. I greatly appreciate Dr. Chris Perrin, Laurie Gustafson, and the whole Classical Academic Press staff for their vision and professionalism.

There are not enough words to express my gratitude to my family for their constant support. My heartfelt appreciation is to the love of my life, Hud Peters, who has prayerfully supported me through it all.

Daniel Coupland, PhD

I am grateful for the *grammarphiles* in my life: Mrs. Linda Tiarks, my elementary school teacher who showed me how to study and love the English language; Dr. Bryan Coupland, my father, who appreciates a well-crafted sentence; and Mrs. Tammy Peters, my coauthor, who is the most talented (and most energetic) grammar teacher I have ever seen. I am also thankful for Marie, our talented content editor, who has helped to make the Well-Ordered Language program even better. And of course, I appreciate Chris, Laurie, and the entire Classical Academic Press team for their tireless effort to get this program in print.

At a Glance

Book A

Chapter	Main Topic	Supplemental Topics
1	Four Kinds of Sentences	
2	Principal Elements, Part 1—Subject and Predicate	
3	Principal Elements, Part 2—Subject and Predicate Verb	Singular and plural subjects with the helping verbs *is* and *are*
4	Adverbs	*Not* and *never* as adverbs; placement of adverbs in sentence order
5	Adjectives	Correct usage of articles *a* and *an*
6	Direct Objects	Word order in sentences
7	Subject Pronouns	Agreement in number: subject pronouns and antecedents; subject pronouns and verbs
8	Interrogative Sentences—Subject Pronouns and Helping Verbs	Contractions: subject pronouns and helping verbs

Book B

Chapter	Main Topic	Supplemental Topics
1	Object Pronouns	Contractions with *not*
2	Pronoun Review	Subject/verb agreement in number and person
3	Prepositional Phrases—Adverbial	Abbreviations for months; capitalization and periods; proper and common nouns
4	Introductory Prepositional Phrases	Revising fragments
5	Compound Subjects	Subject/verb agreement with conjunctions *and, or*
6	Compound Verbs	Synonyms; conjunctions *and, or*
7	Compound Direct Objects	Word order in sentences; proper and common nouns

Table of Contents

Well-Ordered Language

A Classical Approach to English Grammar Instruction

Why Study Grammar?

We study grammar because we wish to master language, and language cannot be easily mastered without grammar. Grammar is the study of what makes language work—the way letters form words, the way words form sentences, the way sentences express human thought.

An educated person wants to understand the rich variety of human thought enshrined in language of all sorts—books from yesterday and the last millennium, books in English and books in other languages as well. An educated person also yearns to express himself clearly, accurately, and completely. It is the study of grammar that yields the capacity to do this, and the student who sees the connection between the study of grammar and the mastery of language will study grammar with zeal.

Learning Grammar, Teaching Grammar

We have designed Well-Ordered Language (WOL) with the understanding that many teachers who will use this book don't know grammar as well as they would like. As a result, we have created a rich teacher's edition that will enable teachers to review and deepen their own understanding of grammar even as they teach students.

We have also worked to provide a clear, incremental presentation of grammar in this series that includes plenty of illustrations, practice, and review. For example, in each chapter, students will memorize through song clear definitions of relevant grammatical concepts. Helpful analogies and attractive graphical illustrations at the beginning of each chapter introduce and complement the concepts in the chapter. Students also will discover emerging from the sentence exercises a story that features characters who appear throughout the text and in the graphical illustrations.

Effective Teaching Methods

The series employs an innovative choral analysis method that makes learning enjoyable and permanent. With clear guidance from the teacher's edition, instructors will easily be able to lead students through the choral analysis of grammar, and through this analysis, students will see grammar embodied in the sentences they study. The program has been layered concept on concept, an approach that aids students in seeing and experiencing how a well-ordered language works and how it increases their understanding and enjoyment of literature, stories, and poetry.

Learning with Delight

We think that the right study of grammar should lead to delight. The traditional study of grammar should be more than mere rote memorization of rules; it must also include opportunities for students to engage language in works of literature and human expression. As students acquire a greater capacity to understand language and use it effectively themselves, they will experience joy and delight. This is one reason we have included for grammatical study beautiful poetry and excerpts from great literature. Students will see that their ongoing study of grammar will open up a deeper understanding of beautiful literature that both instructs and delights.

Compelling Need

In this cultural moment, there is a desperate need for language that is well ordered. Today's discourse is often filled with ambiguity, equivocation, and crudeness. Those who have mastered a well-ordered language not only will stand out as eloquent and clear but also will be able to say well what they mean and to say what others will heed. It will be those with a command of language who will be able to mine the wisdom of the past and to produce eloquence in the future.

Ongoing Support

We have created not only a series of texts but a constellation of products that will help teachers to use WOL effectively. Visit our website at ClassicalAcademicPress.com for additional support for using WOL, including video training (featuring author Tammy Peters), downloadable PDF documents, and other resources.

Thank you for joining us in this most important work of restoring a well-ordered language for the next generation!

Lesson-Planning Options

The Well-Ordered Language series is designed to be flexible, adaptable, and practical. Depending on her needs, the teacher can modify lessons to meet particular classroom expectations. The following options for teaching each chapter assume a 30–40 minute period.

	Option A (4 times per week)	**Option B** (3 times per week)	**Option C** (5 times, one week)
Week One	**Day One** ◇ Chapter Introduction ◇ Introductory Lesson ◇ Introductory Practice	**Day One** ◇ Chapter Introduction ◇ Introductory Lesson ◇ Introductory Practice	**Day One** ◇ Chapter Introduction ◇ Introductory Lesson ◇ Introductory Practice
	Day Two ◇ Lessons to Learn A ◇ Lessons to Practice A	**Day Two** ◇ Lessons to Learn A ◇ Lessons to Practice A	**Day Two** ◇ Lessons to Learn A ◇ Lessons to Practice A
	Day Three ◇ Lessons to Learn B ◇ Lessons to Practice B	**Day Three** ◇ Lessons to Learn B ◇ Lessons to Practice B	**Day Three** ◇ Lessons to Learn B ◇ Lessons to Practice B
	Day Four ◇ Fable* ◇ Fable Sentences (PDF)		**Day Four** ◇ Lessons to Learn C ◇ Lessons to Practice C
			Day Five ◇ Quiz (PDF)
Week Two	**Day Five** ◇ Lessons to Learn C ◇ Lessons to Practice C	**Day Four** ◇ Lessons to Learn C ◇ Lessons to Practice C ***or*** ◇ Lessons to Learn—Review ◇ Lessons to Practice—Review	**From the Sideline:** Option C is an accelerated plan for teachers who want to finish both *WOL1A* and *WOL1B* in one semester. A teacher using Option A or B might find it useful to switch to Option C for a single chapter that is mastered quickly.
	Day Six ◇ Lessons to Learn—Review ◇ Lessons to Practice—Review	**Day Five** ◇ Lessons to Learn—Review ◇ Lessons to Practice—Review ***or*** ◇ Fable*/Fable Sentences (PDF)	
	Day Seven ◇ Poem*/Poem Activity ***or*** ◇ Practice Sheet (PDF)	**Day Six** ◇ Quiz (PDF)	*The fables for chapters 1, 3, 5, 6, 7, and 8 can be found in the downloadable PDF. The poems for chapters 2 and 4 can be found in the PDF.
	Day Eight ◇ Quiz (PDF)		

Introduction to Students

Do you have a favorite word? Most people have favorite words just as they have favorite numbers or colors. So, what is yours?

Maybe it is an exceedingly (very) long word that your friends don't know. Maybe you just like the way its sound rolls off your tongue. Maybe you use it as often as you can, or maybe you save it for special occasions.

We want to share one of our favorite words with you. You probably know what it means already, but you may not have thought of it as an exceptional word. Probably few people would name it as a favorite because it seems so ordinary. It is far from ordinary though. The word is . . . *analyze.*

One reason we love the word *analyze* is because it has interesting grandparents. Its roots are Greek: *ana* meaning "up, throughout" and *lusis* meaning "unloose, release, set free." When you *analyze* something, you break it up into its parts and set them free!

Great thinkers are great analyzers.

Scientists who study bugs are called entomologists. They analyze insects by dissecting them. Sports analysts watch freeze frames of each motion of a single play in football to make sure the referee applied the rules correctly. Detectives analyze every inch of a crime scene, inspecting it for clues. These great thinkers are curious about what is inside an insect, a play, or even a crime.

Great thinkers are always curious. For them, analysis is an adventure.

You are a curious child, and your adventure in this book will be learning how to *analyze* sentences. You will take them apart, unloose their knots, and dissect them. Step by step you will learn the special function of each part of language.

Understanding the parts of something—whether you are a student, scientist, sports analyst, or detective—leads to appreciating the whole thing even more. Once you break something apart, it is natural and right that you should put it back together again. If you take apart a clock to see how it works, you will want to reassemble it so you don't miss dinnertime. Learning how to *analyze* sentences makes you more skilled at *constructing* them too, both in your writing and in your speaking.

The parts of language are words, and words are wonderful.

Introduction to Teachers

In the Well-Ordered Language (WOL) series, grammar instruction is focused, practical, and lively. The curriculum is designed so that teachers and students actively engage with each other and with the grammatical concepts in each lesson, using language skills—reading, writing, speaking, and listening—along with physical movement and song. You and your students will find that the thirty to forty minutes devoted to grammar instruction are among the most dynamic of the school day.

The WOL Marking System—Analyze, Analyze, Analyze

Analysis is the heart and soul of the WOL method. Each chapter includes multiple sentences for students to analyze aloud and on paper, as a class and individually. Students are encouraged from the beginning, as the student introduction illustrates, to consider analysis as the stimulating activity of a curious mind. Just as children naturally enjoy taking things apart and putting them back together, your students will learn that understanding how words in a sentence work together to convey meaning is intriguing and enjoyable.

The unique WOL marking system will help students identify the function of words and the relationship between words in a sentence. In Level 2 and above, WOL teaches classical diagramming alongside this analysis, but the analytic approach in all the levels is extraordinary:

- The teacher explains the concept to students through active engagement with specific, carefully selected sentences.
- The teacher models the structural analysis on the board while the students participate by speaking the analysis in chorus. Scripts are provided for you in the teachers' pages that follow each chapter.
- The structural analysis uses an innovative marking system that builds incrementally, chapter by chapter, preparing the students for sentence diagramming.

◇ The students begin to analyze the sentences themselves, starting with choral analysis and moving to individual analysis.

To emphasize the importance of analysis to the method and to illustrate WOL's marking system, here are sample sentences with complete markings, one taken from early in the curriculum and one from the end:

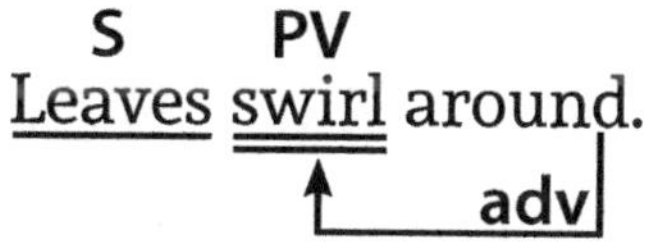

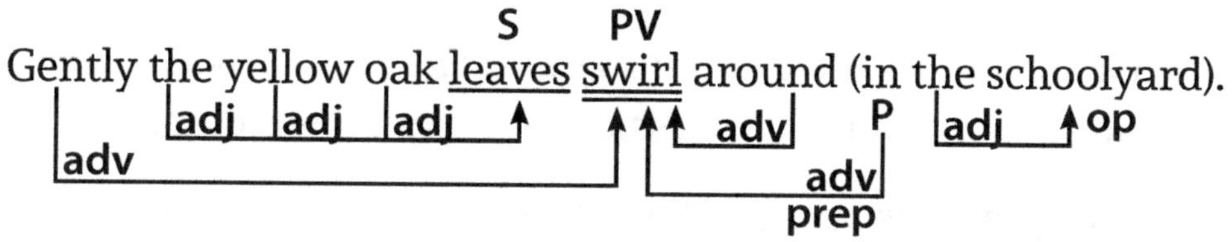

These samples illustrate what would appear on the student's paper during a lesson. But more important than this end product is the lively, unfolding *process*, the progression of markings as the students chorally analyze the grammar. In addition, before analyzing sentences in each lesson, the students already will have enjoyed singing or chanting the definitions of key terms and practicing the grammatical concepts with short games and exercises.

How to Use This Book: Learn, Memorize, Review

Well-Ordered Language offers you a wealth of material—more than you will likely need. In order to teach students to analyze and mark sentences with enthusiastic competence, you can creatively modify the curriculum, adapting it to meet your particular students' needs. The following pages explain the book's structure and suggest a possible daily approach. To assist your lesson planning, we have organized each chapter into four main sections:

Chapter Introduction (first day, ten minutes)

On the first day, ten minutes of the lesson are allotted to acquainting students with the grammatical concepts and important terms covered in the chapter. Then, the students will be ready to participate in a choral analysis of a sentence, which models the focus of the chapter.

- ◇ **Ideas to Understand:** The opening paragraphs introduce the chapter's main focus, using as an example an excerpt from poetry or fiction. (For enrichment beyond the scope of the grammar lessons, a literary appendix containing the complete poems and longer passages from the fiction has been provided as well as appendices containing brief biographical sketches of the authors and bibliographic information for the sources.)
- ◇ **Terms to Remember:** After learning the basic ideas, students are ready to begin memorizing grammatical definitions. Students learn important terms by singing or chanting short, inviting songs or chants that keep this portion of the lesson lighthearted and captivating. Adding movement and hand gestures helps. Each chapter introduces new terms and reviews pertinent terms that students have encountered previously. The book's glossary includes the lyrics for all the songs as well as other pertinent terms and definitions. The songs and chants are available as a recorded CD or downloadable audio files at ClassicalAcademicPress.com.
- ◇ **Sentences to Analyze:** This section is written for teachers to guide the students through an initial sentence analysis and to explain what happens in each step. At this point in the lesson, students recite together the analysis as the teacher models it on the board, marking the sentence with WOL's unique marking system.

Lessons to Learn (daily, fifteen minutes)

This section includes daily lessons, labeled as Introductory, A, B, C, and Review. They are supported in the teacher's edition by extra pages called Well-Ordered Notes. These fifteen-minute lessons are made up of four parts, representing a variety of methods and often including interactive games:

- ◇ **Review It:** The lesson starts with time for singing or chanting key terms along with the CD/audio files. Students absorb the definitions in an enjoyable and memorable way as they stand while singing, do hand motions, and move their bodies.
- ◇ **Practice It:** Next, the teacher warms up the class for the main task—sentence analysis—with a short activity. This section is provided in the teacher's edition only to give the students the opportunity to use the new concept in an oral exercise. The exercises are designed to be lighthearted and quick.
- ◇ **Learn It:** During this portion, the pace is kept lively while further focusing attention. A five-minute lesson reinforces the concept introduced in the chapter or, in some chapters, explains a correlated grammatical concept that will be presented in the Lessons to Practice worksheet. The lesson could be oral, completed on the board together while students mark their books individually, or it could be written and reviewed orally when completed.

- ◇ **Analyze It:** Finally, the lesson climaxes with the students demonstrating the analysis of the grammatical concept, using WOL's unique marking system. You model the analysis using the two example sentences, for which the markings and an analytic script are provided in the teacher's pages. You should expect full participation from the students during choral analysis. The class should complete the analysis vigorously, and you should never allow the analysis to become monotone or dull.

Lessons to Practice (daily, fifteen minutes)

This section corresponds to Lessons to Learn, and the pages are interwoven. Fifteen minutes of the lesson should be allotted daily to Lessons to Practice, which include worksheets for *guided* practice to be done primarily as a class. Choral analysis is to be done in unison. The teacher guides the class through the first part of each worksheet while the second part is to be done independently.

Lessons to Practice should not be considered as merely supplemental. They are an important part of the daily lessons immediately following the Analyze It section. If you find that the abundance of material and exercises provided are more than necessary in a particular chapter, you would do better to omit an entire section—for example, both Lessons to Learn C and Lessons to Practice C—than to skip the Lessons to Practice that correspond to a given Lessons to Learn.

The Extra Practice and Assessments PDF (referred to throughout the book as "downloadable PDF" or "PDF"), available for purchase at ClassicalAcademicPress.com, contains extra fables, poems, and practice sheets for additional classroom lessons or for homework when needed. Please note that quizzes are also provided in the PDF in the same format.

Lessons to Enjoy (weekly option, thirty minutes plus)

This section provides a poem and a fable to read and to discuss as enrichment activities in addition to the daily lessons. It usually requires thirty minutes or a whole class period to complete. For each chapter, either the poem or the fable is found in the students' text and the other is included in the downloadable PDF (and in the teacher's edition). The material that accompanies the literary excerpt not only draws attention to grammar in action, but also provides you with a range of discussion and activity suggestions to help foster the students' love of language. In addition, a page of sentences for analysis, found in the PDF, accompanies the fables. The characters and situations in the sentences match those of the fable. Students will see that well-ordered language plays an important role in creating passages of great beauty and meaning. In this way, as they master the particular grammatical concepts, students can balance detailed language analysis with time spent delighting in language.

Pedagogical Principles and Guidance

The classical tradition has passed down a rich collection of teaching methods that have been successfully used for generations to teach children well. We encourage teachers of WOL to become familiar with and employ these methods while teaching grammar. Below is a list of some key pedagogical principles that come to us from the classical tradition of education. A video overview of these principles is available at http://www.classicalu.com/course/principles-of-classical-pedagogy/. A subscription to ClassicalU.com will grant you access not only to additional videos that cover the nine essential principles in more detail, but also to scores of other online training videos for classical educators.

- *Festina Lente* (Make Haste Slowly)
- *Multum Non Multa* (Much Not Many)
- *Repetitio Mater Memoriae* (Repetition Is the Mother of Memory)
- Embodied Learning
- Songs, Chants, and Jingles
- Wonder and Curiosity
- Educational Virtues
- *Scholé*, Contemplation, Leisure
- *Docendo Discimus* (By Teaching We Learn)

A Side Note about the Side Panels

The *side panels* furnish both the student and the teacher with additional information that stimulates discussion and further learning. There are four types of panels: two for the student (To the Source and Off the Shelf) and two for the teacher that do not appear in the student edition (From the Sidelines and Fewer than Five).

- **To the Source** helps the students understand the etymology of various grammar terms.
- **Off the Shelf** provides more information to the students about books mentioned in the chapters and is there to pique the interest of the reader.
- **From the Sidelines** provides general pedagogical tips from teachers to teacher. It also gives helpful tips about specific content in each chapter.
- **Fewer than Five** provides alternative activities for class sizes smaller than five students, such as homeschool classrooms, tutoring situations, and co-op learning environments.

Notes

From the Sideline: Expect immediate responses. Teach students to complete a task both efficiently and to the best of their ability. We have a saying, "Slow obedience is disobedience."

[A] Write on the board the names of substitute teachers who serve your school. Discuss how the various substitutes serve (i.e., Mrs. Wimple substitutes for you when you are sick or Mr. Michaels substitutes for Coach Howard).

Chapter 1

Object Pronouns[A]

Sometimes teachers need substitutes. Have you ever come to school and discovered your teacher was sick and someone else was standing in for her? You know that the substitute is not your "real" teacher, but you also know that he replaces your teacher and has the authority to teach the class. He is acting in her absence. He takes her place. Having a substitute teacher can be an interesting change from the way things are usually done in your classroom, but for the most part it makes little difference whether your teacher is the regular one or a substitute. They both do the same work in the classroom, and they follow the same rules.

Fewer than Five: The opening metaphor in this chapter assumes a traditional classroom setting. However, if your classroom is different, adapt the metaphor to your situation. Consider substitute instructors in your students' lives, such as coaches, music teachers, den leaders, or Sunday school teachers.

Sometimes substitutes are needed when baking. What if you were baking your favorite treat—chocolate chip cookies—to share at school on your birthday, but one of your friends really doesn't like chocolate? In some of the cookies, you could substitute raisins for chocolate chips. All the treats on the serving plate are still cookies, but there is an assortment, or variety, to choose from. Similarly, when you substitute pronouns for nouns, you add variety to your sentences.

Pronouns■ in a sentence are like substitute teachers in a classroom or substitute ingredients in a recipe—they can replace, or stand in for something. They are used to replace, or stand in for, nouns. Pronouns follow the same rules and behave just like nouns whether they are subjects or direct objects. Like substitute teachers in the classroom, pronouns do the same work in the sentence as the nouns they replace. Like raisins in a chocolate chip cookie recipe, pronouns also add a little variety to sentences.

To the Source:
■ pronoun
The word *pronoun* comes from the Latin word *pronomen*, which literally means "in place of a noun." *Pro* means "in place of" and *nomen* means "name" or "noun."

Off the Shelf: Even if you have already read E.B. White's popular novel *Charlotte's Web*, you'll enjoy reading it again. We can learn a lot from this barnyard society, especially from a clever, caring spider who "spins" a plot to save the life of a beloved pig. Do you remember the colorful character Templeton, the selfish barn rat? Read the longer passage from chapter 6 of *Charlotte's Web* in The Curious Child's Literary Appendix or check out the book at your library.

[B] To establish a context for the quotation used in this chapter, read to the class chapter 6, "Summer Days," from *Charlotte's Web* by E.B. White or refer to the literary appendix for an excerpt. Write Templeton's question and the goose's response on the board and highlight the object pronoun *it*.

Ideas to Understand[B]

There are several types of pronouns, all of which are used in place of nouns. You have already learned about personal subject pronouns (see *WOL1A* chapter 7). You've also heard of the type of pronoun we're going to focus on in this chapter: the object pronoun. An object pronoun is a personal pronoun that is used in the place of a direct object (or **object of the preposition**).

In the novel *Charlotte's Web*, E.B. White uses the object pronoun *it* in place of the word egg when the rat, Templeton, asks for the goose and gander's (male goose) extra "dud" egg:

> "What are you going to do with it?" continued Templeton, his little round beady eyes fixed on the goose.
>
> "You can have it," replied the goose. "Roll it away and add it to that nasty collection of yours."[1]

Templeton's question, "What are you going to do with it?" includes the object pronoun *it* as the object of the preposition *with*. (*With it* is a prepositional phrase. You will learn about prepositional phrases in chapter 3.) The goose's answer, "You can have it," uses the object pronoun *it* as the direct object. The goose's next sentence (which is an imperative sentence, by the way) also uses *it* twice as a direct object—*roll it* and *add it*. E.B. White uses pronouns to help his story flow better. (You learned about how pronouns help the flow of a sentence or story in chapter 7 of *WOL1A*.) Without pronouns, the sentences would be choppy: *What are you going to do with* ***the egg****? You can have* ***the egg****. Roll* ***the egg*** *away and add* ***the egg*** *to that nasty collection.* That's too many eggs!

Do you remember how pronouns are classified? We classify them according to how they function in a sentence. So, an object pronoun functions as either a direct object or an object of the preposition. We also classify pronouns according to their person (first, second, or third) and number (singular or plural). The following chart will help you understand how object pronouns are organized:

1. E.B. White, "Summer Days," *Charlotte's Web* (New York: HarperTrophy, 1980), pp. 45–46.

Object Pronouns[C]

	Singular	Plural
First Person	me	us
Second Person	you	you
Third Person	him, her, it	them

[C]To reinforce students' understanding of person, have them chant:
First: speaking (Use your thumbs and point to yourself.)
Second: spoken to (Point your index fingers straight out.)
Third: spoken of (Point your thumbs over your right shoulder.)

Terms to Remember[D]

[D]Play the appropriate CD tracks/audio files and have students sing/chant along. Remind students to commit the songs to memory by listening to these tracks/files at other times as well.

It is very important to memorize the object pronouns and be able to distinguish them from the subject pronouns. By doing so, you can avoid the many grammatical mistakes that happen when speakers or writers use an object pronoun when they should use a subject pronoun and vice versa. Just as distinguishing an insect from a spider is a very basic and necessary skill in entomology (the study of insects), so is distinguishing the different kinds of pronouns in sentence analysis.

Pronoun *(1–11)*

A pronoun is a part of speech
used in place of a noun or nouns.
A pronoun is a part of speech
used in place of a noun or nouns.
A pronoun is a part of speech.

Subject Pronouns *(1–12)*

Subject pronouns are in the nominative case:
I, you, he, she, it, we, you, they *(repeat)*.
Subject pronouns are in the nominative case:
I, you, he, she, it, we, you, they *(repeat)*.

Antecedents *(1–13)*

The antecedent is a noun, clause, or phrase
to which a pronoun refers.
If the antecedent is singular,
then the pronoun is singular too.

But if the noun, clause, or phrase is plural,
then the pronoun must be plural too.
The antecedent determines which pronoun is used.

NEW! **Object Pronouns** *(1–15)*

Object pronouns are in the objective case.
Me, you, him, her, it, us, you, them
Me, you, him, her, it, us, you, them.
Object pronouns are in the objective case.
Me, you, him, her, it, us, you, them
Me, you, him, her, it, us, you, them
Me, you, him, her, it, us, you, them.

A Sentence to Analyze[E]

[E] As you did in *WOL1A*, model how to mark the sentence while the students chorally analyze it. The class should say in chorus the words in gray.

Now it's time to include object pronouns in sentence analysis. As with subject pronouns, object pronouns are easy to analyze because they behave like nouns. You didn't forget how to analyze sentences, did you?

With your teacher's guidance, use the following steps to analyze the sentence. Speak the words in gray along with your teacher and pay close attention to what she is writing. When your teacher is finished, the sentence will look like this:

S PV
Templeton wants (it).
do

a. First, read the sentence aloud. "Templeton wants it."

b. "This is a sentence and it is declarative."

c. "This sentence is about *Templeton*. So, Templeton is the subject because it is what the sentence is about." (Since *Templeton* is the subject, underline it and place a capital letter *S* above it.)

d. "This sentence tells us that Templeton *wants*. So, *wants* is the predicate because it is what the sentence tells us about *Templeton*." (Since *wants* tells something about Templeton, double underline it and place a capital letter *P* above it.) "It is a predicate verb because it shows action. There is no linking verb because predicate verbs do not need linking verbs." (Since *wants* shows action, place a capital letter *V* to the right of the letter *P* above the predicate.)

e. "*It* tells us what Templeton wants." (Since *it* tells us what Templeton wants, draw a circle around it.)

f. "So, *it* is an objective element because it completes the meaning of an action verb. It is a direct object because it tells what Templeton wants." (Write *do* in lowercase letters beneath the direct object.)

Even if you love chocolate chip cookies, raisin cookies do the trick when you want something sweet and need to replace the chocolate. Even if you really like your teacher, you probably welcome having substitutes sometimes. They bring variety to a school day, and they make sure you don't miss anything important in the absence of your teacher. Even when you use a great noun, you may need to replace it with an object pronoun in the next sentence. Object pronouns don't just stand in for nouns. They also get rid of unnecessary repetition. Sentences flow more smoothly and with more variety when object pronouns fill in for nouns as direct objects or objects of prepositions.

From the Sideline: The most important lesson of this chapter is that the students learn to correctly choose object pronouns for objective elements. Some of the transitive verbs in this chapter, such as *ask*, *tell*, and *show*, are completed by object pronouns that might seem to be indirect objects rather than direct objects: "ask them," "told me," and "show him," but we have marked them all with *do*. Because each of these objects answers the question *what* or *whom* and because it is the only object receiving the action of the verb, it is a direct object. A sentence cannot have an indirect object without a direct object. The pronouns are indirect objects only when followed by a direct object, such as in "ask them a question," "tell me a story," or "show him a picture." We will analyze constructions like these in *WOL Level 3* when indirect objects are taught.

Do you remember the Clark family: Mom, Dad, Winston, Heidi, Fritz, and their mischievous dog, Rex? What about their cousins—Theo, Peggy, and Lucy—and the rest of the extended family—Aunt Gabby, Uncle Ulysses, Grandma, and Grandpa? In the sentences you'll be studying throughout this book, you'll continue reading about some of their adventures as a family.

Study the illustration at the beginning of this chapter. How many cookies, baked and unbaked, can you see? How many dozen is that? Do you think Rex should get one too?

Well-Ordered Notes Introductory

Practice It

Draw the structure (the lines and the column and row headings) of the object pronoun chart on the board.

Review person by leading the students in the person chant:

First: speaking (Use your thumbs and point to yourself.)

Second: spoken to (Point your index fingers straight out.)

Third: spoken of (Point your thumbs over your right shoulder.)

Then, ask volunteers one by one to fill in a space in the chart, calling for the pronouns in random order.

Example:

> **Teacher: "Please fill in the third-person plural object pronoun."**
> **Student writes *them* in the correct space in the chart.**

While each student is approaching the board and writing on it, the rest of the class should do the object pronoun chant together, repeating it until the chart is complete. Then, to reinforce their memorization, reverse the exercise, asking individual students to erase particular pronouns while the entire class continues to repeat the chant.

Object Pronouns

	Singular	Plural
First Person	me	us
Second Person	you	you
Third Person	him, her, it	them

Analyze It

As a class, analyze the following sentences (*S* = subject; *PV* = predicate verb; *hv* = helping verb; *adv* = adverb; *adj* = adjective; *do* = direct object). Write the sentences on the board. Have the students analyze the sentences, reciting the analysis aloud using the following script. While the students recite, you will mark the sentence on the board.

S hv PV

1. Uncle Ulysses will not read (it) tonight.

adv do

adv

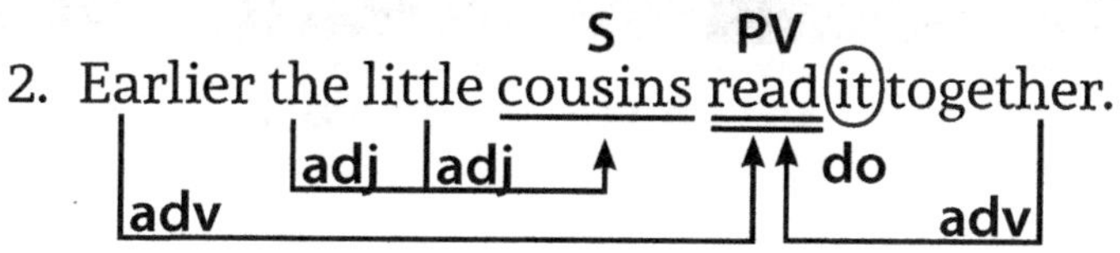

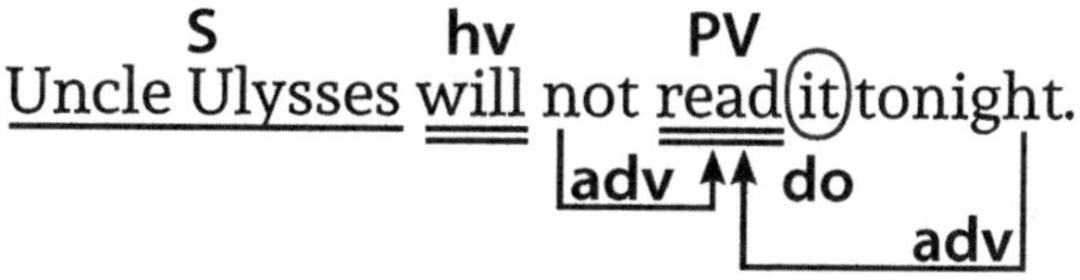

a. (First, read the sentence aloud.) "Uncle Ulysses will not read it tonight."

b. "This is a sentence and it is declarative."

c. "This sentence is about *Uncle Ulysses*." (Underline the subject.) "So, *Uncle Ulysses* is the subject because it is what the sentence is about." (Place a capital letter *S* above the subject.)

d. "This sentence tells us that Uncle Ulysses *will read*." (Double underline the helping verb and the predicate.) "So, *will read* is the predicate because it is what the sentence tells us about *Uncle Ulysses*." (Place a capital letter *P* above the action verb.) "It is a predicate verb because it shows action." (Place a capital letter *V* to the right of the *P*.) "There is no linking verb because predicate verbs do not need linking verbs. *Will* is the helping verb." (Place a lowercase *hv* above the helping verb.)

e. "*It* tells us what Uncle Ulysses will read." (Draw a circle around the word.) "So, *it* is an objective element because it completes the meaning of the action verb. It is a direct object because it tells *what* Uncle Ulysses will read." (Write *do* in lowercase letters beneath the direct object.)

f. "*Tonight* tells us *when* Uncle Ulysses will read." (Draw a straight line down from the adverb, then a horizontal line toward the word that it modifies, and then a straight line with an arrow pointing to the word it modifies.) "So, *tonight* is an adverbial element because it modifies a verb. It is an adverb." (Write *adv* in lowercase letters in the elbow opposite the line with the arrow.)

g. "*Not* tells us *how* Uncle Ulysses will read." (Draw a straight line down from the adverb, then a horizontal line toward the word that it modifies, and then a straight line with an arrow pointing to the word it modifies.) "So, *not* is an adverbial element because it modifies a verb. It is an adverb." (Write *adv* in lowercase letters in the elbow opposite the line with the arrow.)

For the analysis of the second sentence, adjust the script accordingly.

Introductory Lesson
Object Pronouns

The order of the lesson is: **Review It**, **Practice It**, **Learn It**, and **Analyze It**.

Review It: Write the five grammar terms on the board. Have the students recite the definitions for all five terms.

Review It

Can you define the following five grammar terms from memory?

Direct objects

Antecedents

Object pronouns

Pronouns

Subject pronouns

Practice It: For this warm-up, see Well-Ordered Notes Introductory.

From the Sidelines: Contractions were introduced in chapter 8 of *WOL1A* when the students learned about subject pronouns. We emphasized making contractions with subject pronouns and verbs and only touched on making contractions with verbs and the adverb *not*. To follow up in this chapter, we emphasize making contractions with *not*. Contractions are not a complicated part of grammar instruction, but we find that children do need to practice which letter to drop and where to place the apostrophe.

Learn It

Do you remember what contractions are? Contractions are abbreviated words created by eliminating letters (sounds) and inserting apostrophes in their places. You probably also remember that in addition to making contractions with subject pronouns and verbs such as *is*, *are*, *will*, *would*, *have*, *has*, and *had*, we can make contractions with verbs and the adverb *not*. When you form a contraction with the adverb *not*, it makes the original meaning of a verb negative. We form the contraction by deleting the space between the verb and *not* and replacing the *o* in *not* with an apostrophe. The word *cannot* is unusual because the verb and *not* are already one word, so the apostrophe replaces one *n* and the *o* like this: *can't*. The contraction for *will not* is also irregular: *won't*.

On the blanks provided, write the contractions for the following words.

Example: ***is not*** **= isn't**

1. do not ______ **don't** ______
2. does not ______ **doesn't** ______
3. did not ______ **didn't** ______
4. cannot ______ **can't** ______

5. could not couldn't

6. should not shouldn't

7. will not won't

8. must not mustn't

Analyze It

Analyze the following sentences (*S* = subject; *PV* = predicate verb; *hv* = helping verb; *adv* = adverb; *adj* = adjective; *do* = direct object).

Analyze it: This is the essential part of the lesson. See Well-Ordered Notes Introductory.

1. Uncle Ulysses (S) will (hv) not (adv) read (PV) it (do) tonight (adv).

2. Earlier (adv) the little (adj) cousins (S) read (PV) it (do) together (adv).

Introductory Practice
Object Pronouns

1. Analyze the following sentences (*S* = subject; *PV* = predicate verb; *hv* = helping verb; *adv* = adverb; *adj* = adjective; *do* = direct object).

   a. S PV
   The cold winter winds blew (it) away.
   adj adj adj do adv

   b. S PV
   The slushy sleet covered (them).
   adj adj do

   c. hv S PV
   Will Winston chase (it) now?
   do adv

   d. S PV
   Suddenly Grandpa calls (us) back.
   adv do adv

2. Fill in the following chart with the correct object pronouns.

Object Pronouns

	Singular	Plural
First Person	me	us
Second Person	you	you
Third Person	him, her, it	them

3. Remember, contractions are shortened versions of words created by taking out letters (sounds) and inserting apostrophes (') in their places. On the blanks provided, write the contractions for the following words.

   a. did not ____**didn't**____

   b. must not ____**mustn't**____

   c. cannot ____**can't**____

   d. should not ____**shouldn't**____

   e. do not ____**don't**____

   f. might not ____**mightn't**____

Well-Ordered Notes A

Practice It

Play Split the Word. Divide the class into pairs and give each pair ten blank index cards. Have each group neatly write down the following words, one word per card: *I, you, he, she, it, we, they, am, is, are.* Say the following contractions to the class and have each pair of students hold up the two words that make up the original contraction. Whichever team first holds up the words wins that round.

> **Fewer than Five:** Play Split the Word as individuals rather than in pairs. Have each student neatly write down the pronouns and verbs, one word per card. When you say a contraction, each student holds up the two words that make it up. Whichever student first holds up the words wins that round.

You can add more contractions to this game too. If you do so, you will need to give the students more cards and have them write the following words: *was, were, have, has, had, will, would, not.*

Example:

Teacher: "he's"
Student 1: "*he*"
Student 2: "*is*"

I'm: I am

you're: you are

he's: he is

she's: she is

it's: it is

we're: we are

you're: you are

they're: they are

Analyze It

As a class, analyze the following sentences (*S* = subject; *PV* = predicate verb; *hv* = helping verb; *adv* = adverb; *adj* = adjective; *do* = direct object). Write the sentences on the board. Have the students analyze the sentences, reciting the analysis aloud using the following script. While the students recite, you will mark the sentence on the board.

1. Grandma (S) warmly (adv) greeted (PV) her (do).

2. Grandpa (S) lifted (PV) her (do) high (adv) too (adv).

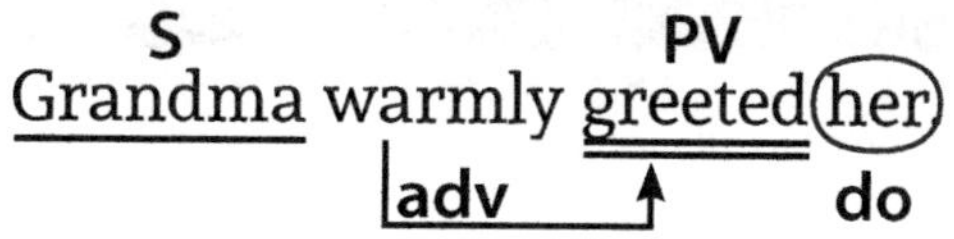

a. (First, read the sentence aloud.) "Grandma warmly greeted her."

b. "This is a sentence and it is declarative."

c. "This sentence is about *Grandma*." (Underline the subject.) "So, *Grandma* is the subject because it is what the sentence is about." (Place a capital letter *S* above the subject.)

d. "This sentence tells us that Grandma *greeted*." (Double underline the predicate.) "So, *greeted* is the predicate because it is what the sentence tells us about *Grandma*." (Place a capital letter *P* above the predicate.) "It is a predicate verb because it shows action." (Place a capital letter *V* to the right of the *P*.) "There is no linking verb because predicate verbs do not need linking verbs."

e. "*Her* tells us whom Grandma greeted." (Draw a circle around the word.) "So, *her* is an objective element because it completes the meaning of the action verb. It is a direct object because it tells *whom* Grandma greeted." (Write *do* in lowercase letters beneath the direct object.)

f. "*Warmly* tells us *how* Grandma greeted." (Draw a straight line down from the adverb, then a horizontal line toward the word that it modifies, and then a straight line with an arrow pointing to the word it modifies.) "So, *warmly* is an adverbial element because it modifies a verb. It is an adverb." (Write *adv* in lowercase letters in the elbow opposite the line with the arrow.)

For the analysis of the second sentence, adjust the script accordingly.

Lessons to Learn
Object Pronouns

A

The order of the lesson is: **Review It**, **Practice It**, **Learn It**, and **Analyze It**.

Review It: Sing/chant and review definitions as a class. Keep this review fresh by varying the pace and loudness of the singing, sometimes having the students sing slowly and quietly and other times having them sing quickly and sing loudly. You can also ask students to narrate back to you the meaning of the definitions or have them expand on some aspect of the definition.

Learn It: Draw the structure (the lines and the column and row headings) of the object pronoun chart on the board. Have the students say aloud the object pronoun chant. Then, call out the person and number of each object pronoun and complete the chart on the board as the students fill in their own charts.

Review It

As you learned in *WOL1A*, mastering definitions requires reviewing them often.

List the eight subject pronouns.

List the eight object pronouns.

Which pronouns are singular?

Which pronouns are plural?

Practice It: For this warm-up, see Well-Ordered Notes A on p. a of the teacher's pages for this chapter.

Learn It

Listen while your teacher directs you to fill in the following object pronoun chart.

Example:

Teacher: "Please fill in the first-person plural object pronoun." Students write *us* in the correct space on the chart.

	Singular	Plural
First Person	me	us
Second Person	you	you
Third Person	him, her, it	them

A Lessons to Learn

Object Pronouns

Analyze It

> **Analyze It:** This is the essential part of the lesson. See Well-Ordered Notes A.

1. Grandma warmly greeted her.
   (S: Grandma; PV: greeted; adv: warmly; do: her)

2. Grandpa lifted her high too.
   (S: Grandpa; PV: lifted; do: her; adv: high; adv: too)

Lessons to Practice A
Object Pronouns

1. Analyze the following sentences (*S* = subject; *PV* = predicate verb; *hv* = helping verb; *adv* = adverb; *adj* = adjective; *do* = direct object).

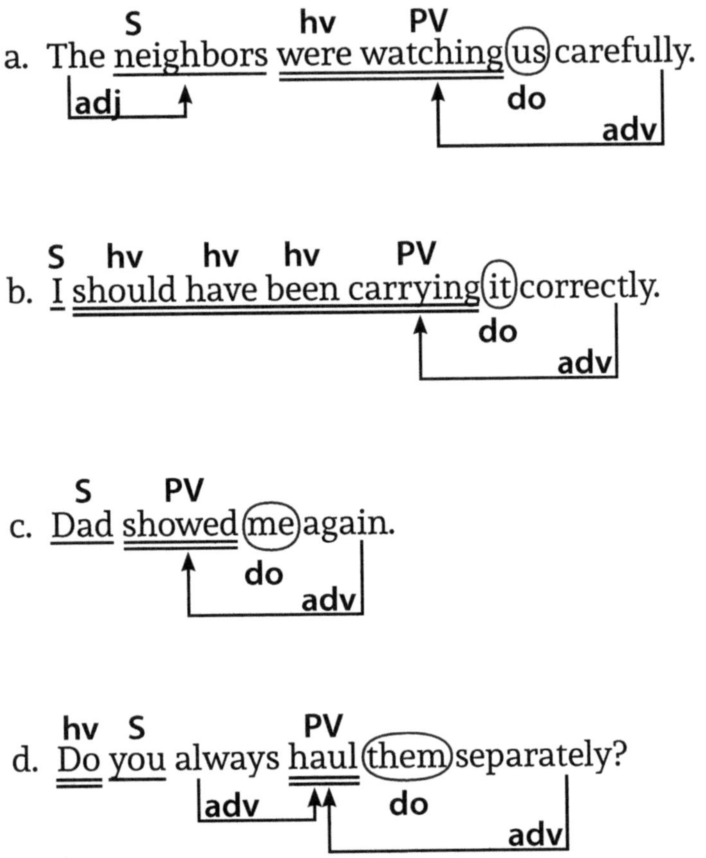

haul: move or transport a heavy load

2. Fill in the following chart with the correct object pronouns.

Object Pronouns

	Singular	Plural
First Person	me	us
Second Person	you	you
Third Person	him, her, it	them

3. Fill in the blanks with the two words that make up each of the following contractions. (Hint: There are two contractions in this list that could be split into two different sets of words.)

   a. it's ___**it is, it has**___

   b. we're ___**we are**___

   c. I'm ___**I am**___

   d. he's ___**he is; he has**___

   e. they're ___**they are**___

   f. you're ___**you are**___

Well-Ordered Notes B

Practice It

Play Stage a Contraction. Call on four or five volunteers (or as many as are needed to represent letters in a word) to stage a contraction. Have the volunteers stand shoulder to shoulder at the front of the room, each holding an index card with his specific letter on it. The first student holds the *first letter* of the word, the second student holds the *second*, and so forth. Make sure one student holds an apostrophe card.

Example: Have the volunteers spell out *don't*. (The first student is the letter *d*, the second student is the letter *o*, the third student is the letter *n*, the fourth student is an apostrophe, and the fifth student is the letter *t*.)

Then have the volunteers rearrange themselves to make two words by extracting the apostrophe, adding the missing letter, and making a space between the letters.

Example: Have the students change from spelling *don't* to spelling *do not* (first student is the letter *d*, second student is the letter *o*, leave a space, third student begins the next word with the letter *n*, fourth student is the letter *o*, fifth student is the letter *t*).

couldn't (could not)	can't (cannot)
mustn't (must not)	shouldn't (should not)
won't (will not)	mightn't (might not)
didn't (did not)	aren't (are not)

Analyze It

As a class, analyze the following sentences (*S* = subject; *PV* = predicate verb; *hv* = helping verb; *adv* = adverb; *adj* = adjective; *do* = direct object). Write the sentences on the board. Have the students analyze the sentences, reciting the analysis aloud using the following script. While the students recite, you will mark the sentence on the board.

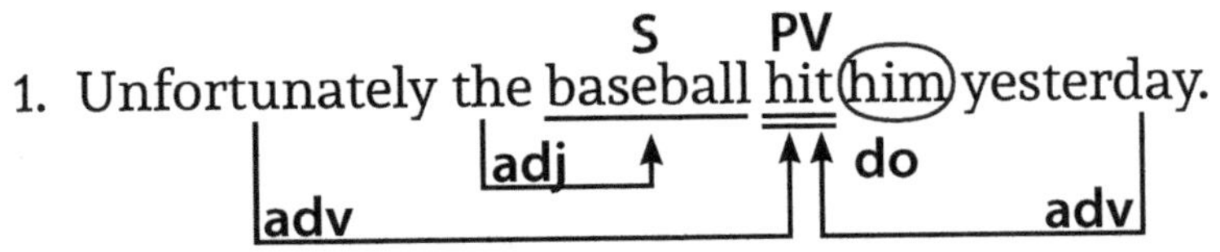

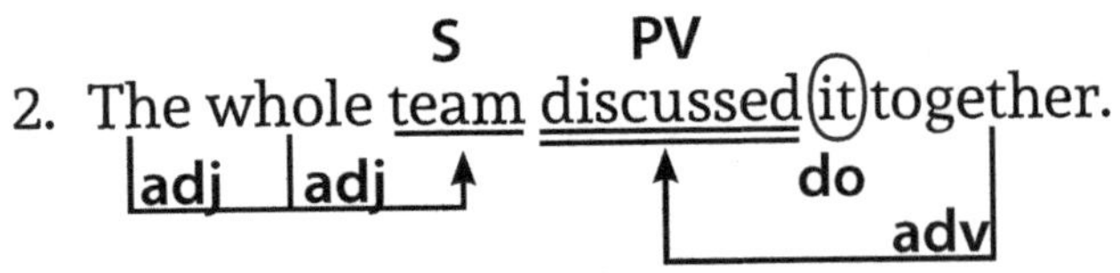

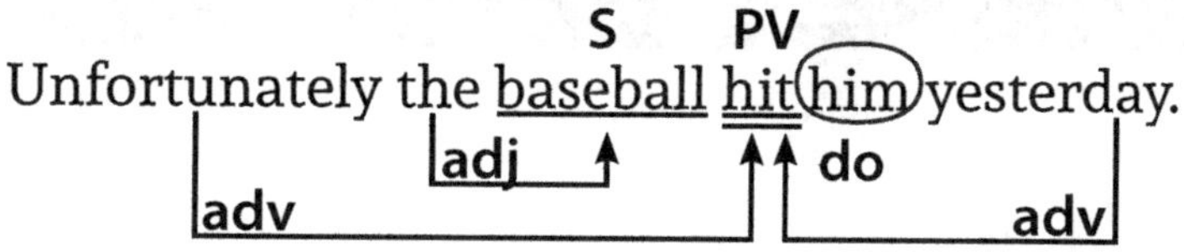

a. (First, read the sentence aloud.) "Unfortunately the baseball hit him yesterday."

b. "This is a sentence and it is declarative."

c. "This sentence is about *baseball*." (Underline the subject.) "So, *baseball* is the subject because it is what the sentence is about." (Place a capital letter *S* above the subject.)

d. "This sentence tells us that baseball *hit*." (Double underline the predicate.) "So, *hit* is the predicate because it is what the sentence tells us about *baseball*." (Place a capital letter *P* above the predicate.) "It is a predicate verb because it shows action." (Place a capital letter *V* to the right of the *P*.) "There is no linking verb because predicate verbs do not need linking verbs."

e. "*Him* tells us whom baseball hit." (Draw a circle around the word.) "So, *him* is an objective element because it completes the meaning of the action verb. It is a direct object because it tells *whom* baseball hit." (Write *do* in lowercase letters beneath the direct object.)

f. "*Yesterday* tells us *when* the baseball hit." (Draw a straight line down from the adverb, then a horizontal line toward the word that it modifies, and then a straight line with an arrow pointing to the word it modifies.) "So, *yesterday* is an adverbial element because it modifies a verb. It is an adverb." (Write *adv* in lowercase letters in the elbow opposite the line with the arrow.)

g. "*The* tells us *which* baseball." (Draw a straight line down from the adjective, then a horizontal line toward the word that it modifies, and then a straight line with an arrow pointing to the word it modifies.) "So, *the* is an adjective element because it modifies a noun. It is an adjective."[1] (Write *adj* in lowercase letters in the elbow opposite the line with the arrow.)

h. "*Unfortunately* tells us *how* the baseball hit." (Draw a straight line down from the adverb, then a horizontal line toward the word that it modifies, and then a straight line with an arrow pointing to the word it modifies.) "So, *unfortunately* is an adverbial element because it modifies a verb. It is an adverb." (Write *adv* in lowercase letters in the elbow opposite the line with the arrow.)

For the analysis of the second sentence, adjust the script accordingly.

1. The words *article adjective* can be substituted in place of the word *adjective*.

Lessons to Learn B
Object Pronouns

The order of the lesson is: **Review It**, **Practice It**, **Learn It**, and **Analyze It**.

Review It: Sing and review definitions as a class.

Review it

Answers the following review questions.

What is a verb?

What are the four classes of verbs?

What is an intransitive verb?

What is a direct object?

What is a transitive verb?

What is a helping verb?

Practice It: For this warm-up, see Well-Ordered Notes B.

Learn It

Pronouns behave like the nouns they represent. In the following sentences, underline the noun that is behaving like a direct object and then rewrite the sentence with the correct object pronoun. Keep on your toes! Notice how the article, and sometimes the adjective, is replaced along with the direct object when an object pronoun is substituted.

Example: Fritz spotted some bats. **Fritz spotted *them*.**

1. Aunt Gabby saw the sunset. **Aunt Gabby saw it.**

2. The sky displayed rosy clouds. **The sky displayed them.**

3. Dad brought Winston and me along. **Dad brought us along.**

4. Fritz spotted a meteorite. **Fritz spotted it.**

meteorite: a rock or pieces of rock that fall from an asteroid or comet and reaches the surface of the earth

5. Rex just watched <u>Fritz</u>. **Rex just watched him.**

____

Analyze It

Analyze the following sentences (*S* = subject; *PV* = predicate verb; *hv* = helping verb; *adv* = adverb; *adj* = adjective; *do* = direct object).

> **Analyze It:** This is the essential part of the lesson. See Well-Ordered Notes B.

1. Unfortunately the baseball hit (him) yesterday.

   S: baseball; **PV**: hit; **do**: him; **adj**: the → baseball; **adv**: Unfortunately → hit; **adv**: yesterday → hit

2. The whole team discussed (it) together.

   S: team; **PV**: discussed; **do**: it; **adj**: The → team; **adj**: whole → team; **adv**: together → discussed

Lessons to Practice
Object Pronouns

1. Analyze the following sentences (*S* = subject; *PV* = predicate verb; *hv* = helping verb; *adv* = adverb; *adj* = adjective; *do* = direct object).

   a. The vessel should have brought us too.
   (S: vessel; hv: should; hv: have; PV: brought; do: us; adj: The; adv: too)

   vessel: ship

   b. Suddenly the sailor spotted him.
   (S: sailor; PV: spotted; do: him; adj: the; adv: Suddenly)

   c. The whale might accidentally spray them.
   (S: whale; hv: might; PV: spray; do: them; adj: The; adv: accidentally)

   d. Will you snap it quickly?
   (hv: Will; S: you; PV: snap; do: it; adv: quickly)

2. Fill in the following chart with the correct object pronouns.

Object Pronouns

	Singular	Plural
First Person	me	us
Second Person	you	you
Third Person	him, her, it	them

3. Fill in the blanks with the two words that make up each of the following contractions.

   a. haven't **have not**

   b. won't **will not**

   c. isn't **is not**

   d. aren't **are not**

   e. hadn't **had not**

   f. weren't **were not**

Well-Ordered Notes C

Practice It

This activity is called Write on White and uses mini whiteboards. Supply each student with a mini whiteboard. Before starting the activity, remind students that antecedents are the nouns to which a pronoun refers. Read aloud each of the following sets of two sentences, emphasizing the antecedent (italicized) in the first sentence. Have the students write on their boards the pronoun that is missing from the second sentence and hold up their answers. You will be able to quickly see if students have selected the correct pronoun for each sentence.

Example: The kids baked the *cupcakes*. They frosted ____ them ____ too.

1. Do you have the *gift*? Yes, I have ____ **it** ____.
2. *Lucy* called two friends. They didn't answer ____ **her** ____.
3. Secretly the *girls* came over. Theo hid ____ **them** ____ underneath the bed.
4. Theo had a *surprise*. He wrapped ____ **it** ____ up.
5. Later the *friends* jumped out. ____ **They** ____ surprised Lucy.
6. *Rex* barked excitedly. Theo chased ____ **him** ____ around.

Analyze It

As a class, analyze the following sentences (*S* = subject; *PV* = predicate verb; *hv* = helping verb; *adv* = adverb; *adj* = adjective; *do* = direct object). Write the sentences on the board. Have the students analyze the sentences, reciting the analysis aloud using the following script. While the students recite, you will mark the sentence on the board.

1. Did the children find him afterward?

   hv: Did; S: children; PV: find; adj: the; do: him; adv: afterward

2. Curiously Winston asked them again.

   S: Winston; PV: asked; adv: Curiously; do: them; adv: again

From the Sideline: The sentence "Curiously Winston asked them again" implies that Winston asked a question to *them*, so you or your students may wonder how *them* is a direct object. In fact, if the sentence were "Curiously, Winston asked them a question again," the direct object would be *question*, and *them* (as we will learn in *WOL Level 3*) would be the indirect object. However, the word *question* does not appear in our sentence here, and a sentence cannot have an indirect object without a direct object. Therefore, despite seeming to receive the action indirectly, *them* is the direct object in this sentence. Similar questions may arise for other transitive verbs in this chapter, such as *tell* and *show* and the same principle applies.

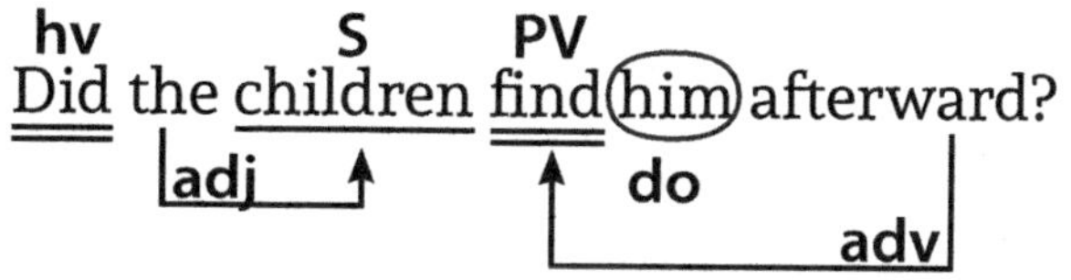

a. (First, read the sentence aloud.) "Did the children find him afterward?"

b. "This is a sentence and it is interrogative."

c. "This sentence is about *children*." (Underline the subject.) "So, *children* is the subject because it is what the sentence is about." (Place a capital letter *S* above the subject.)

d. "This sentence tells us that children *did find*." (Double underline the helping verb and the predicate verb.) "So, *did find* is the predicate because it is what the sentence tells us about *children*." (Place a capital letter *P* above the action verb.) "It is a predicate verb because it shows action." (Place a capital letter *V* to the right of the *P*.) "There is no linking verb because predicate verbs do not need linking verbs. *Did* is the helping verb." (Place a lowercase *hv* above the helping verb.)

e. "*Him* tells us whom children did find." (Draw a circle around the word.) "So, *him* is an objective element because it completes the meaning of the action verb. It is a direct object because it tells *whom* the children did find." (Write *do* in lowercase letters beneath the direct object.)

f. "*Afterward* tells us *when* the children did find." (Draw a straight line down from the adverb, then a horizontal line toward the word that it modifies, and then a straight line with an arrow pointing to the word it modifies.) "So, *afterward* is an adverbial element because it modifies a verb. It is an adverb." (Write *adv* in lowercase letters in the elbow opposite the line with the arrow.)

g. "*The* tells us *which* children." (Draw a straight line down from the adjective, then a horizontal line toward the word that it modifies, and then a straight line with an arrow pointing to the word it modifies.) "So, *the* is an adjective element because it modifies a noun. It is an adjective."[1] (Write *adj* in lowercase letters in the elbow opposite the line with the arrow.)

For the analysis of the second sentence, adjust the script accordingly.

1. The words *article adjective* can be substituted in place of the word *adjective*.

Lessons to Learn
Object Pronouns

C

The order of the lesson is: **Review It**, **Practice It**, **Learn It**, and **Analyze It**.

Review It: Sing/chant and review definitions as a class. Consider adding freshness by varying speed and volume or by asking individual students to paraphrase the meaning of a definition.

Review It

Grammar terms are the building blocks of learning. Have you memorized the answers to the following questions yet?

What is a pronoun?

What are the subject pronouns?

What are the object pronouns?

What is an antecedent?

Practice It: For this warm-up, see Well-Ordered Notes C.

Learn It

As you know, contractions are two words shortened into a single word by taking out letters (sounds) and inserting apostrophes (') in their places. When you form a contraction with the adverb *not*, it makes the original meaning of a verb negative. Fill in the blanks with the two words that make up each of the following contractions.

Example: isn't = is not

1. aren't **are not**
2. wasn't **was not**
3. weren't **were not**
4. haven't **have not**
5. hadn't **had not**
6. hasn't **has not**
7. won't **will not**
8. wouldn't **would not**

C Lessons to Learn
Object Pronouns

Analyze It

Analyze the following sentences (*S* = subject; *PV* = predicate verb; *hv* = helping verb; *adv* = adverb; *adj* = adjective; *do* = direct object).

Analyze It: This is the essential part of the lesson. See Well-Ordered Notes C.

1. Did (hv) the (adj) children (S) find (PV) him (do) afterward (adv)?

2. Curiously (adv) Winston (S) asked (PV) them (do) again (adv).

Lessons to Practice C
Object Pronouns

1. Analyze the following sentences (*S* = subject; *PV* = predicate verb; *hv* = helping verb; *adv* = adverb; *adj* = adjective; *do* = direct object).

    a. Winston quietly told (me)
    S: Winston; PV: told; adv: quietly → told; do: me

    b. Did that naughty dog scamper off again?
    hv: Did; S: dog; PV: scamper; adj: that → dog; adj: naughty → dog; adv: off → scamper; adv: again → scamper

    c. Kindly Grandma Lola scrubbed (him)
    S: Grandma Lola; PV: scrubbed; adv: Kindly → scrubbed; do: him

    d. Unhappily Rex endured (it)
    S: Rex; PV: endured; adv: Unhappily → endured; do: it

    endured: dealt with or accepted

2. Fill in the following chart with the correct object pronouns.

Object Pronouns

	Singular	Plural
First Person	me	us
Second Person	you	you
Third Person	him, her, it	them

3. Fill in the blanks with the two words that make up each of the following contractions.

   a. didn't ______did not______

   b. shouldn't ______should not______

   c. can't ______cannot______

   d. mustn't ______must not______

   e. don't ______do not______

   f. mightn't ______might not______

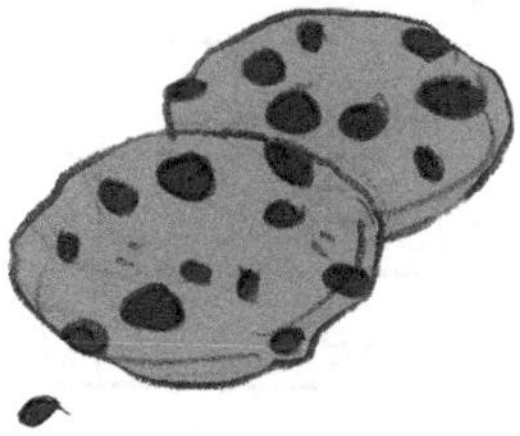

Lessons to Learn—Review
Object Pronouns

Review It: Write the questions on the board. Sing/chant and review definitions as a class.

Review It

How good is your memory? Let's test it!

What is a direct object? Think of a sentence with a direct object.

What is a pronoun?

What is an antecedent?

List eight subject pronouns.

List eight object pronouns.

Learn It: This part of the lesson can be an oral exercise completed on the board together while students mark their books individually or it can be an individual written exercise that is reviewed orally as a class when finished.

Learn It

Construct sentences using the following transitive verbs and object pronouns. Remember, a transitive verb is a verb that takes an objective element.

Example:

Verb: catch
Pronoun: him
Sentence: Fritz will *catch him*.

Verbs	Object Pronouns
catch(es)	me
help(s)	you
gather(s)	him
knead(s)	her
swat(s)	it
scratch(es)	us
follow(s)	you
choose(s)	them

Verbs	Object Pronouns
share(s)	
change(s)	
write(s)	
wash(es)	
doubt(s)	

1. Winston helps them. ______________________

____

2. Rex scratches it. ______________________

____

3. Lucy swats him. ______________________

____

4. Dad will follow her. ______________________

____

5. Uncle Ulysses chooses us. ______________________

____

Lessons to Practice—Review
Object Pronouns

1. Analyze the following sentences (*S* = subject; *PV* = predicate verb; *hv* = helping verb; *adv* = adverb; *adj* = adjective; *do* = direct object).

   a. hv S PV
Does the coach drill (them) regularly?
adj do adv

   b. S hv PV
Coach Howard is now calling (her) over.
adv do adv

   c. S PV
The grateful player regarded (him) respectfully.
adj adj do adv

   d. S PV
Playfully the team threw (it) high.
adj do adv adv

2. Fill in the following chart with the correct object pronouns.

Object Pronouns

	Singular	Plural
First Person	me	us
Second Person	you	you
Third Person	him, her, it	them

3. Fill in the blanks with the two words that make up each of the following contractions. (Hint: There is one contraction in this list that could be split into two different sets of words.)

   a. you're ____**you are**____

   b. doesn't ____**does not**____

   c. they're ____**they are**____

   d. she's ____**she is; she has**____

   e. hadn't ____**had not**____

   f. can't ____**cannot**____

Sometimes the solution to a problem may not be as easy as it seems. In this fable, a large family of mice must solve a problem with a pesky cat. Read to find out how the impossible task is to be performed and by whom.

The Mice in Council

by Aesop

dread: fear

fearsome: causing fear

bell (verb): to put a bell on

Something had to be done about the Cat! Hardly a day went by that the Mice didn't hear of some brother or sister, aunt or uncle, having gotten gobbled down by the Cat. The Mice lived in such constant dread of her claws that they hardly dared to stir from their dens by night or day. Finally they called a meeting to decide on a plan to free themselves from their fearsome enemy.

Many plans were discussed, but none of them sounded good enough. At last, a very Young Mouse got up and said, "I have a plan that seems very simple, but I know it will be successful. All we have to do is to hang a bell about the Cat's neck. When we hear the bell ringing, we will know immediately that our enemy is coming."

All the Mice were much surprised that they had not thought of such a plan before. "Hurrah for the Young Mouse!" they shouted.

As they were cheering and rejoicing over their good fortune, an Old Mouse stood up. Shaking a finger at the gathering, he said, "I will say that the plan of the Young Mouse is very good. But let me ask one question: Who will bell the Cat?"

Moral: It is one thing to say that something should be done, but quite a different matter to do it.[1]

1. Aesop, "The Mice in Council," in *Writing & Rhetoric Book 1: Fable*, by Paul Kortepeter (Camp Hill, PA: Classical Academic Press, 2013), p. 60.

Questions to Ponder

1. What do the Mice want?
2. What does it mean to live in "constant dread"?
3. How would you put in your own words what the wise old Mouse says at the end of the fable?
4. What does the old Mouse's statement have to do with the moral of the fable?

Extras: Please note that the teacher's pages for this chapter include more material for extra practice, a quiz, and another Lessons to Enjoy section with discussion questions and activities. All this material, in reproducible form, is also included in the PDF that accompanies the textbook.

From the Sideline: For possible answers to these discussion questions, see p. a of the teacher's pages. For even more suggestions for discussion and for enrichment activities related to the poem, see p. b.

Lessons to Enjoy—Fable

Questions to Ponder

1. What do the Mice want?

   Like humans, the Mice want security and the freedom to carry on their activities without fearing for the safety of their loved ones. Their civilization mirrors that of humans, including meetings, plans for the future, and communication with each other. They simply want it to continue in peace.

2. What does it mean to live in "constant dread"?

   Within the fable, living in "constant dread" for the Mice means that they are frightened for their lives because of the Cat. Living with this fear keeps them confined to their dens instead of experiencing full mousey freedom. Consider that this may be a complex question for students who are becoming aware of political, economic, and environmental problems in the world. You may want to ask the students the following question: Are there humans who live in "constant dread"?

3. How would you put in your own words what the wise old Mouse says at the end of the fable?

   The old Mouse reveals that the seemingly simple solution to the problem requires someone to take a huge, life-threatening risk. Draw students' attention to the unusual use of *bell* as a verb. Ask students why this language choice is better than "Who will *put a bell* on the Cat?" It is more concise, like a punch line that emphasizes the irony of the plan.

4. What does the old Mouse's statement have to do with the moral of the fable?

   The old Mouse's statement is about the particular situation of the mice. If the Cat were belled, their problem would be solved. But the idea itself poses a problem: it requires a Mouse brave enough to take the risk. The moral of the fable extends the story to everyday human life, suggesting that solving problems for a community requires an individual's courage. Plans and solutions that may appear easy when stated or written often need someone very special to accomplish them.

Well-Ordered Notes—Fable

Read

- Have the students enjoy reading the fable to themselves as they listen to music, such as Aaron Copland's "The Cat and the Mouse."
- Have the students sing the definition of a fable (Fable, 1–14).

Retell

- Discuss the tale using the questions at the end of the fable.
- Make cookie mice puppets according to the directions below. Retell the story to the students using the cookie puppets they have made, or have them perform the puppet show themselves. Ask the students which character is most like them—the unnamed fearful mice, the Young Mouse, the Old Mouse, or even the Cat. Clean up . . . by letting the students eat their puppets!

Record

- Have each student write his own version of the fable. Perhaps have students change the characters in the fable (e.g., wolf and the sheep).

Cookie Mice Puppets Instructions

Ingredients

chocolate sandwich cookies

mini chocolate sandwich cookies

Popsicle sticks

Twist open mini sandwich cookies and scrape off the white frosting. Slide the two mini chocolate cookies into the top of a regular-sized sandwich as ears. Insert a Popsicle stick in the bottom.

Variation: Add frosting dollops to secure mini chocolate candies or mini chocolate chips for eyes. Use frosting to create whiskers.

Fable Sentences
Object Pronouns

ANSWERS

Analyze the following sentences (*S* = subject; *PV* = predicate verb; *hv* = helping verb; *adv* = adverb; *adj* = adjective; *do* = direct object).

S PV
1. Sadly many helpless mice disappeared.
adj adj
adv

S hv PV
2. The cat was devouring them.
adj do

S PV
3. They finally had it.
adv do

S PV
4. The elder mice called them together.
adj adj do adv

S hv PV
5. Many plans were discussed.
adj

S PV
6. A young mouse called them.
adj adj do

S hv PV
7. They must get a (bell)
do
adj

S hv PV
8. The cat shall wear (it)
adj do

S hv PV
9. Cheers were suddenly stopped.
adv

S PV
10. One final question needed an (answer)
adj adj do
adj

Practice Sheet
Object Pronouns

ANSWERS

Analyze the following sentences (*S* = subject; *PV* = predicate verb; *hv* = helping verb; *adv* = adverb; *adj* = adjective; *do* = direct object).

S hv PV
1. We were watching (it) intently.
do adv

S PV
2. Slowly the heavy rains drenched (us).
adj adj do
adv

drenched: soaked

S PV
3. Then some players knocked (her) over.
adj do adv
adv

hv S PV
4. Did those two girls see (her)?
adj adj do

S hv PV
5. Coach Howard is now signaling (them).
adv do

S PV
6. Suddenly lightning stopped (it).
adv do

7. Mom frantically called (us) back.
S: Mom; PV: called; do: us; adv: frantically; adv: back

frantically: fearfully

8. Eagerly Fritz held (her) tightly.
S: Fritz; PV: held; do: her; adv: Eagerly; adv: tightly

9. Will the referees call (it) now?
hv: Will; S: referees; PV: call; do: it; adj: the; adv: now

10. The three wet girls will not play (them) again today.
S: girls; hv: will; PV: play; do: them; adj: The; adj: three; adj: wet; adv: not; adv: again; adv: today

Quiz
Object Pronouns

ANSWERS

1. Analyze the following sentences (*S* = subject; *PV* = predicate verb; *hv* = helping verb; *adv* = adverb; *adj* = adjective; *do* = direct object).

   a. Should (hv) the cousins (S) open (PV) it (do) now (adv)?
      - the → adj (modifies cousins)
      - now → adv (modifies open)

   b. She (S) gently held (PV) them (do).
      - gently → adv (modifies held)

   c. One tiny hamster (S) scratched (PV) her (do).
      - One → adj; tiny → adj (modify hamster)

   d. Accidentally Heidi (S) dropped (PV) it (do).
      - Accidentally → adv (modifies dropped)

2. Fill in the following chart with the correct object pronouns.

Object Pronouns

	Singular	Plural
First Person	me	us
Second Person	you	you
Third Person	him, her, it	them

3. Fill in the blanks with the two words that make up the following contractions. (Hint: There is one contraction in this list that could be split into two different sets of words.)

   a. they're **they are**

   b. shouldn't **should not**

   c. she's **she is; she has**

   d. doesn't **does not**

   e. you're **you are**

   f. I'm **I am**

George Pope Morris was an American editor and songwriter, but he became well-known with his poem "Woodman, Spare That Tree." It was first titled "The Oak" and was later changed to its current title. Have you ever wanted to save something that was dear to you? Read what this character does.

Woodman, Spare That Tree

by George Pope Morris (1802–1864)

woodman: a woodcutter

'twas: contraction for *it was*
forefather's: ancestor's
cot: a small house, cottage
renown: fame

o'er: poetic form of *over*
hew: chop
forbear: hold back
thy: your
wouldst thou: would you

Woodman, spare that tree!
Touch not a single bough!
In youth it sheltered me,
And I'll protect it now.
'Twas my forefather's hand
That placed it near his cot;
There, woodman, let it stand,
Thy axe shall harm it not!

That old familiar tree,
Whose glory and renown
Are spread o'er land and sea,
And wouldst thou hew it down?
Woodman, forbear thy stroke!
Cut not its earth-bound ties;
Oh, spare that aged oak
Now towering to the skies!

When but an idle boy
I sought its grateful shade;
In all their gushing joy,
Here, too, my sisters played.
My mother kissed me here;

My father pressed my hand—
Forgive this foolish tear,
But let that old oak stand!

My heart-strings round thee cling,
Close as thy bark, old friend!
Here shall the wild-bird sing,
And still thy branches bend.
Old tree! the storm still brave!
And, woodman, leave the spot;
While I've a hand to save;
Thy axe shall harm it not.[1]

heart-strings: deepest feelings
thee: you

Questions to Ponder

1. What is the poet describing in the first stanza?
2. What does " 'Twas my forefather's hand / that placed it near his cot" mean?
3. What were some special memories the speaker had near the tree?
4. What is the plea in this poem?

1. George Pope Morris, "Woodman, Spare That Tree," *Favorite Poems Old and New*, ed. Helen Ferris (New York: Doubleday & Company, Inc., 1957), pp. 546–547.

Lessons to Enjoy—Poem

Questions to Ponder

1. What is the poet describing in the first stanza?

   From the poet's description, students will readily imagine a woodcutter set to chop down an old, gnarled oak, only to have the speaker of the poem rush in to save it, calling on the rich memories of his childhood and family history that it evokes.

2. What does "'Twas my forefather's hand / that placed it near his cot" mean?

   It means that one of the poet's ancestors planted the tree near his cottage with his own hands. The speaker of the poem is proud of the fact that the tree was planted by one of his ancestors. The fact that the forefather planted it near the cottage suggests that it was done with care. Presumably, the planter of the tree is dead and gone, but the tree—and the planter's descendants—are still thriving.

3. What were some special memories the speaker had near the tree?

   The memories include being sheltered and shaded by the tree, watching his sisters playing under it, being kissed by his mother near it, and shaking his father's hand by it. Ask the students if their families have special memory spots within their homes or yards.

4. What is the plea in this poem?

   The speaker begs the woodcutter not to cut down the tree. He wants the grand old tree to remain standing because it represents important memories he wants to preserve.

Well-Ordered Notes—Poem

Recite

- Enjoy reading the poem with the students.
- Ask the students to memorize the first stanza of the poem.

Retell

- Discuss the poem using the provided questions.
- Tell the students to circle the word *it* when used as an object pronoun, warning them to be careful not to circle *it* when used as a subject pronoun. (Note: In this poem, *it* is an object pronoun every time it appears except in the third line—"it sheltered me"—and in the contraction "'Twas" when it acts as the subject of the sentences. Don't let the students get confused with *its*, which appears twice in the poem.)

From the Sideline: Challenge the students to find two more object pronouns in the poem. They will probably notice the direct object *me* in "In youth it sheltered *me*" and in "My mother kissed *me* here," but you can tease their brains, giving them clues to find the archaic *thee*, which is the object of the unusual preposition *round*.

Record

- Have the students write about an adventure the main character of the poem might have had with his tree.
- Read *The Giving Tree* by Shel Silverstein with the students and have the students list similarities and differences between it and Morris's poem.

From the Sideline: Keep it organized. Help the students organize their desks. Instruct them where to place their notebooks, supply box, and books. That way time devoted to tidying is minimized. We have a saying, "It's your seat; keep it neat."

Chapter 2

Pronoun Review[A]

In your house you probably have a kitchen drawer where your parents keep all sorts of utensils, such as spatulas, whisks, a corkscrew, a rolling pin, and other interesting gadgets. Each kitchen tool has a different job. You wouldn't whisk eggs with a spatula, stir soup with a corkscrew, or flip a pancake with a rolling pin. Knowing to use the right tool for the right job just makes sense.

Pronouns are like tools you can pull out of your grammar gadget drawer to help you whip up an interesting sentence. You have already learned what the different pronouns are—which ones are subject pronouns and which ones are object pronouns—and how they stand in for specific nouns in a sentence. Now it is time to practice choosing the right pronoun tool for the right job in a sentence. For instance, when you use a subject pronoun, it determines whether the verb in the sentence is singular or plural. Then, another thing to consider is that placing a subject pronoun between the helping verb and the main verb signals that the sentence is interrogative. Finally, some pronouns can be used only as objects, and it's important not to confuse them with subject pronouns.

There are many types of pronouns, just as there are many tools in a kitchen. In this chapter we are reviewing subject pronouns and object pronouns. All this may sound tricky, but you are becoming more and more skilled in the grammar kitchen. Let's open our gadget drawer, review the personal pronouns, and see what we can create!

[A]Having introduced your students to subject and object pronouns separately in previous chapters, you now can ensure a strong foundation in pronoun usage by reviewing subject and object pronouns together, reinforcing their similarities and differences. Bring in a spatula, whisk, corkscrew, and other kitchen utensils to help you illustrate our opening metaphor of choosing the proper gadgets.

Ideas to Understand[B]

The first tools to take out of the drawer are the subject pronouns. Pronouns enable the speaker or writer to communicate meaning without using the nouns over and over again. In the tale "The Beginning of the Armadillos" from *Just So Stories*, author Rudyard Kipling tells about a conversation between a tortoise and a small jaguar cub named Painted Jaguar. The tortoise, named Slow-and-Solid, is discussing with Painted Jaguar what the cub's mother had told him earlier about how to eat a tortoise. Slow-and-Solid shrewdly relies on pronouns to trick Painted Jaguar into forgetting his mother's instructions:

> Well, suppose you say that I said that she said something quite different, I don't see that it makes any difference; because if she said what you said I said she said, it's just the same as if I said what she said she said.[1]

This passage is meant to be light and humorous. Slow-and-Solid is trying to confuse Painted Jaguar. Let's replace the pronouns with their proper noun antecedents to test whether the tortoise got them all right:

> Well, suppose *Painted Jaguar* says that *Slow-and-Solid* said that *Mother Painted Jaguar* said something quite different, *Slow-and-Solid* doesn't see that it makes any difference; because if *Mother Painted Jaguar* said what *Painted Jaguar* said *Slow-and-Solid* said *Mother Painted Jaguar* said, it's just the same as if *Slow-and-Solid* said what *Mother Painted Jaguar* said *Mother Painted Jaguar* said.

He did it! Such repetition of pronouns makes the text awkward and very confusing, but that is Kipling's joke. Nonetheless, he cleverly and correctly uses the subject pronouns *I*, *you*, and *she* to replace a proper noun as the subject of a verb.

Off the Shelf: Rudyard Kipling's *Just So Stories* are called *pourquoi* stories. *Pourquoi* is the French word for *why*. These stories are fanciful tales of *why* certain animals have trunks or humps or spots or other characteristics shared only by their own species (kind). "The Beginning of the Armadillos" tells the story of how the turtle and the hedgehog transformed into the first armadillo. You can find a longer passage of the story in The Curious Child's Literary Appendix. Do you want to read the whole story? Take it off the shelf and check it out at your library.

> [B]Read chapter 7, "The Beginning of the Armadillos," from *Just So Stories* by Rudyard Kipling to the class. Write Slow-and-Solid's humorous, pronoun-filled sentence (quoted above) on the board and highlight the subject pronouns. Note: Do not highlight "it" or "it's" because they are used here as indefinite pronouns, which will be taught later.

1. Rudyard Kipling, "The Beginning of the Armadillos," *Just So Stories* (New York: Doubleday, 1952), p. 39.

Subject Pronouns

	Singular	Plural
First Person	I	we
Second Person	you	you
Third Person	he, she, it	they

Now, back to the kitchen. The "recipe" for a correct sentence using pronouns demands that you choose a verb that agrees in number and in person with the subject pronoun. This is called **subject-verb agreement**. If the pronoun is singular, then the verb must be singular; if the pronoun is plural, then the verb must be plural. Depending on the person of the pronoun, the verb may change form too. Notice in the examples below how the pronouns *I*, *you*, *we*, and *they* use the same verb—*say*—while the third-person singular pronouns *he*, *she*, and *it* use a slightly different form of the verb—*says*.

	Singular	Plural
First Person	I *say* it.	We *say* it.
Second Person	You *say* it.	You *say* it.
Third Person	He ***says*** it./She ***says*** it./It ***says*** it.	They *say* it.

While we are talking about subject pronouns, and comparing them to kitchen gadgets, do you remember that there is a special "recipe" for an interrogative sentence with a subject pronoun? This recipe calls for the subject pronoun to come between the helping verb and the main verb. This order signals that the sentence is a question before you even see the question mark. *Do* (helping verb) *you* (subject pronoun) *remember* (main verb)?

The next set of gadgets in our grammar gadget drawer is our collection of object pronouns. After Slow-and-Solid tricks Painted Jaguar into releasing him into the water, Slow-and-Solid tells his prickly hedgehog friend what happened. Notice Kipling's object pronouns in this passage, which we have put in *italics*:

> I told *him* truthfully that I was a truthful Tortoise, but he wouldn't believe *it*, and he made *me* jump into the river to see if I was, and I was, and he is surprised. Now he's gone to tell his Mummy. Listen to *him*!

Here Kipling chooses only object pronouns for the objects in the sentences. If the recipe is to turn out right, object pronouns must be used as objects and subject pronouns must be used as subjects. It would be nonsense for Kipling to have written "I told he" and "listen to he" because he would have chosen subject pronouns for a direct object and an object of a preposition.

Object Pronouns

	Singular	Plural
First Person	me	us
Second Person	you	you
Third Person	him, her, it	them

[C]Remind students to commit the songs to memory by listening to the CD tracks/audio files at other times as well.

Terms to Remember[C]

When people make mistakes in grammar, the problem is often their choice of pronouns. This is why it is important to review the basic tools of grammar.

Eight Parts of Speech *(1–1)*

The eight parts of speech are classes of words
with the same kind of meaning and use.
They are: nouns, verbs, adjectives, adverbs,
prepositions, pronouns, conjunctions, interjections.
These are the eight parts of speech,
classes of words with the same kind of meaning and use. *(Repeat.)*

Sentence *(1–2)*

A sentence is a group of words expressing a complete thought.
There are four kinds of sentences:
Declarative sentence—makes a statement.
Interrogative sentence—asks a question.
Imperative sentence—gives a command.
Exclamatory sentence—expresses strong feelings.

A sentence is a group of words expressing a complete thought.
There are four kinds of sentences. *(Repeat.)*

Principal Elements *(1–3)*

Principal elements are the parts of the sentence
that are needed for the sentence to be completed.
Subject and predicate are those two parts.

Subject Pronouns *(1–12)*

Subject pronouns are in the nominative case:
I, you, he, she, it, we, you, they *(repeat).*
Subject pronouns are in the nominative case:
I, you, he, she, it, we, you, they *(repeat).*

Object Pronouns *(1–15)*

Object pronouns are in the objective case.
Me, you, him, her, it, us, you, them
Me, you, him, her, it, us, you, them.
Object pronouns are in the objective case.
Me, you, him, her, it, us, you, them
Me, you, him, her, it, us, you, them
Me, you, him, her, it, us, you, them.

A Sentence to Analyze[D]

Remember to say the analysis aloud, with expression, while you mark the sentence neatly.

S PV
We saw (her)
do

[D]Continue to model how to mark the sentence while the students chorally analyze each sentence. The class should say in chorus the words in gray.

a. (First, read the sentence aloud.) "We saw her."

b. "This is a sentence and it is declarative."

c. "This sentence is about *we*. So, *we* is the subject because it is what the sentence is about." (Since *we* is the subject, underline it and place a capital letter *S* above it.)

d. "This sentence tells us that we *saw*. So, *saw* is the predicate because it is what the sentence tells us about *we*." (Since *saw* tells us something about *we*, double underline it and place a capital letter *P* above it.) "It is a predicate verb because it shows action. There is no linking verb because predicate verbs do not need linking verbs." (Since *saw* shows action, place a capital letter *V* to the right of the letter *P* above the predicate.)

e. "*Her* tells us what we saw." (Since *her* tells what we saw, draw a circle around *her*.)

f. "So, *her* is an objective element because it completes the meaning of an action verb. It is a direct object because it tells *what* we saw." (Write *do* in lowercase letters beneath the direct object.)

Usually your ear naturally distinguishes between pronouns, and you choose correctly between subject and object pronouns and between singular and plural verbs. But when you start writing more complicated sentences, just like a chef creating more complicated recipes, you will be glad that you have memorized and analyzed the basic ingredients and that you have practiced choosing the best sentence tools.

Notes

Well-Ordered Notes Introductory

Practice It

Draw the structures (the lines and the column and row headings) of the subject and object pronoun charts on the board. First, review person, by leading the students in the person chant:

First: speaking (Use your thumbs and point to yourself.)

Second: spoken to (Point your index fingers straight out.)

Third: spoken of (Point your thumbs over your right shoulder.)

Then, ask volunteers one by one to fill in a space in one of the charts, calling for the pronouns in random order.

Example:

Teacher: "Please fill in the first-person plural object pronoun."
Student 1 writes *us* in the object pronoun chart.
Teacher: "Please fill in the second-person singular subject pronoun."
Student 2 writes *you* in the subject pronoun chart.

While each student is approaching the board and writing on it, the rest of the class should alternate between reciting the subject pronoun chant and the object pronoun chant, repeating them over and over until the two charts are complete. Then, to reinforce their memorization, reverse the exercise, asking individual students to erase particular pronouns while the entire class continues to repeat the chants.

Subject Pronouns

	Singular	Plural
First Person	I	we
Second Person	you	you
Third Person	he, she, it	they

Object Pronouns

	Singular	Plural
First Person	me	us
Second Person	you	you
Third Person	him, her, it	them

Analyze It

As a class, analyze the following sentences (*S* = subject; *PV* = predicate verb; *hv* = helping verb; *adv* = adverb; *adj* = adjective; *do* = direct object). Write the sentences on the board. Have the students analyze the sentences, reciting the analysis aloud using the following script. While the students recite, you will mark the sentence on the board.

1. 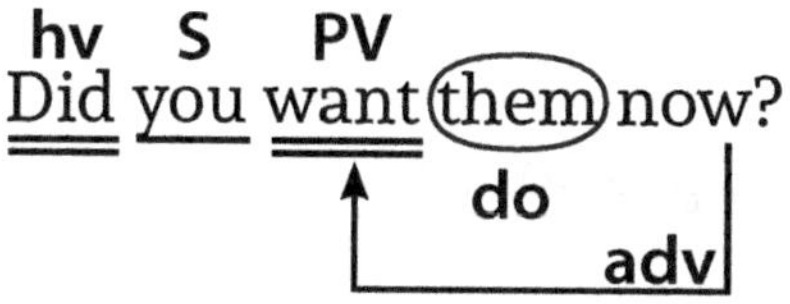

2. 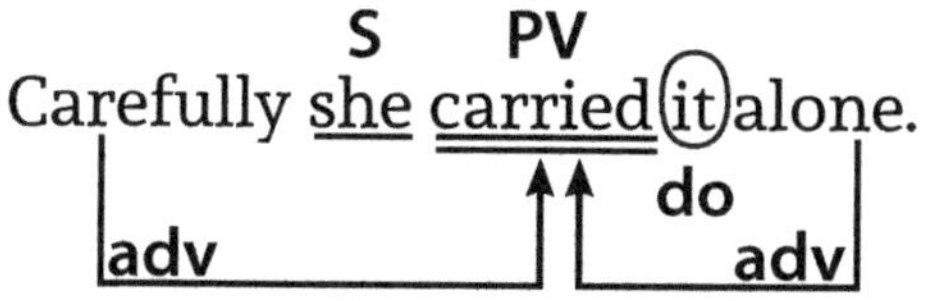

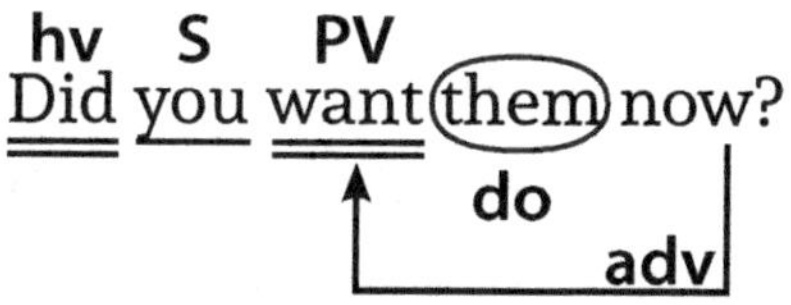

a. (First, read the sentence aloud.) "Did you want them now?"

b. "This is a sentence and it is interrogative."

c. "This sentence is about *you*." (Underline the subject.) "So, *you* is the subject because it is what the sentence is about." (Place a capital letter *S* above the subject.)

d. "This sentence tells us that you *did want*." (Double underline the helping verb and the predicate verb.) "So, *did want* is the predicate because it is what the sentence tells us about *you*." (Place a capital letter *P* above the action verb.) "It is a predicate verb because it shows action. There is no linking verb because predicate verbs do not need linking verbs." (Place a capital letter *V* to the right of the letter *P*.) "*Did* is the helping verb because it helps the verb." (Place a lowercase *hv* above the helping verb.)

e. "*Them* tells us whom you did want." (Draw a circle around the word.) "So, *them* is an objective element because it completes the meaning of the action verb. It is a direct object because it tells *whom* you did want." (Write *do* in lowercase letters beneath the direct object.)

f. "*Now* tells us *when* you did want." (Draw a straight line down from the adverb, then a horizontal line toward the word that it modifies, and then a straight line with an arrow pointing to the word it modifies.) "So, *now* is an adverbial element because it modifies a verb. It is an adverb." (Write *adv* in lowercase letters in the elbow opposite the line with the arrow.)

For the analysis of the second sentence, adjust the script accordingly.

Introductory Lesson
Pronoun Review

The order of the lesson is: **Review It**, **Practice It**, **Learn It**, and **Analyze It**.

Review It: Have the students recite the definitions for all five terms.

Review It

What are the definitions of the following terms?

Eight parts of speech

Sentence

Principal Elements

Subject pronouns

Object pronouns

Practice It: For this warm-up, see Well-Ordered Notes Introductory.

Learn It: This can be an oral or written exercise.

From the Sidelines: As mentioned earlier, object pronouns can also replace objects of the preposition. Prepositional phrases will be covered in the next chapter.

Learn It

Although subject pronouns and object pronouns are both personal pronouns, they have different roles in a sentence. Subject pronouns can replace subject nouns, while object pronouns can replace direct objects.

In the following sentences, circle the correct pronoun.

Example: Did (we / us) bring the picnic basket?

1. (She / Her) sang the songs softly.
2. The tender mother returned (he / him) gently.
3. Unfortunately (they / them) slammed the door.
4. (He / Him) suddenly woke up.

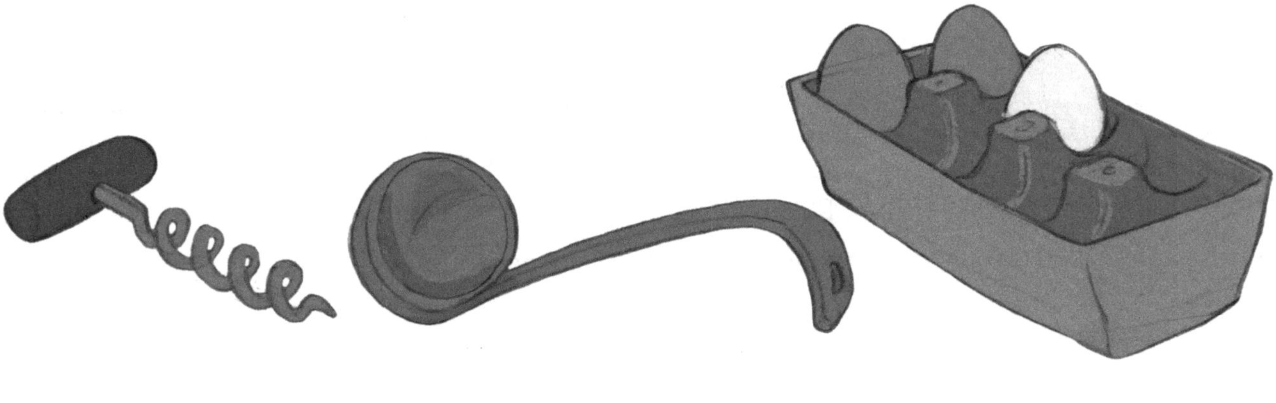

Analyze It

Analyze the following sentences (*S* = subject; *PV* = predicate verb; *hv* = helping verb; *adv* = adverb; *adj* = adjective; *do* = direct object).

1. Did (hv) you (S) want (PV) them (do) now (adv)?

2. Carefully (adv) she (S) carried (PV) it (do) alone (adv).

> **Analyze It:** This is the essential part of the lesson. See Well-Ordered Notes Introductory.

Introductory Practice

Pronoun Review

1. Analyze the following sentences (*S* = subject; *PV* = predicate verb; *hv* = helping verb; *adv* = adverb; *adj* = adjective; *do* = direct object).

   a. S PV
   They brought them over yesterday.
   do adv adv

   b. S PV
   He usually helps her
   adv do

   c. S hv PV
   Next we were building it
   adv do

   d. hv S PV
   Will you help us later?
   do adv

2. What is a *pronoun*? **A pronoun is a part of speech used in place of a noun or of more than one noun.**

3. In the following sentences, circle the correct pronoun.

   a. The neighbors heard (I / me).

   b. Later (we / us) filled wicker baskets.

   c. Will (your / you) help afterward?

   d. (Her / She) will cut all the tree branches.

4. Imagine that Heidi and Fritz are in the garage and Heidi is trying to help Fritz get his bike helmet adjusted to fit properly. Then write a sentence about the two of them using both a *subject pronoun* and an *object pronoun.*

   She helped him.

Well-Ordered Notes A

Practice It

Remind students that when using subject pronouns, the verbs must agree with the subjects in number and in person. See page 33 in Ideas to Understand for explanation and examples.

Play Write What's Right. Divide the class into two or three teams. Have one representative from each team come to the board. Read one of the following sentences aloud, with the blank, and state the two verb options. Then say "Write what's right," which will signal the students to write. The first student who writes the correct verb neatly gets the point. Insist on legible writing; otherwise, no point will be given. Just because it is a race doesn't mean that sloppy work is acceptable. To keep crowd control, if any team member says anything while the representative is writing, the whole team will lose a point.

> **Fewer than Five:** You can use a stopwatch to time how quickly the correct verb can be written neatly, combining the grammar lesson with penmanship.

Example: We ____bring____ lunches along. (bring / brings)

1. He ______________ me over. (call / (calls))
2. They ______________ more hot dog buns downstairs. ((need) / needs)
3. She ______________ them again. (tell / (tells))
4. Later we ______________ the back panel. ((open) / opens)
5. It seldom ______________ the music now. (play / (plays))
6. I ______________ more ketchup. ((want) / wants)

Analyze It

As a class, analyze the following sentences (*S* = subject; *PV* = predicate verb; *hv* = helping verb; *adv* = adverb; *adj* = adjective; *do* = direct object). Write the sentences on the board. Have the students analyze the sentences, reciting the analysis aloud using the following script. While the students recite, you will mark the sentence on the board.

1. They (S) might (hv) not (adv) show (PV) (him) (do) later (adv).

hv S PV
2. Will he tell (us) soon?
do
adv

S hv PV
They might not show (him) later.
adv do
adv

a. (First, read the sentence aloud.) "They might not show him later."

b. "This is a sentence and it is declarative."

c. "This sentence is about *they*." (Underline the subject.) "So, *they* is the subject because it is what the sentence is about." (Place a capital letter *S* above the subject.)

d. "This sentence tells us that they *might show*." (Double underline the helping verb and the predicate verb.) "So, *might show* is the predicate because it is what the sentence tells us about *they*." (Place a capital letter *P* above the action verb.) "It is a predicate verb because it shows action." (Place a capital letter *V* to the right of the *P*.) "There is no linking verb because predicate verbs do not need linking verbs. *Might* is the helping verb because it helps the verb." (Place a lowercase *hv* above the helping verb.)

e. "*Him* tells us whom they might show." (Draw a circle around the word.) "So, *him* is an objective element because it completes the meaning of the action verb. It is a direct object because it tells whom they might show." (Write *do* in lowercase letters beneath the direct object.)

f. "*Later* tells us *when* they might show." (Draw a straight line down from the adverb, then a horizontal line toward the word that it modifies, and then a straight line with an arrow pointing to the word it modifies.) "So, *later* is an adverbial element because it modifies a verb. It is an adverb." (Write *adv* in lowercase letters in the elbow opposite the line with the arrow.)

g. "*Not* tells us *how* they might show." (Draw a straight line down from the adverb, then a horizontal line toward the word that it modifies, and then a straight line with an arrow pointing to the word it modifies.) "So, *not* is an adverbial element because it modifies a verb. It is an adverb." (Write *adv* in lowercase letters in the elbow opposite the line with the arrow.)

For the analysis of the second sentence, adjust the script accordingly.

Lessons to Learn
Pronoun Review

A

The order of the lesson is: **Review It**, **Practice It**, **Learn It**, and **Analyze It**.

Review It: Sing/chant and review definitions as a class. Consider adding freshness by varying speed and volume or by asking individual students to paraphrase the meaning of a definition.

Learn It: This can be an oral or written exercise. Write the following sentences on the board or read them aloud. Have the students complete them in their books. Discuss how the antecedent determines which object pronoun is missing.

Review It

Can you list the eight subject pronouns from memory? Which ones are singular? Which ones are plural? Can you list the eight object pronouns? Which ones are singular? Which ones are plural?

Practice It: For this warm-up, see Well-Ordered Notes A.

Learn It

1. In the following pairs of sentences, fill in the missing pronouns. Each pronoun should replace the noun antecedent that is in the first sentence in each pair.

Example: Sunflower seeds covered the ground. The cardinals ate __them__.

a. The two sparrows flew down. We fed __**them**__.

b. I watched a blue jay. __**He or It**__ attacked the others.

c. The birds flew upward. Theo chased __**them**__.

d. Lucy flapped her arms. __**She**__ chased the blue jay away.

e. Grandpa threw more seeds. __**They**__ blanketed the ground.

2. To continue the story of the sparrows and the blue jay, construct two sentences. Be sure to include both a subject pronoun and an object pronoun.

The hungry birds flew back. They eagerly pecked it.

____

Analyze It

Analyze the following sentences (*S* = subject; *PV* = predicate verb; *hv* = helping verb; *adv* = adverb; *adj* = adjective; *do* = direct object).

> **Analyze It:** This is the essential part of the lesson. See Well-Ordered Notes A.

1. They (S) might (hv) not (adv) show (PV) him (do) later (adv).

2. Will (hv) he (S) tell (PV) us (do) soon (adv)?

Lessons to Practice
Pronoun Review

A

1. Analyze the following sentences (*S* = subject; *PV* = predicate verb; *hv* = helping verb; *adv* = adverb; *adj* = adjective; *do* = direct object).

   a. Gently he carted them back.
   S: he; PV: carted; do: them; adv: Gently; adv: back

   b. We cheered her along too.
   S: We; PV: cheered; do: her; adv: along; adv: too

   c. Have you carried it before?
   hv: Have; S: you; PV: carried; do: it; adv: before

   d. I will not run that obstacle course again.
   S: I; hv: will; PV: run; adv: not; adj: that; adj: obstacle; do: course; adv: again

2. Fill in the following chart with the correct object pronouns.

Object Pronouns

	Singular	Plural
First Person	me	us
Second Person	you	you
Third Person	him, her, it	them

3. In the following sentences circle the correct pronoun.
   a. Have (you / your) washed (he / him) before?
   b. (We / Us) usually fill the washtub together.
   c. (I / Me) can't find the scrub brush.
   d. Rex always hides (it / its) somewhere.
4. Imagine that you are washing Rex with the other children, and then write a sentence about it using both a *subject pronoun* and an *object pronoun*.

   He did not wash him before.

Well-Ordered Notes B

Practice It

Play Around the Class. Have the students stand beside their desks. Ask each student the following question, using one of the example nouns that have been supplied: What is the *subject pronoun* form of __________? Then ask another student the following question using the same example noun you used in the first question: What is the *object pronoun* form of __________? If the student answers correctly, she may be seated; if not, she remains standing until you ask her another question. Select students in a random "popcorn" fashion to encourage students to be on their game. This is a fast, lively game. Keep it that way.

Fewer than Five: Skip the standing and sitting part of the instructions and ask the students to use each pronoun they provide in a sentence spoken about the antecedent.

Example:

Teacher: "What is the *subject pronoun* form of *football player*."
Student 1: "He."
Teacher: "What is the *object pronoun* form of *football player*."
Student 2: "Him."

	Subject Pronoun	Object Pronoun
A waitress	she	her
Two farmers	they	them
A sailor	he	him
You and I	we	us
A nephew	he	him
The evening sunset	it	it
A group of people being spoken to	you	you
A daughter	she	her
One pinecone	it	it
A woman	she	her
A person being spoken to	you	you
Grandpa and I	we	us
A person speaking	I	me
The Duke of York	he	him

Analyze It

As a class, analyze the following sentences (*S* = subject; *PV* = predicate verb; *hv* = helping verb; *adv* = adverb; *adj* = adjective; *do* = direct object). Write the sentences on the board. Have the students analyze the sentences, reciting the analysis aloud using the following script. While the students recite, you will mark the sentence on the board.

S hv hv PV
1. Soon we should be returning him
adv do

hv S PV
2. Will you recount them again?
do
adv

S hv hv PV
Soon we should be returning him
adv do

a. (First, read the sentence aloud.) "Soon we should be returning him."

b. "This is a sentence and it is declarative."

c. "This sentence is about *we*." (Underline the subject.) "So, *we* is the subject because it is what the sentence is about." (Place a capital letter *S* above the subject.)

d. "This sentence tells us that we *should be returning*." (Double underline the helping verb and the predicate verb.) "So, *should be returning* is the predicate because it is what the sentence tells us about *we*." (Place a capital letter *P* above the action verb.) "It is a predicate verb because it shows action." (Place a capital letter *V* to the right of the *P*.) "There is no linking verb because predicate verbs do not need linking verbs. *Should* is a helping verb. *Be* is a helping verb." (Place a lowercase *hv* above the helping verb.)

e. "*Him* tells us whom we should be returning." (Draw a circle around the word.) "So, *him* is an objective element because it completes the meaning of the action verb. It is a direct object because it tells *whom* we should be returning." (Write *do* in lowercase letters beneath the direct object.)

f. "*Soon* tells us *when* we should be returning." (Draw a straight line down from the adverb, then a horizontal line toward the word that it modifies, and then a straight line with an arrow pointing to the word it modifies.) "So, *soon* is an adverbial element because it modifies a verb. It is an adverb." (Write *adv* in lowercase letters in the elbow opposite the line with the arrow.)

For the analysis of the second sentence, adjust the script accordingly.

Lessons to Learn

Pronoun Review

B

The order of the lesson is: **Review It**, **Practice It**, **Learn It**, and **Analyze It**.

Review It: Sing/chant and review definitions as a class.

Review It

Reviewing is at the heart of learning. See if you can answer the following questions.

What are the eight parts of speech?

What are the principal elements?

What is a sentence?

What are the four kinds of sentences?

Can you give an example of a declarative sentence?

Can you give an example of an interrogative sentence?

Practice It: For this warm-up, see Well-Ordered Notes B.

Learn It: Draw the structures (the lines and the column and row headings) of the subject and object pronoun charts on the board. Review the two pronoun chants. Then call on students to tell you what to write in each block. The pronouns should be called out in random order. While you are filling in the charts on the board, students should be completing the charts in their own books.

Learn It

Your teacher will direct you to fill in the blanks in the following charts with the correct subject and object pronouns.

Example:

Teacher: "What should I write here?" pointing to the third-person plural object pronoun.
Student 1 says "*them*." While your teacher writes *them* in the correct place on the board, you should fill in that space in your book.

Subject Pronouns

	Singular	Plural
First Person	I	we
Second Person	you	you
Third Person	he, she, it	they

B Lessons to Learn
Pronoun Review

Object Pronouns

	Singular	Plural
First Person	me	us
Second Person	you	you
Third Person	him, her, it	them

Analyze It

> **Analyze It:** This is the essential part of the lesson. See Well-Ordered Notes B.

Analyze the following sentences (*S* = subject; *PV* = predicate verb; *hv* = helping verb; *adv* = adverb; *adj* = adjective; *do* = direct object).

S hv hv PV
1. Soon we should be returning him.
adv do

hv S PV
2. Will you recount them again?
do adv

Lessons to Practice B
Pronoun Review

1. Analyze the following sentences (*S* = subject; *PV* = predicate verb; *hv* = helping verb; *adv* = adverb; *adj* = adjective; *do* = direct object).

   a. I did not ask them earlier.
   (I = S; did = hv; ask = PV; not = adv; them = do; earlier = adv)

   b. Quietly they whispered together.
   (they = S; whispered = PV; Quietly = adv; together = adv)

   c. Did we want her along anyway?
   (Did = hv; we = S; want = PV; her = do; along = adv; anyway = adv)

   d. She should have stayed behind.
   (She = S; should = hv; have = hv; stayed = PV; behind = adv)

2. Fill in the following chart with the correct subject pronouns.

Subject Pronouns

	Singular	Plural
First Person	I	we
Second Person	you	you
Third Person	he, she, it	they

3. In the following sentences, circle the correct pronoun.

   a. Are (your / you) going tomorrow?

   b. (Her / She) left earlier today.

   c. (I / Me) will play soccer afterwards.

   d. Later the coach called (we / us) together.

4. Imagine that you're part of the soccer team and the coach called you over. Then, write a sentence using both a *subject pronoun* and an *object pronoun*.

   He drilled us again.

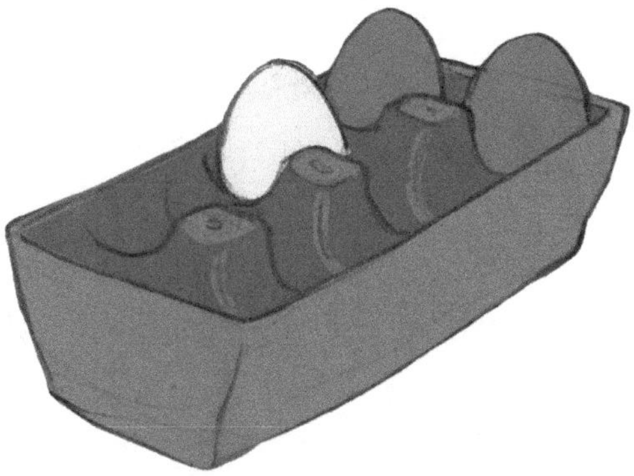

Well-Ordered Notes C

Practice It

Remind students that when using subject pronouns, the verbs must agree with the subjects in number and in person. See page 33 in Ideas to Understand for explanation and examples. Lead the class in the activity Write on White using mini whiteboards. Read each of the following sentences with the two subject pronoun options. Have the students write the missing pronoun on their personal boards and hold up their answers.

Example: ______She______ fills the kitchen cupboards. (She / We)

1. ______________ twist the tops off. (They / She)
2. ______________ spreads peanut butter evenly. (We / He)
3. ______________ chews the graham cracker noisily. (I / He)
4. Quietly ______________ nibble crackers. (you / she)
5. ______________ drink mocha chocolate milk. (They / It)
6. ______________ likes lemonade instead. (You / She)

Analyze It

As a class, analyze the following sentences (*S* = subject; *PV* = predicate verb; *hv* = helping verb; *adv* = adverb; *adj* = adjective; *do* = direct object). Write the sentences on the board. Have the students analyze the sentences, reciting the analysis aloud using the following script. While the students recite, you will mark the sentence on the board.

1. Must (hv) we (S) always (adv) wear (PV) them (do)?

2. I (S) did (hv) not (adv) wear (PV) it (do) yesterday (adv).

hv S PV
Must we always wear them?
adv do

a. (First, read the sentence aloud.) "Must we always wear them?"

b. "This is a sentence and it is interrogative."

c. "This sentence is about *we*." (Underline the subject.) "So, *we* is the subject because it is what the sentence is about." (Place a capital letter *S* above the subject.)

d. "This sentence tells us that we *must wear*." (Double underline the helping verb and the predicate verb.) "So, *must wear* is the predicate because it is what the sentence tells us about *we*." (Place a capital letter *P* above the action verb.) "It is a predicate verb because it shows action." (Place a capital letter *V* to the right of the *P*.) "There is no linking verb because predicate verbs do not need linking verbs. *Must* is the helping verb." (Place a lowercase *hv* above the helping verb.)

e. "*Them* tells us what we must wear." (Draw a circle around the word.) "So, *them* is an objective element because it completes the meaning of the action verb. It is a direct object because it tells *what* we must wear." (Write *do* in lowercase letters beneath the direct object.)

f. "*Always* tells us *when* we must wear." (Draw a straight line down from the adverb, then a horizontal line toward the word that it modifies, and then a straight line with an arrow pointing to the word it modifies.) "So, *always* is an adverbial element because it modifies a verb. It is an adverb." (Write *adv* in lowercase letters in the elbow opposite the line with the arrow.)

For the analysis of the second sentence, adjust the script accordingly.

Lessons to Learn
Pronoun Review

C

The order of the lesson is: **Review It**, **Practice It**, **Learn It**, and **Analyze It**.

Review It: Sing/chant and review definitions as a class. Consider adding freshness by varying speed and volume or by asking individual students to paraphrase the meaning of a definition.

Learn It: Discuss the reorganized subject/object pronoun chart. It contains the same information as the pronoun charts with which students are already familiar, but the information is presented in a slightly different way. Fill in the chart together on the board as the students complete it in their own books.

Review It

Have you memorized the answers to the following questions yet? What is a pronoun? What are the subject pronouns? What are the object pronouns? What is an antecedent?

Practice It: For this warm-up, see Well-Ordered Notes C.

Learn It

1. The following chart organizes subject pronouns and object pronouns in a different way than you're used to seeing. This chart includes **gender**, which refers to whether the pronoun replaces a male, female, or **neuter** antecedent. Something that is neuter is neither male nor female. See if you can fill in the missing pronouns in the chart.

Number	Person	Gender	Subject Pronoun	Object Pronoun
Singular	first	male/female	I	me
	second	male/female	you	you
	third	male	he	him
		female	she	her
		neuter	it	it
Plural	first	male/female	we	us
	second	male/female	you	you
	third	male/female/neuter	they	them

2. Imagine Heidi in art class holding a paintbrush and working on the clay pot she made. Then, write a sentence about it, being sure to include both a subject pronoun and an object pronoun.

She has not painted it before.

Analyze It

Analyze the following sentences (*S* = subject; *PV* = predicate verb; *hv* = helping verb; *adv* = adverb; *adj* = adjective; *do* = direct object).

> **Analyze It:** This is the essential part of the lesson. See Well-Ordered Notes C.

1. Must (hv) we (S) always (adv) wear (PV) them (do)?

2. I (S) did (hv) not (adv) wear (PV) it (do) yesterday (adv).

Lessons to Practice
Pronoun Review

1. Analyze the following sentences (*S* = subject; *PV* = predicate verb; *hv* = helping verb; *adv* = adverb; *adj* = adjective; *do* = direct object).

   hv S PV
   a. Will you help her now?
   do adv

   S PV
   b. She carelessly colored them
   adv do

   S hv PV
   c. They should not criticize her!
   adv do

   S PV
   d. We painted them over again.
   do adv adv

2. What is a pronoun?

   A pronoun is a part of speech used in place of a noun or of more than one noun.

3. In the following sentences, circle the correct pronoun
   a. (I / He) shoots the basketball well.
   b. (They / Them) cheer loudly together.
   c. (You / He) usually sit alone.
   d. (We / She) carefully watches the game.
4. Imagine Winston shooting baskets with the basketball team, and then write an interrogative sentence about it using both a subject pronoun and an object pronoun.

   Will we see him too?

   ____

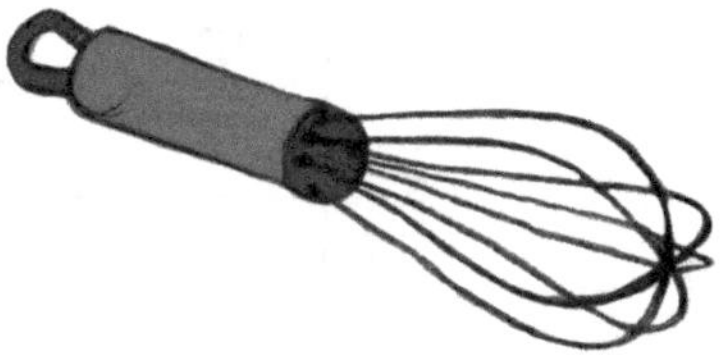

Review It

Answer the following review questions.

What are the eight parts of speech?

What is a sentence?

What is a declarative sentence?

What is an interrogative sentence?

What is an imperative sentence?

What is an exclamatory sentence?

What are the eight subject pronouns?

What are the eight object pronouns?

Learn It: Have students use the chart to make as many sentences as possible. If needed, you can add more transitive verbs to the list.

Learn It

Construct three sentences using the pronouns and transitive verbs listed in the following chart. Make sure that each sentence has a subject, verb, and direct object. You may also add more words, such as helping verbs or adverbs, to your sentences. Tell a mini story by making the topics of your sentences related. For an extra challenge, make one sentence declarative, one interrogative, and one exclamatory.

Example: *I* (subject pronoun), *remove* (verb), *it* (object pronoun).
Sentence: May *I remove it* now?

Subject Pronouns	Verbs	Object Pronouns
I	remove	me
you	shake	you
he	command	him
she	recount	her
it	fry	it
we	respect	us

Subject Pronouns	Verbs	Object Pronouns
you	draw	you
they	fill	them
	answer	
	choose	
	write	

1. First he will shake them.

2. Then they will fry them.

3. We should fill it up again.

Lessons to Practice—Review

Pronoun Review

1. Analyze the following sentences (*S* = subject; *PV* = predicate verb; *hv* = helping verb; *adv* = adverb; *adj* = adjective; *do* = direct object).

   a. He roughly put it down.
   (S: He; PV: put; do: it; adv: roughly; adv: down)

   b. We should have cared too.
   (S: We; hv: should; hv: have; PV: cared; adv: too)

   c. Could you put them safely away?
   (hv: Could; S: you; PV: put; do: them; adv: safely; adv: away)

   d. Yesterday I accidentally broke them.
   (S: I; PV: broke; do: them; adv: Yesterday; adv: accidentally)

2. Fill in the following chart with the correct object pronouns.

Object Pronouns

	Singular	Plural
First Person	me	us
Second Person	you	you
Third Person	him, her, it	them

3. In the following sentences, circle the correct pronoun.
   a. Did (us / we) read that same book last summer?
   b. Peggy whispers (he / it) softly.
   c. (Her / She) had a reason.
   d. Will (they / them) read (us / it) together again?
4. Imagine that you are with Peggy in class and you are reading the same book. Write a sentence about it using both a *subject pronoun* and an *object pronoun.*

   We liked it.

Lessons to Enjoy—Poem
Pronoun Review

Some poems use silly words, and some poems use unusual ones. This poem, "Calico Pie," is a nonsense poem; it really doesn't make sense, but it's clever. Edward Lear, the British author, penned many such nonsensical poems that were whimsical (playful) and imaginative. Calico is a type of spotted cat or cotton cloth with a pattern printed on it. Do you think this poem is about a cat?

Calico Pie

by Edward Lear (1812–1888)

Calico Pie,
The little Birds fly
Down to the calico tree,
Their wings were blue,
And they sang, "Tilly-loo!"
Till away they flew—
And they never came back to me!
They never came back!
They never came back!
They never came back to me!

Calico Jam,
The little Fish swam
Over the syllabub sea,
He took off his hat,
To the Sole and the Sprat,
And the Willeby-wat—
But he never came back to me!
He never came back!
He never came back!
He never came back to me!

syllabub: a drink made with milk or cream mixed and sweetened with cider or wine

Calico Ban,
The little Mice ran,
To be ready in time for tea,
Flippity flup,
They drank it all up,
And danced in the cup—
But they never came back to me!
They never came back!
They never came back!
They never came back to me!

Calico Drum,
The Grasshoppers come,
The Butterfly, Beetle, and Bee,
Over the ground,
Around and around,
With a hop and a bound—
But they never came back to me!
They never came back!
They never came back![1]

Extras: Please note that the teacher's pages for this chapter include more material for extra practice, a quiz, and another Lessons to Enjoy section with discussion questions and activities. All this material, in reproducible form, is also included in the PDF that accompanies the textbook.

bound: jump forward

Questions to Ponder

From the Sideline: For possible answers to these discussion questions, see p. a of the teacher's pages. For even more suggestions for discussion and for enrichment activities related to the poem, see p. b.

1. What kinds of animals never return?
2. What are "the Sole and the Sprat"?
3. What do you think a "Willeby-wat" is?
4. What are the pronouns in the poem?

1. Edward Lear, "Calico Pie," *The Golden Treasury of Poetry*, ed. Louis Untermeyer (New York: Golden Books Publishing, 1998), p. 211.

Lessons to Enjoy—Poem

Questions to Ponder

1. What kinds of animals never return?

   The animals that don't return are the little Birds, the little Fish, the little Mice, and the Grasshoppers, Butterfly, Beetle, and Bee. The poem includes a broad range of creatures. They all entertain the speaker and then leave. They also all happen to be animals that cats like to chase. Here are some follow-up questions you could ask your students: Is the poem told from the perspective of a calico cat? Does the escape of the animals add to the poem's lightheartedness and nonsensical humor or does it create a note of loneliness or abandonment?

2. What are "the Sole and the Sprat"?

   Sole and sprat are both species of fish.

3. What do you think a "Willeby-wat" is?

   The Willeby-wat seems to be Lear's own nonsensical creation. Point out to the students how its name fits the rhythm and the rhyme of the poem. Ask them to describe what they think the creature looks like. You can find Lear's illustrations for the poem at http://www.nonsenselit.org/Lear/ns/calico.html. Have students point out other interesting rhythms and rhymes in the poem.

4. What are the pronouns in the poem?

   Each stanza uses subject pronouns with clear antecedents. In the first, third, and fourth stanzas the subject pronoun *they* stands in for *Birds*, *Mice*, and *Grasshoppers*, *Butterfly*, *Beetle*, and *Bee*. In the second stanza, *Fish* is replaced with *he*. Note that the noun antecedents begin with uppercase letters as if they are proper nouns, personifying the creatures or making them seem human. While these animals are all curiosities, it is the object pronoun *me* repeated throughout the poem that is perhaps the most perplexing. Who is *me*? Is he sad or happy-go-lucky? Does he feel abandoned? Is he a calico cat fascinated with birds, fish, mice, and insects? Perhaps the poem is about nothing more than how fun it is to say the word *calico* and spin off from it other interesting sounds!

Well-Ordered Notes—Poem

Read

- Enjoy reading the poem with the students several times, using your voice to exaggerate the rhythms and rhymes or the sadness in the "never came back" lines. Bring in Reese's Peanut Butter Cups and call them "little pies" as a snack to enjoy while reading the poem (be sure to be aware of any food allergies).
- Play for the students the folk-song version of "Calico Pie" sung by Natalie Merchant (www.youtube.com/watch?v=KZ5yxytTO-g). This particular video animates Edward Lear's original illustrations for the poem.

Retell

- Discuss the poem using the provided questions.
- Read the poem aloud, replacing all the subject pronouns with their antecedents. (See the answer to the last Question to Ponder for guidance.) Discuss the awkwardness and redundancy of using only nouns in the poem. Point out how the rhythm of the poem therefore depends on pronouns.

Record

- Have the students copy a favorite stanza in their copybooks.
- Ask the students to draw or paint a picture of one of the stanzas.

Practice Sheet
Pronoun Review

ANSWERS

Analyze the following sentences (*S* = subject; *PV* = predicate verb; *hv* = helping verb; *adv* = adverb; *adj* = adjective; *do* = direct object).

1. Did (hv) you (S) see (PV) them (do) earlier (adv → see)?

2. She (S) scrubbed (PV) it (do).

3. He (S) washed (PV) them (do) thoroughly (adv → washed).

4. They (S) helped (PV) him (do) too (adv → helped).

5. Should (hv) she (S) use (PV) it (do) now (adv → use)?

6. Did (hv) he (S) ask (PV) him (do)?

hv S PV
7. Can I sort them?
do

S PV
8. He threw them out.
do
adv

S hv hv PV
9. They will be coming later.
adv

hv S PV
10. Will we join them?
do

Quiz
Pronoun Review

ANSWERS

1. Analyze the following sentences (*S* = subject; *PV* = predicate verb; *hv* = helping verb; *adv* = adverb; *adj* = adjective; *do* = direct object).

    a. Foolishly they placed them together.
    (S: they; PV: placed; do: them; adv: Foolishly → placed; adv: together → placed)

    b. He bumped her playfully.
    (S: He; PV: bumped; do: her; adv: playfully → bumped)

    c. Then she shoved him over.
    (S: she; PV: shoved; do: him; adv: Then → shoved; adv: over → shoved)

    d. Quickly they separated them again.
    (S: they; PV: separated; do: them; adv: Quickly → separated; adv: again → separated)

2. What is a *pronoun*?

    A pronoun is a part of speech used in place of a noun or of more than one noun.

3. In the following sentences, circle the correct pronoun.

    a. (**We** / Us) brought popcorn along.

    b. Can (**she** / her) swim too?

    c. Today Grandpa will watch (they / **them**).

d. ((He)/ They) cheers very loudly.

4. Imagine that Grandpa is sitting at the edge of the pool near where the kids are playing, and then write a sentence about it using both a *subject pronoun* and an *object pronoun*.

They will splash him.

Lessons to Enjoy—Fable
Pronoun Review

Have you ever wanted another scoop of ice cream even though you had a giant, two-scoop cone in your hands? Greed is the desire for something else or something more when you have enough. This fable tells of a Dog that is jealous of another Dog that has a butcher bone too. Or is she jealous of only a reflection? Read and find out what such greed will do.

The Dog and Her Reflection

by Aesop

swiped: grabbed with a sweeping motion

A Dog had swiped a bone from a butcher's shop, and she was hurrying home with her prize as fast as she could go. As the Dog crossed a narrow footbridge, she happened to look down. She saw herself reflected in the quiet water as if in a mirror. But the greedy Dog did not recognize herself. She thought she saw another Dog carrying a bone much bigger than her own and she felt extremely desirous.

desirous: having a wish or longing for something

viciously: ferociously

If the Dog had stopped to think, she would have known better, but instead she started growling viciously. "I want that big bone," she thought. Her fur stood up on the back of her neck and she bared her fangs. The Dog in the river also bared her fangs. In a rage, the Dog dropped her bone and sprang at her reflection, only to find herself swimming for dear life. At last, the Dog managed to reach the shore and scramble out. As she shook the water from her coat, the Dog remembered the lost bone. "Oh, what a silly Dog I've been!" she cried.

Moral: It is very foolish to be greedy.[1]

1. Aesop, "The Dog and Her Reflection," *Writing & Rhetoric Book 1: Fable*, by Paul Kortepeter (Camp Hill, PA: Classical Academic Press, 2013), p. 71.

Questions to Ponder

1. What does the dog swipe?
2. Why does the dog not recognize herself in the reflection?
3. What does "she felt extremely desirous" mean?
4. What happened to the bone at the end?

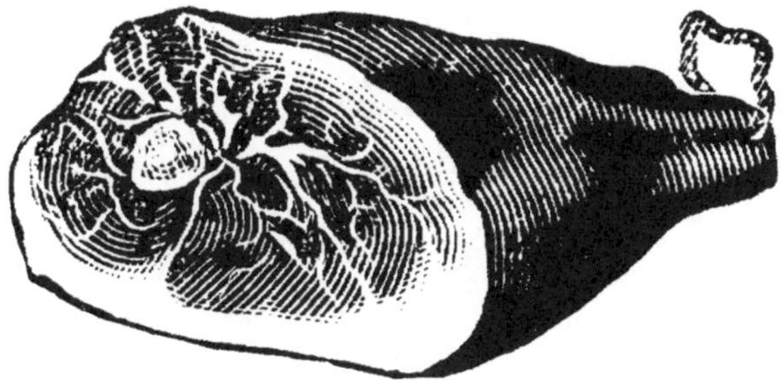

Lessons to Enjoy—Fable

Questions to Ponder

1. What does the dog swipe?

   The dog swipes a bone, which is described as a "prize," so it must be very pleasing to the dog. Note to students that the reflection of the bone would make it look bigger and therefore all the more desirable.

2. Why does the dog not recognize herself in the reflection?

   The dog does not recognize herself because she's focused on the bone. It is as if she's blinded by the belief that a bigger prize than her own is held by another. When she reacts viciously, she is further blinded to the truth, thinking the other dog is ready to attack.

3. What does "she felt extremely desirous" mean?

   To be "desirous" is to be filled with desire or longing. Ask the students if they have ever wished for something so much that they were obsessed with it, blinded to other things or people.

4. What happened to the bone at the end?

   Because of the dog's great, foolish greed, the bone is lost, sunk to the bottom of the river and out of reach.

Well-Ordered Notes—Fable

Read

- Encourage the students to enjoy reading the fable aloud together. Bring in a stuffed dog, bone, and a mirror and use them to retell the story.
- Sing with the students the definition of a fable (*Fable*, 1–14).

Retell

- Discuss the fable using the provided questions.
- Reread the tale, replacing the subject pronoun *she* with the antecedent *a dog* to illustrate how pronouns are necessary and natural sounding.

Record

- Have the students copy the fable into a copybook and illustrate it. They can glue aluminum foil on the picture to represent the water.

Fable Sentences

Pronoun Review

ANSWERS

Analyze the following sentences (*S* = subject; *PV* = predicate verb; *hv* = helping verb; *adv* = adverb; *adj* = adjective; *do* = direct object).

S PV
1. The dog swiped it.
adj do

S hv PV
2. She was hurrying along.
adv

S PV
3. Soon she crossed a narrow footbridge.
adv adj adj do

S PV
4. She saw the reflection.
adj do

S PV
5. Viciously she growled.
adv

hv S PV
6. Did she want it?
do

hv S PV
7. Must she have (it) too?
do
adv

S PV
8. Suddenly she sprang forward.
adv adv

S PV
9. She helplessly swam around.
adv adv

S PV
10. The foolish dog lost (it).
adj adj do

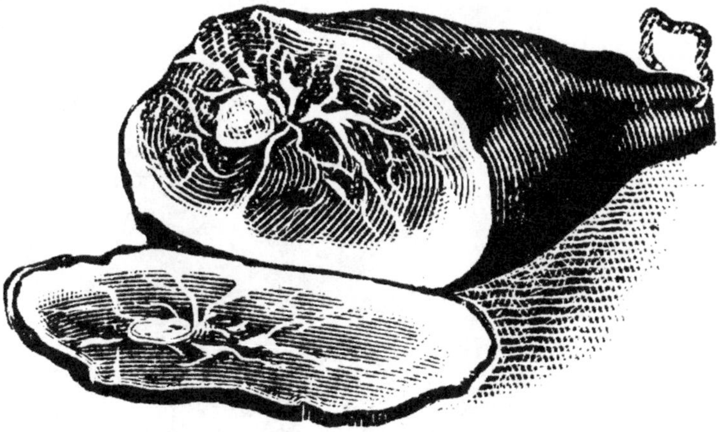

From the Sideline: Establish a routine. Have an efficient procedure for passing out papers, getting books, and lining up. We have the students silently "peel off" one at a time from their desk row when it's time to line up at the door. This is an orderly way for each student to leave his seat and quietly line up.

Chapter 3

Prepositional Phrases—Adverbial[A]

Imagine plump apples hanging on tree branches in an orchard. If you could picture one tree from that orchard, thoughts of dozens of reddish-green apples clustering all over its leafy boughs might come to mind. Think about all that luscious (very delicious) fruit clinging to the branches. How is it attached to the tree? Each fleshy, round apple is connected to the tree by a slender stem. But if you subtract that stem, the apple falls to the ground with a thud. It is interesting to think that such a little twig could be so important, but without those itty-bitty stems, the tree would be fruitless.

[A]Bring in pictures of heavy-laden apple tree boughs. Or bring in an apple with a stem still attached to it. Pass out apple slices and share as a snack.

Now imagine that a sentence is like that apple tree. You know a lot about the parts of this tree because you already have studied five of the eight parts of speech—nouns, verbs, adjectives, adverbs, and pronouns. In this chapter, you will learn about prepositions. A **preposition** connects a noun or pronoun to another word in the sentence, telling us something more about it. You can imagine the preposition as that important little stem that connects an apple (a noun or pronoun) to the branch (another word in the sentence).

Ideas to Understand[B]

Before we define "preposition" further, take a peek at a list of some of the most common prepositions, and you will find them very familiar. You use them all the time to connect words within your sentences:

[B]Write the excerpt of the poem "Moon Folly" by Fannie Stearns Davis on the board. You may want to read the whole poem (available in The Curious Child's Literary Appendix) or play the song arrangement for your students. In recent years, Jan Luby put the poem "Moon Folly" to music. It is available at: http://janluby.com/track/350052/moon-folly.

aboard	about	above	across	after
against	along	among	around	at
before	behind	below	beneath	beside
between	beyond	by	down	during
except	for	from	inside	in
into	near	of	off	on
out	outside	over	past	since
through	throughout	to	toward	under
up	until	upon	with	within
without	underneath			

To the Source:
■ preposition
In Latin, the word *preposition* is *praeponere*, which literally means "put before," with *prae* meaning "before" and *ponere* meaning "to put, set, or place."

A preposition■ is a word placed before a noun or pronoun (called the object of the preposition). Together they form a **prepositional phrase**. The preposition connects its object to another word in the sentence, often the verb. The preposition shows the relationship between the two words. That relationship might have to do with location: Mom put the apple pie (where?) *on the table*. It might have to do with time: We ate dessert (when?) *during the movie*. It might have to do with manner: We smacked our lips (how?) *with delight*. Whatever the relationship, the entire prepositional phrase modifies the word to which it is connected, such as the verb *put*, *ate*, or *smacked* in our sample sentences. In this way, the prepositional phrase behaves like a single part of speech. In *WOL Level 1*, we will be looking at prepositional phrases that behave like adverbs modifying verbs, and in *WOL Level 2*, we will include prepositional phrases behaving like adjectives.

Let's see how prepositional phrases function in an excerpt from the poem "Moon Folly" by Fannie Stearns Davis. (You can find the whole poem in The Curious Child's Literary Appendix.) The poet uses prepositional phrases that behave like adverbs, or **adverbial prepositional phrases**, to describe a night journey to capture the moon:

> I will go up the mountain after the Moon:
> She is caught in a dead fir-tree.
> Like a great pale apple of silver and pearl,
> Like a great pale apple is she.

I will leap and will clasp her with quick cold hands
And carry her home in my sack.
I will set her down safe on the oaken bench
That stands at the chimney-back.

And then I will sit by the fire all night,
And sit by the fire all day.
I will gnaw at the Moon to my heart's delight,
Till I gnaw her slowly away.[1]

Did you see any adverbial prepositional phrases in this portion of the poem? "With quick cold hands" describes *how* the poet will catch the moon, and "in my sack" describes *where* the poet carries the moon. If she had included "during the night," she would have told *when* the journey happened. These phrases are called adverbial prepositional phrases. Each one includes a preposition—*with*, *in*, or *during*—which we imagine to be like the connecting stem of an apple. Each preposition is followed by a noun, which is the object of the preposition—*hands*, *sack*, or *night*—which we have compared to the apple itself. Each phrase contains adjectives—*quick*, *cold*, *my*, *the*—which are a bit like the apple's leaves attached to an apple stem. What does the stem connect the apple to? In each of these examples, the stem connects the apple to a verb. That means each entire prepositional phrase functions as an adverb modifying the verb.

Keep in mind that the noun or pronoun in a prepositional phrase is called the object of the preposition. Most objects of the preposition are common nouns. **Common nouns** name any person, place, thing, or idea. *Apple* and *hands* are common nouns because they name a nonspecific person or thing. Some objects of the prepositions are proper nouns. **Proper nouns**, such as the months of the year, refer to a particular person, place, thing, or idea; they begin with a capital letter.

Your goal for this lesson is to learn to identify prepositions, their objects, and what they modify in sentences. The prepositions listed on the previous page are the most common ones used in English. Being able to recognize them at a glance is a handy analytic skill, so you will need to memorize them.

From the Sidelines: Here is a complete list of adverbial prepositional phrases that appear in these three stanzas of "Moon Folly": *up the mountain*, *after the Moon*, *in a dead fir-tree*, *with quick cold hands*, *in my sack*, *on the oaken bench*, *at the chimney-back*, *by the fire*, *at the Moon*, and *to my heart's delight*. All of them modify verbs and answer the questions *where* or *how*.

From the Sidelines: The poet also uses prepositional phrases that behave like adjectives, such as *like a great pale apple* and *of silver and pearl*. **Adjectival prepositional phrases** modify nouns and answer the questions *how many*, *whose*, *which one*, or *what kind*. (Students will learn more about adjectival prepositional phrases in *WOL Level 2*.)

1. Fannie Stearns Davis, "Moon Folly" from *In Poetry*, vol. I, ed. Harriet Monroe (New York: A.M.S. Reprint CO, Vol. 1, No. 6, March 1912–1913), pp. 183–184. Available at: https://books.google.com/books?id=9MARAAAAYAAJ.

[c]Play the appropriate CD tracks/audio files and have students sing/chant along. Remind students to commit the songs to memory by listening to these tracks/files at other times as well.

Terms to Remember[c]

By now you know that music is one of the best tools for memorizing. The long list of prepositions and the related definitions will be a snap once you learn the tunes.

NEW! **Preposition** *(1–16)*

A preposition *(a preposition)*
is a part of speech *(is a part of speech)*
used to show the relationship
between certain words in a sentence *(in a sentence). (Repeat.)*

NEW! **List of Prepositions** *(1–17)*

Aboard, about, above, across, after, against, along, among, around
Preposition Words
Before, behind, below, beneath, beside, between, beyond, at, by
Preposition Words
Down, during, except, for, from, inside, in, into, near
Preposition Words
Of, off, on, out, outside, over, past, since, through
Preposition Words
Throughout, to, toward,
Under, up, until,
Upon, with, within,
Without, underneath
Preposition Words
Preposition Words
Preposition Words!

NEW! **Phrase** *(1–18)*

A phrase is a group of words
behaving like one part of speech
not containing a subject or a predicate. *(Repeat.)*

NEW! **Object of the Preposition** *(1–19)*

The object of the preposition
The object of the preposition
is the noun or pronoun
after the preposition. *(Repeat.)*

> [D] There is a slight shift in analysis now that the sentences include prepositional phrases. Make sure you rehearse the order of analysis chant with the students. Phrases need to be identified first because a phrase acts as a single part of speech within a sentence. All markings within the phrases are completed before the analysis of the principal elements. Then, the function of the phrase as a whole is marked along with other modifiers. Though clauses will be discussed later in the Well-Ordered Language program, it is important to include clauses now as the second step of analysis to accustom students to an approach that is consistent both for simple sentences and for more sophisticated sentence structures.

A Sentence to Analyze[D]

In this chapter, we are adding another level of analysis that comes *before* the steps that you are used to doing. When you are analyzing sentences that contain prepositional phrases, you need to first mark the parts of a prepositional phrase—the preposition, the object of the preposition, any adjectives within the phrase—so that you can analyze the whole phrase as a modifier within the sentence.

So, from now on your analysis of sentences will follow what we call the **order of analysis**. The order is phrases, clauses, principal elements, and modifiers. As you say the analysis aloud and mark the sentence, the order of analysis falls into two parts:

Part 1: Identify the *phrases*. (You will learn how to identify *clauses* later in *WOL Level 2*.)

Part 2: Identify the *principal elements* and *modifiers*.

After you read aloud the sentence to analyze, recite the following chant to help you remember this organizing principle: "The order of analysis is phrases, clauses, principal elements, modifiers."

Part 1: Identify Phrases

Winston paddled(to the island)
p adj op

a. (First, read the sentence aloud.) "Winston paddled to the island."

b. Chant: "The order of analysis is phrases, clauses, principal elements, modifiers."

c. "Are there any prepositional phrases?" (Choral response: "Yes, sir." Since there is one in this sentence, you can answer *yes.*)

d. "*To the island* is a prepositional phrase." (Since *to the island* is a prepositional phrase, put parentheses around the phrase.)

e. "*To* is the preposition." (Since *to* is a preposition, you can place a lowercase letter *p* underneath it.)
"*Island* is the object of the preposition." (Since *island* is a noun and is connected to the preposition, making it the object of the preposition, you can place the lowercase letters *op* underneath it.)

f. "*The* is an adjective."[2] (Since *the* tells *which* island, it is an adjective. You can draw a straight line down from the adjective, then a horizontal line toward the word it modifies, and then a straight line with an arrow pointing to *island*. Write *adj* in lowercase letters in the elbow opposite the line with the arrow.)

Part 2: Identify Principal Elements and Modifiers

S PV
Winston paddled (to the island)
p adj op

a. (Read the sentence again aloud.) "Winston paddled to the island."

b. "This is a sentence and it is declarative."

c. "This sentence is about *Winston*. So, Winston is the subject because it is what the sentence is about." (Since *Winston* is the subject, underline the word and place a capital letter *S* above it.)

d. "This sentence tells us that Winston *paddled*. So, *paddled* is the predicate because it is what the sentence tells us about *Winston*." (Since *paddled* tells us something about Winston, double underline the predicate and place a capital letter *P* above it.)

e. "It is a predicate verb because it shows action. There is no linking verb because predicate verbs do not need linking verbs." (Since *paddled* shows action, place a capital letter *V* to the right of the letter *P* above the predicate.)

2. The words *article adjective* can be substituted in place of the word *adjective*.

f. "*To the island* tells us *where* Winston paddled." (Since *to the island* tells *where* Winston paddled, you can draw a straight line down from the letter *p* that's under the preposition, then a horizontal line toward the word that it modifies, and then a straight line with an arrow pointing to *paddled*.)

g. "So, *to the island* is an adverbial element because it modifies a verb. It is an adverbial prepositional phrase." (Since the prepositional phrase is behaving like an adverb, write *adv* in lowercase letters in the elbow opposite the line with the arrow. Since the phrase is a prepositional phrase, you can write *prep* in lowercase letters directly below the *adv*, underneath the modifier line.)[E]

If you first identify and analyze in a sentence the prepositional phrases with their slender stems (the preposition) and their apples (the noun/pronoun as object of the preposition), you can identify the principal elements of the sentence more promptly.

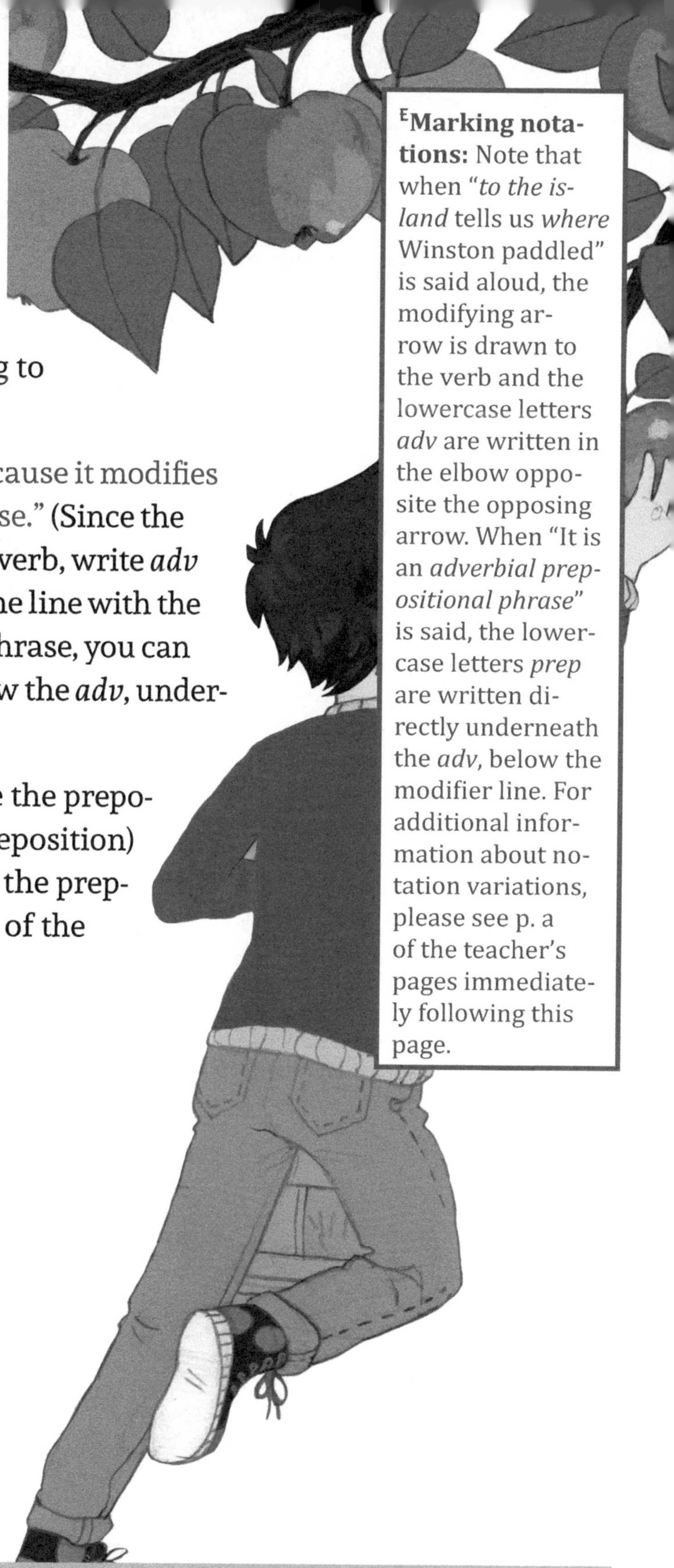

[E]**Marking notations:** Note that when "*to the island* tells us *where* Winston paddled" is said aloud, the modifying arrow is drawn to the verb and the lowercase letters *adv* are written in the elbow opposite the opposing arrow. When "It is an *adverbial prepositional phrase*" is said, the lowercase letters *prep* are written directly underneath the *adv*, below the modifier line. For additional information about notation variations, please see p. a of the teacher's pages immediately following this page.

Turn back to the illustration of the three siblings under an apple tree. Did you notice the wooden bench? Do you think the children are picking apples in the park or are they somewhere else? Where are apples usually grown? Have you ever picked apples?

Chapter 3: Prepositional Phrases—Adverbial

[E]From p. 67. **Notation variations:**

a. **Two or more adverbial elements:** If a sentence has more than one type of adverbial element, the modifier lines must be separated and not crossed. For example, in the sentence "Winston paddled to the island yesterday," the modifier lines do not cross one another. The modifier line for *yesterday* is written below the adverbial prepositional modifier line.

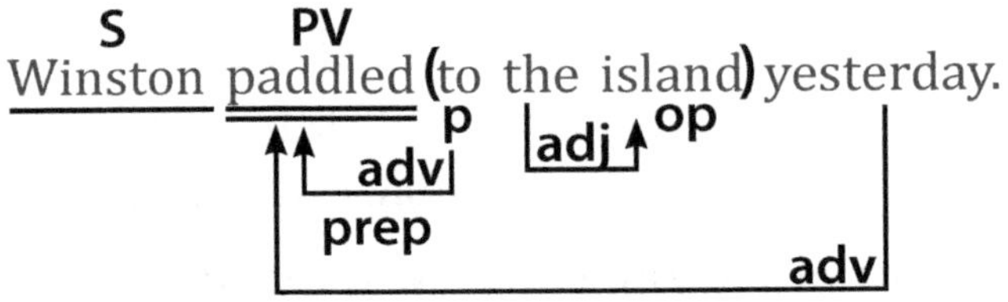

b. **Two or more adverbial prepositional phrases after the verb:** If a sentence has more than one adverbial prepositional phrase after the verb, then the modifier lines can be joined. For example, in the sentence "Winston paddled to the island in a sailboat," the modifier lines are joined. The lines become one line modifying the same verb: *paddled.*

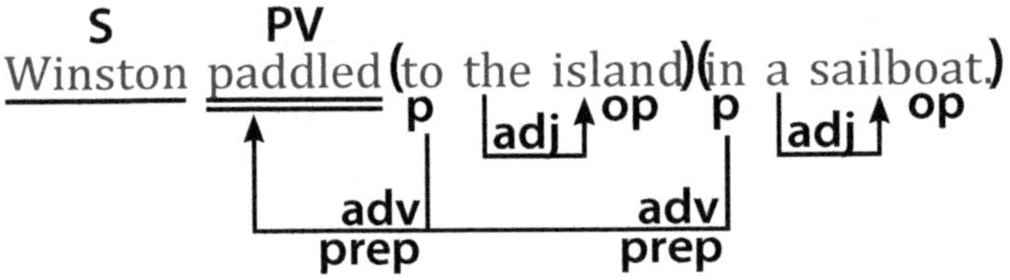

c. **Object pronouns as the object of the preposition:** If the object of the preposition is an object pronoun, the marking is the same as if the object of the preposition were a noun.

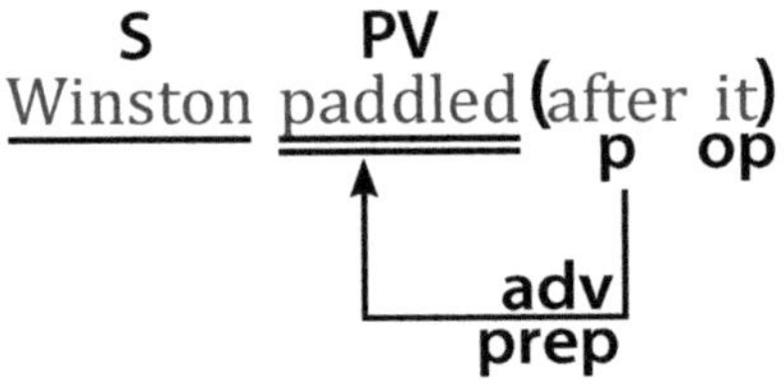

Notes

Well-Ordered Notes Introductory

Practice It

When the name of a month appears in a sentence, it is often part of a prepositional phrase, such as *in January*, *next October*, or *after December*. Therefore, this chapter provides an opportunity for the students to practice the order of the months and their abbreviations.

Write the months of the year in order on the board. Have the students chant them in order while marching in place. Review proper nouns and capitalizations.

Then, explain that an abbreviation shortens a word and ends with a period. Add the months' abbreviations on the board. Point out that months with four letters or fewer (May, June, and July) are not abbreviated.

Use mini whiteboards to reinforce the month abbreviations. Say a month and ask the students to write the abbreviation on their mini whiteboards. The students should hold up their mini whiteboards to show their answers. Continue until every month has been reviewed.

Example:

Teacher: "October."
Students write *Oct.*

January	Jan.	July	July
February	Feb.	August	Aug.
March	Mar.	September	Sept.
April	Apr.	October	Oct.
May	May	November	Nov.
June	June	December	Dec.

Analyze It

As a class, analyze the following sentences (*S* = subject; *PV* = predicate verb; *hv* = helping verb; *adv* = adverb; *adj* = adjective; *do* = direct object; *p* = preposition; *op* = object of the preposition; *prep* = prepositional phrase). Write the sentences on the board. Have the students analyze the sentences, reciting the analysis aloud using the following script. While the students recite, you will mark the sentence on the board.

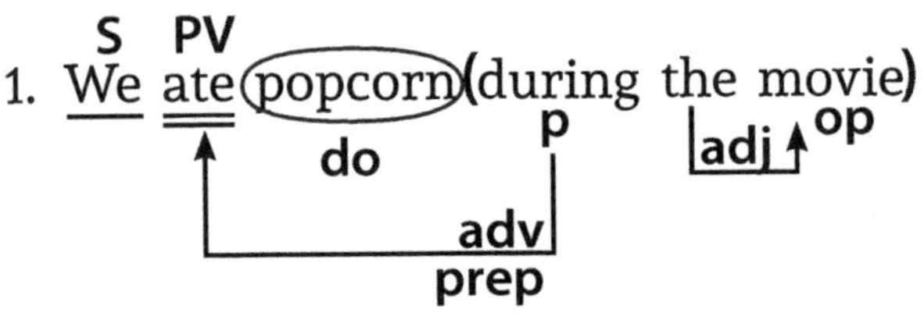

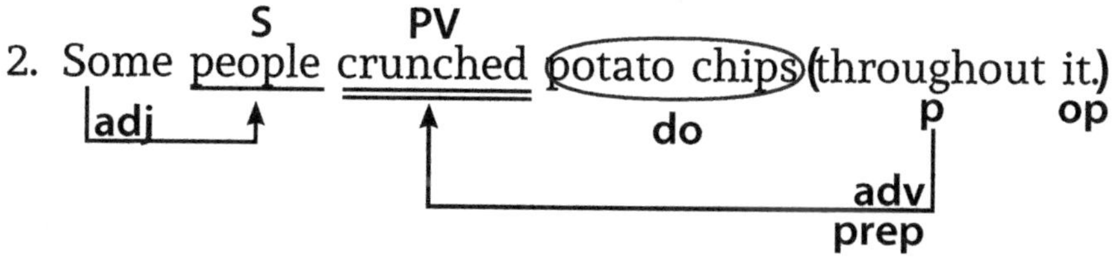

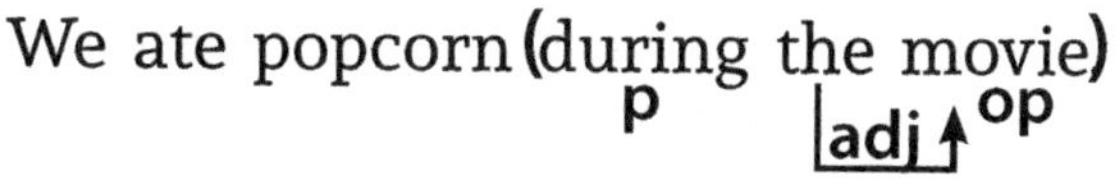

Part 1: Identify Phrases

a. (First, read the sentence aloud.) "We ate popcorn during the movie."

b. Chant: "The order of analysis is phrases, clauses, principal elements, modifiers."

c. "Are there any prepositional phrases?" (Choral response: "Yes, sir.")

d. "*During the movie* is a prepositional phrase." (Place parentheses around the prepositional phrase.)

e. "*During* is the preposition." (Place a lowercase *p* underneath the preposition.)

f. "*Movie* is the object of the preposition." (Place a lowercase *op* underneath the object of the preposition.)

g. "*The* is an adjective."[1] (Draw a straight line down from the adjective, then a horizontal line toward the word that it modifies, and then a straight line with an arrow pointing to the word it modifies. Write *adj* in lowercase letters in the elbow opposite the line with the arrow.)

Part 2: Identify Principal Elements and Modifiers

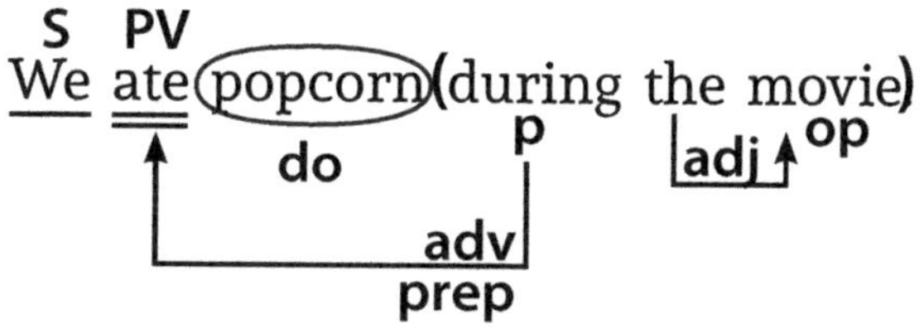

a. (Read the sentence aloud again.) "We ate popcorn during the movie."

b. "This is a sentence and it is declarative."

c. "This sentence is about *we*." (Underline the subject.) "So, *we* is the subject because it is what the sentence is about." (Place a capital letter *S* above the subject.)

d. "This sentence tells us that we *ate*." (Double underline the predicate.) "So, *ate* is the predicate because it is what the sentence tells us about *we*." (Place a capital letter *P* above the predicate.) "It is a

1. The words *article adjective* can be substituted in place of the word *adjective*.

predicate verb because it shows action." (Place a capital letter *V* to the right of the letter *P* above the predicate.) "There is no linking verb because predicate verbs do not need linking verbs."

e. "*Popcorn* tells us what we ate." (Draw a circle around the word.) "So, *popcorn* is an objective element because it completes the meaning of the action verb. It is a direct object because it tells *what* we ate." (Write *do* in lowercase letters beneath the direct object.)

f. "*During the movie* tells us when we ate." (Draw a straight line down from the letter *p* that's under the preposition, then a horizontal line toward the word that it modifies, and then a straight line with an arrow pointing to the word it modifies.) "So, *during the movie* is an adverbial element because it modifies a verb. It is an adverbial prepositional phrase." (Write *adv* in lowercase letters in the elbow opposite the line with the arrow. Write *prep* in lowercase letters directly below the *adv*, underneath the modifier line.)

For the analysis of the second sentence, adjust the script accordingly.

Notes

Introductory Lesson
Prepositional Phrases—Adverbial

The order of the lesson is: **Review It**, **Practice It**, **Learn It**, and **Analyze It**.

Review It: Challenge the students to rely less and less on the list of prepositions in their books each time they review the chant.

Review It

Can you name the forty-seven prepositions you have learned in this chapter? Learn the song and you will be able to say all of them by heart.

aboard	about	above	across	after
against	along	among	around	at
before	behind	below	beneath	beside
between	beyond	by	down	during
except	for	from	inside	in
into	near	of	off	on
out	outside	over	past	since
through	throughout	to	toward	under
up	until	upon	with	within
without	underneath			

Practice It: For this warm-up, see Well-Ordered Notes Introductory.

Learn It: This part of the lesson can be completed individually and then reviewed orally as a class.

Learn It

Knowing the prepositions will make it easier for you to find prepositional phrases in sentences. In the following sentences, find the prepositions and then put parentheses around the prepositional phrases.

Example: The dark gray clouds filled the sky (in the west).

1. The green banners decorated the gate (with school colors.)
2. Peggy is now playing soccer (with Heidi) (after school.)
3. The coach might run (with the team) tonight.
4. Unfortunately an unforeseen storm drove them (into the shelter.)

Analyze It

Analyze the following sentences (*S* = subject; *PV* = predicate verb; *hv* = helping verb; *adv* = adverb; *adj* = adjective; *do* = direct object; *p* = preposition; *op* = object of the preposition; *prep* = prepositional phrase).

> **Analyze It:** This is the essential part of the lesson. See Well-Ordered Notes Introductory.

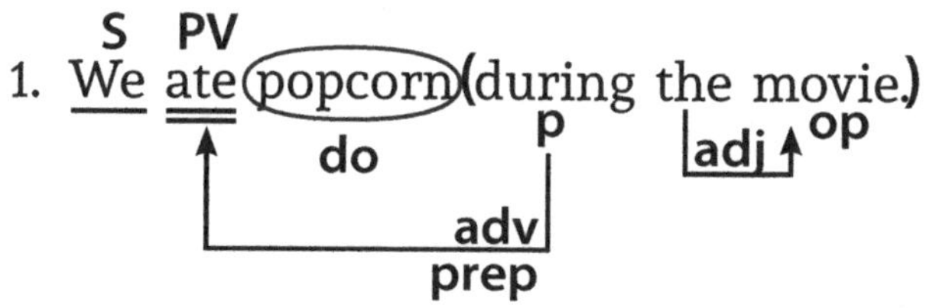

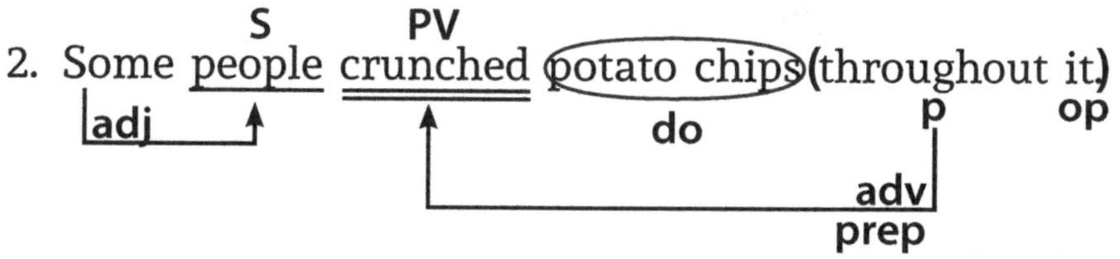

Introductory Practice
Prepositional Phrases—Adverbial

1. Analyze the following sentences (*S* = subject; *PV* = predicate verb; *hv* = helping verb; *adv* = adverb; *adj* = adjective; *do* = direct object; *p* = preposition; *op* = object of the preposition; *prep* = prepositional phrase).

   S hv PV
   a. We were swinging (at the playground.)
   p adj op
   adv prep

   S PV
   b. Earlier Grandpa Fred watched (us) (in the park.)
   adv do p adj op
   adv prep

   S PV
   c. The big boys hid (from the little boys) (after the game.)
   adj adj p adj adj op p adj op
   adv prep adv prep

   S PV
   d. Afterward the kids strolled together (to the ice cream store.)
   adj adv p adj adj op
   adv adv prep

2. What is a *preposition*? **A preposition is a part of speech used to show the relationship between certain words in a sentence.**

3. List nine prepositions that begin with the letter *a*.
   Answers may vary. All ten of the prepositions beginning with the letter *a* are listed here: aboard, about, above, across, after, against, along, among, around, at.

Notes

Well-Ordered Notes A

Practice It

Play Lightning, a review game that requires students to think quickly. Have the students stand beside their desks and be seated when they have constructed their prepositional phrases. To begin the game, say a preposition to the first student. He has five seconds to supply a prepositional phrase using that preposition. If he supplies a phrase, he may sit down; if not, he is to remain standing until you return to him. The Lightning review game is to be fast moving and light, so prepositions, which can show positional relationship to an object, work particularly well. Such prepositions are listed below.

Variation: Use a beanbag or some object in the classroom as a prop to help the students come up with a sentence containing a prepositional phrase (i.e., under: The beanbag is *under the desk*).

> **Fewer than Five:** A student can stand to give the first prepositional phrase, sit for the next, stand, sit, and so on. The student should not change her position unless she successfully gives the phrase. The idea is to review the prepositions quickly both to reinforce the concept and to enjoy playing with language.

Example:

Teacher: "beneath"
Student: "*beneath the bench*"

above	across	against
around	behind	below
beneath	beside	between
inside	in	into
near	out	outside
over	through	under
upon	with	within
without	underneath	

Analyze It

As a class, analyze the following sentences (*S* = subject; *PV* = predicate verb; *hv* = helping verb; *adv* = adverb; *adj* = adjective; *do* = direct object; *p* = preposition; *op* = object of the preposition; *prep* = prepositional phrase). Write the sentences on the board. Have the students analyze the sentences, reciting the analysis aloud using the following script. While the students recite, you will mark the sentence on the board.

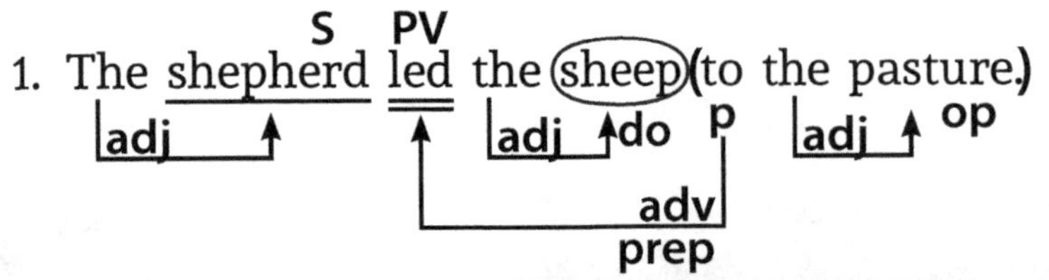

S PV

2. Foolishly the boy planned a mean trick (during the afternoon.)

adj, adj, adj, do, p, adj, op, adv, adv prep

The shepherd led the sheep (to the pasture.)

p, adj, op

Part 1: Identify Phrases

a. (First, read the sentence aloud.) "The shepherd led the sheep to the pasture."

b. Chant: "The order of analysis is phrases, clauses, principal elements, modifiers."

c. "Are there any prepositional phrases?" (Choral response: "Yes, sir.")

d. "*To the pasture* is a prepositional phrase." (Put parentheses around the phrase.)

e. "*To* is the preposition." (Place a lowercase *p* underneath the preposition.)

f. "*Pasture* is the object of the preposition." (Place a lowercase *op* underneath the object of the preposition.)

g. "*The* is an adjective."[1] (Draw a straight line down from the adjective, then a horizontal line toward the word that it modifies, and then a straight line with an arrow pointing to the word it modifies. Write *adj* in lowercase letters in the elbow opposite the line with the arrow.)

Part 2: Identify Principal Elements and Modifiers

S PV

The shepherd led the sheep (to the pasture.)

adj, adj, do, p, adj, op, adv prep

a. (Read the sentence aloud again.) "The shepherd led the sheep to the pasture."

b. "This is a sentence and it is declarative."

c. "This sentence is about *shepherd*." (Underline the subject.) "So, *shepherd* is the subject because it is what the sentence is about." (Place a capital letter *S* above the subject.)

d. "This sentence tells us that shepherd *led*." (Double underline the predicate.) "So, *led* is the predicate because it is what the sentence tells us about *shepherd*." (Place a capital letter *P* above the predicate.)

---

1. The words *article adjective* can be substituted in place of the word *adjective*.

"It is a predicate verb because it shows action." (Place a capital letter *V* to the right of the letter *P* above the predicate.) "There is no linking verb because predicate verbs do not need linking verbs."

e. "*Sheep* tells us what the shepherd led." (Draw a circle around the word.) "So, *sheep* is an objective element because it completes the meaning of the action verb. It is a direct object because it tells *what* the shepherd led." (Write *do* in lowercase letters beneath the direct object.)

f. "*To the pasture* tells us *where* the shepherd led." (Draw a straight line down from the letter *p* that's under the preposition, then a horizontal line toward the word that it modifies, and then a straight line with an arrow pointing to the word it modifies.) "So, *to the pasture* is an adverbial element because it modifies a verb. It is an adverbial prepositional phrase." (Write *adv* in lowercase letters in the elbow opposite the line with the arrow. Write *prep* in lowercase letters directly below the *adv*, underneath the modifier line.)

g. "*The* is an adjective."[2] (Draw a straight line down from the adjective, then a horizontal line toward the word that it modifies, and then a straight line with an arrow pointing to the word it modifies. Write *adj* in lowercase letters in the elbow opposite the line with the arrow.)

For the analysis of the second sentence, adjust the script accordingly.

2. The words *article adjective* can be substituted in place of the word *adjective*.

Notes

Lessons to Learn
Prepositional Phrases—Adverbial

A

The order of the lesson is: **Review It**, **Practice It**, **Learn It**, and **Analyze It**.

Review It: Sing/chant and review definitions as a class. Consider adding freshness by varying speed and volume or by asking individual students to paraphrase the meaning of a definition.

Review It

Prepositions are little words, but they are very important in our English language. What is a preposition? Can you name all the prepositions that begin with the letter *a*? What about listing the ones beginning with the letter *b*? What is a phrase? What is an object of the preposition?

Practice It: For this warm-up, see Well-Ordered Notes A.

Learn It: Students can write in their own books while a different volunteer corrects each sentence on the board.

Learn It

Each sentence below is missing two things that every sentence should have: a capital letter at the beginning and a period at the end. Since they contain at least one month of the year, these particular sentences are also missing something in the middle: a capital letter at the beginning of that proper noun. On the lines provided, correct all of the following sentences by rewriting them with the proper capitalization and punctuation.

Example: school begins in september
School begins in September.

1. the month of september has thirty days

   The month of September has thirty days.

2. april also has the same number of days as september

   April also has the same number of days as September.

3. remember the number of days in april is the same as in june

*R*emember the number of days in *A*pril is the same as in *J*une.

4. is the number of days in november the same as in june too

*I*s the number of days in *N*ovember the same as in *J*une too*?*

Analyze It

Analyze the following sentences (*S* = subject; *PV* = predicate verb; *hv* = helping verb; *adv* = adverb; *adj* = adjective; *do* = direct object; *p* = preposition; *op* = object of the preposition; *prep* = prepositional phrase).

1. The shepherd led the (sheep) (to the pasture)

S: shepherd; PV: led; The → adj; the → adj; sheep → do; to → p; the → adj; pasture → op; (to the pasture) → adv prep

2. Foolishly the boy planned a mean (trick) (during the afternoon)

S: boy; PV: planned; Foolishly → adv; the → adj; a → adj; mean → adj; trick → do; during → p; the → adj; afternoon → op; (during the afternoon) → adv prep

Analyze It: This is the essential part of the lesson. See Well-Ordered Notes A.

From the Sideline: Please note that these sentences complement the fable for this chapter, which you can find in the teacher's edition and in the PDF material.

Lessons to Practice A

Prepositional Phrases—Adverbial

1. Analyze the following sentences (*S* = subject; *PV* = predicate verb; *hv* = helping verb; *adv* = adverb; *adj* = adjective; *do* = direct object; *p* = preposition; *op* = object of the preposition; *prep* = prepositional phrase).

   S hv PV
   a. Lucy will not leave (for school) (without the note.)
   adv p op p adj op
   adv prep adv prep

   S PV
   b. Earlier she forgot the envelope (on the counter.)
   adv adj do p adj op
   adv prep

   S PV
   c. Mom reminded her again (about the note.)
   do adv p adj op
   adv prep

   S PV
   d. Cleverly she placed it (in the lunchbox.)
   adv do p adj op
   adv prep

2. On the lines provided, correct all of the following sentences by rewriting them with the proper capitalization and punctuation. Remember that the months of the year are proper nouns.

   a. gentle april showers often bring may flowers

   Gentle *April* showers often bring *May* flowers.

b. do goldenrods and sword lilies dot the august gardens

Do goldenrods and sword lilies dot the *A*ugust gardens?

c. yellow mums are also called painted daisies in september

***Y*ellow mums are also called painted daisies in *S*eptember.**

d. february displays her ice crystals and snow dainties

***F*ebruary displays her ice crystals and snow dainties.**

3. Imagine that at lunchtime Lucy finds the note she was looking for. Now write a sentence about it, being sure to include a prepositional phrase.

Lucy discovered the note in the lunchbox.

Well-Ordered Notes B

Practice It

Lead the class in the activity Stage a Sentence:

- Using four or five volunteers (or as many as are needed to represent each of the words in a sentence), have the students "stage" a sentence. Have two of the volunteers stand at the front of the room with enough space between them for another person to fit.
- Have one student hold up a tagboard strip with the first part of the sentence written on it, which you have prepared in advance (e.g., *He stared*).
- The next student holds up another tagboard strip with the rest of the prepositional phrase (e.g., *the window*) on it. Make sure this student is standing far enough away from the first student that another student will be able to stand between them.
- Then have three student volunteers stand to the side of the two students holding the parts of the sentence, each holding a tagboard strip with a different preposition (e.g., *out*, *in*, *at*) on it. (You'll want to make sure that the prepositions you choose will work with the two parts of the sentence.)
- Have the students holding the prepositions take turns standing between the students holding the two parts of the sentence. Discuss as a class how each preposition changes the meaning of the sentence (e.g., *He stared* ***out*** *the window*; *He stared* ***in*** *the window*; *He stared* ***at*** *the window*).
- Repeat this process with each of the following sentences.

> **Fewer than Five:** You can use labeled index cards or craft sticks to represent the two parts of the sentences and the prepositions.

1. The gray hawk flew ____________________ the branches. (above, under, around)
2. Uncle Ulysses hid it ____________________ the shutters. (inside, beneath, between)
3. Wildly Rex ran ____________________ the children. (toward, near, around)
4. Six cousins giggled ____________________ Rex. (at, behind, near)
5. The dog played ____________________ Uncle Ulysses. (with, beside, near)
6. Grandpa watched the children ____________________ the window. (from, under, through)

Analyze It

As a class, analyze the following sentences (*S* = subject; *PV* = predicate verb; *hv* = helping verb; *adv* = adverb; *adj* = adjective; *do* = direct object; *p* = preposition; *op* = object of the preposition; *prep* = prepositional phrase). Write the sentences on the board. Have the students analyze the sentences, reciting the analysis aloud using the following script. While the students recite, you will mark the sentence on the board.

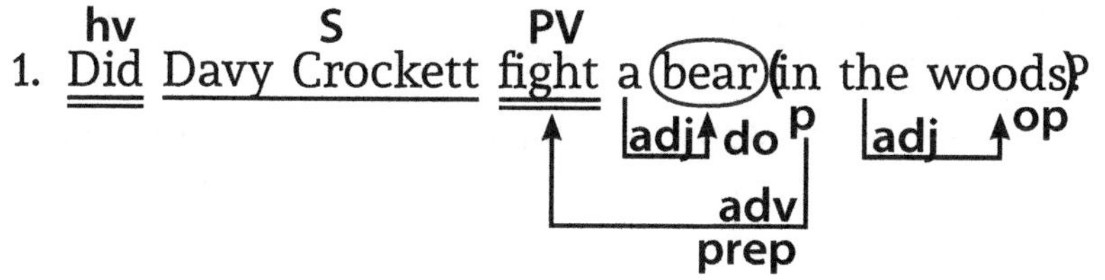

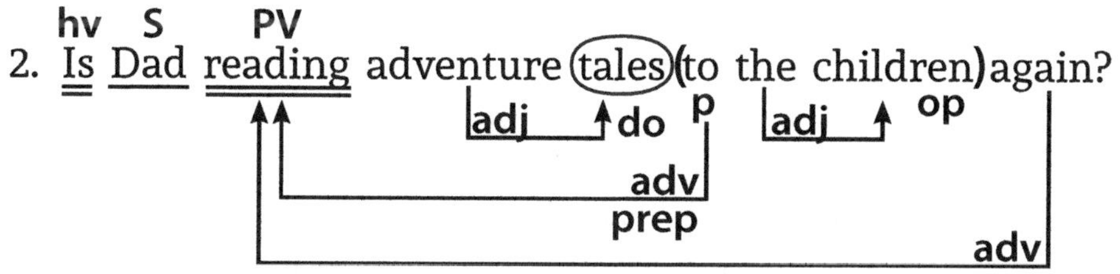

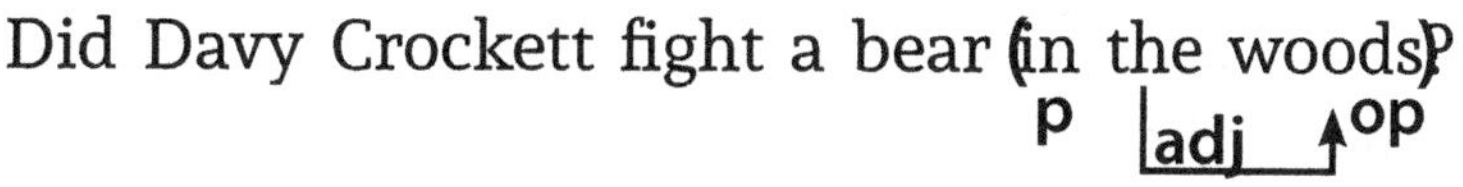

Part 1: Identify Phrases

a. (First, read the sentence aloud.) "Did Davy Crockett fight a bear in the woods?"

b. Chant: "The order of analysis is phrases, clauses, principal elements, modifiers."

c. "Are there any prepositional phrases?" (Choral response: "Yes, sir.")

d. "*In the woods* is a prepositional phrase." (Place parentheses around the prepositional phrase.)

e. "*In* is the preposition." (Place a lowercase *p* underneath the preposition.)

f. "*Woods* is the object of the preposition." (Place a lowercase *op* underneath the object of the preposition.)

g. "*The* is an adjective."[1] (Draw a straight line down from the adjective, then a horizontal line toward the word that it modifies, and then a straight line with an arrow pointing to the word it modifies. Write *adj* in lowercase letters in the elbow opposite the line with the arrow.)

Part 2: Identify Principal Elements and Modifiers

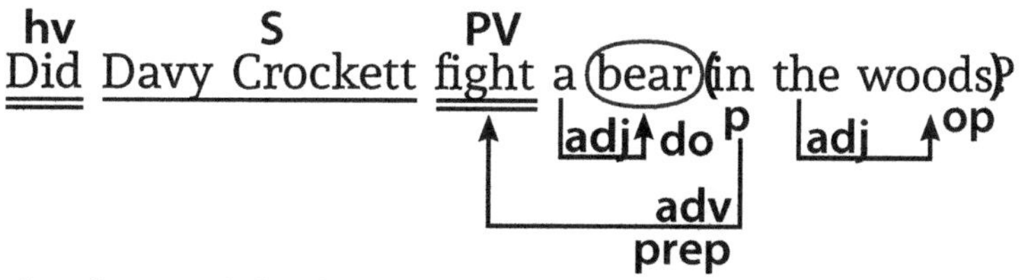

a. (Read the sentence aloud again.) "Did Davy Crockett fight a bear in the woods?"

b. "This is a sentence and it is interrogative."

1. The words *article adjective* can be substituted in place of the word *adjective*.

c. "This sentence is about *Davy Crockett*." (Underline the subject.) "So, *Davy Crockett* is the subject because it is what the sentence is about." (Place a capital letter *S* above the subject.)

d. "This sentence tells us that Davy Crockett *did fight*." (Double underline the helping verb and the predicate verb.) "So, *did fight* is the predicate because it is what the sentence tells us about *Davy Crockett*." (Place a capital letter *P* above the action verb.) "It is a predicate verb because it shows action." (Place a capital letter *V* to the right of the letter *P*.) "There is no linking verb because predicate verbs do not need linking verbs. *Did* is the helping verb." (Place a lowercase *hv* above the helping verb.)

e. "*Bear* tells us what Davy Crockett did fight." (Draw a circle around the word.) "So, *bear* is an objective element because it completes the meaning of the action verb. It is a direct object because it tells *what* Davy Crockett did fight." (Write *do* in lowercase letters beneath the direct object.)

f. "*In the woods* tells us *where* Davy Crockett did fight." (Draw a straight line down from the letter *p* that's under the preposition, then a horizontal line toward the word that it modifies, and then a straight line with an arrow pointing to the word it modifies.) "So, *in the woods* is an adverbial element because it modifies a verb. It is an adverbial prepositional phrase." (Write *adv* in lowercase letters in the elbow opposite the line with the arrow. Write *prep* in lowercase letters directly below the *adv*, underneath the modifier line.)

g. "*A* tells us *how many* bears." (Draw a straight line down from the adjective, then a horizontal line toward the word that it modifies, and then a straight line toward the word it modifies.) "So, *a* is an adjective element because it modifies a noun. It is an adjective."[2] (Write *adj* in lowercase letters in the elbow opposite the line with the arrow.)

For the analysis of the second sentence, adjust the script accordingly.

2. The words *article adjective* can be substituted in place of the word *adjective*.

Notes

Lessons to Learn
Prepositional Phrases—Adverbial

B

The order of the lesson is: **Review It**, **Practice It**, **Learn It**, and **Analyze It**.

Review It: Sing/chant and review definitions as a class.

Review It

Practice makes perfect. Can you answer the following questions?

What is a preposition?

What is an object of the preposition?

What is a phrase?

What are the forty-seven prepositions you've learned in this chapter?

Practice It: For this warm-up, see Well-Ordered Notes B.

Learn It: This part of the lesson can be an oral exercise completed while students mark their books individually. Write the sentences on the board.

From the Sideline: Here's an opportunity to point out to the students that while the months are always proper nouns, the seasons are not—spring, summer, autumn or fall, and winter. Exception: Seasons are capitalized when they are part of titles, as in Winter Olympics or Summer Clearance Sale.

Learn It

On the lines provided, correct all of the following sentences by rewriting them with the proper capitalization and punctuation. Remember that the months of the year are proper nouns.

Example: spring begins in march **_S_pring begins in _M_arch.**

1. january has thirty-one days

   _J_anuary has thirty-one days.

2. december and july both have as many days as january

   _D_ecember and _J_uly both have as many days as _J_anuary.

3. march and may have as many days as august and july

   _M_arch and _M_ay have as many days as _A_ugust and _J_uly.

4. curiously february only has twenty-eight days

Curiously *F*ebruary only has twenty-eight days.

5. february has twenty-nine days every four years

***F*ebruary has twenty-nine days every four years.**

Analyze It

> **Analyze It:** This is the essential part of the lesson. See Well-Ordered Notes B.

Analyze the following sentences (*S* = subject; *PV* = predicate verb; *hv* = helping verb; *adv* = adverb; *adj* = adjective; *do* = direct object; *p* = preposition; *op* = object of the preposition; *prep* = prepositional phrase).

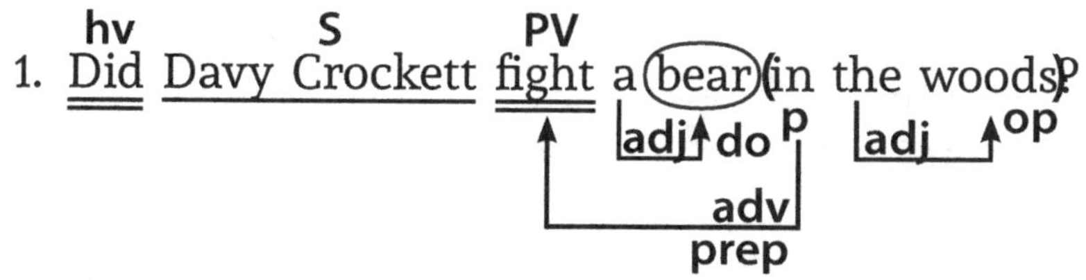

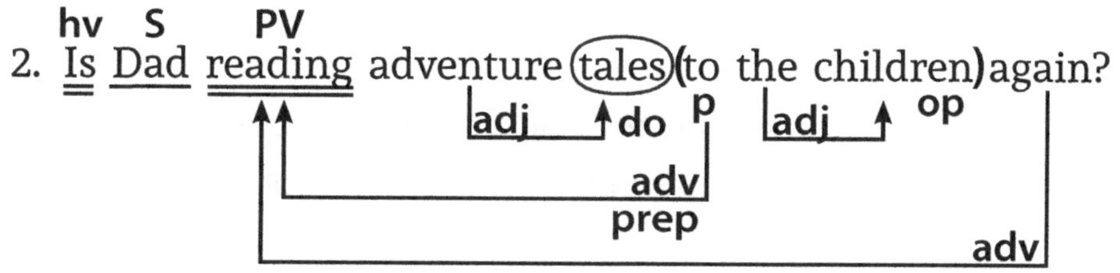

Lessons to Practice B
Prepositional Phrases—Adverbial

1. Analyze the following sentences (*S* = subject; *PV* = predicate verb; *hv* = helping verb; *adv* = adverb; *adj* = adjective; *do* = direct object; *p* = preposition; *op* = object of the preposition; *prep* = prepositional phrase).

   a. The farmer carefully drove the old tractor (from the barn) (to the field)

   S: farmer; PV: drove; adj: The; adv: carefully; adj: the, old; do: tractor; p: from; adj: the; op: barn; p: to; adj: the; op: field; adv prep: from the barn; adv prep: to the field

   b. Quickly four mice scurried (through the grass) (to the farm shed)

   S: mice; PV: scurried; adv: Quickly; adj: four; p: through; adj: the; op: grass; p: to; adj: the, farm; op: shed; adv prep: through the grass; adv prep: to the farm shed

   c. Two mice families live (underneath the front porch.)

   S: families; PV: live; adj: Two, mice; p: underneath; adj: the, front; op: porch; adv prep: underneath the front porch

   d. Those tiny, furry creatures ate all the seeds (under the birdfeeder.)

   S: creatures; PV: ate; adj: Those, tiny, furry; adj: all, the; do: seeds; p: under; adj: the; op: birdfeeder; adv prep: under the birdfeeder

2. On the lines provided, correct all of the following sentences by rewriting them with the proper capitalization and punctuation. Remember that the months of the year are proper nouns.

   a. are the trees and flowers really sleeping in january

   Are the trees and flowers really sleeping in January?

b. november winds blow oak leaves and ash leaves about

November winds blow oak leaves and ash leaves about.

c. tulips and crocuses grow in march

Tulips and crocuses grow in March.

d. lily pads and water lilies float on the quiet pond in july

Lily pads and water lilies float on the quiet pond in July.

3. List nine prepositions that *do not* begin with the letter *a*.

Answers will vary. The following is a list of the prepositions that students have learned in this chapter that do not begin with the letter *a*:

before	**down**	**near**	**since**	**upon**
behind	**during**	**of**	**through**	**with**
below	**except**	**off**	**throughout**	**within**
beneath	**for**	**on**	**to**	**without**
beside	**from**	**out**	**toward**	**underneath**
between	**inside**	**outside**	**under**	
beyond	**in**	**over**	**up**	
by	**into**	**past**	**until**	

Well-Ordered Notes C

Practice It

Lead the class in the activity Construct It. Divide the class into groups of two or three students. Each group should choose someone to be the group's recorder. Have each group use the following prepositions to come up with as many sentences as they can. The recorder should write on a piece of paper all of the group's sentences. Have each group share the sentences they construct.

Example: ***to the store***
Aunt Gabby went *to the store* alone.

to Philadelphia	after school	over the bridge
near the fountain	at the station	inside the tunnel
since yesterday	under the porch	through the yard
on Wednesday	above the trees	without them

Analyze It

As a class, analyze the following sentences (*S* = subject; *PV* = predicate verb; *hv* = helping verb; *adv* = adverb; *adj* = adjective; *do* = direct object; *p* = preposition; *op* = object of the preposition; *prep* = prepositional phrase). Write the sentences on the board. Have the students analyze the sentences, reciting the analysis aloud using the following script. While the students recite, you will mark the sentence on the board.

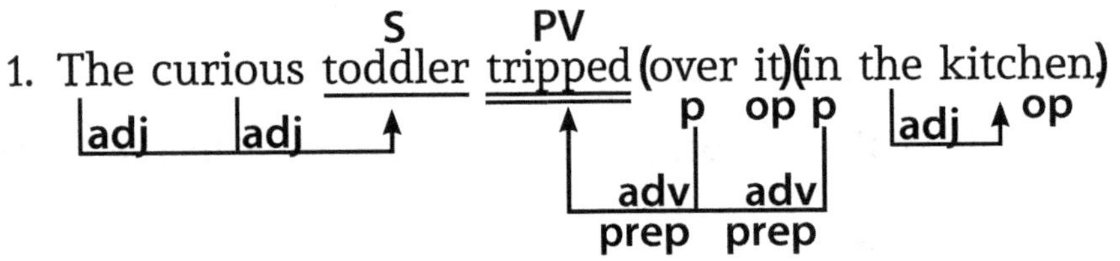

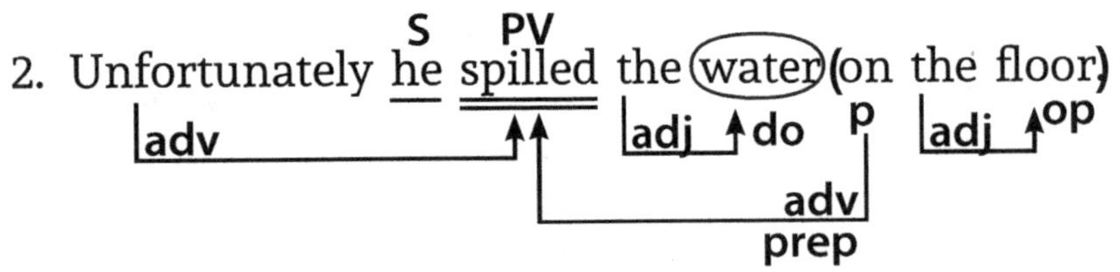

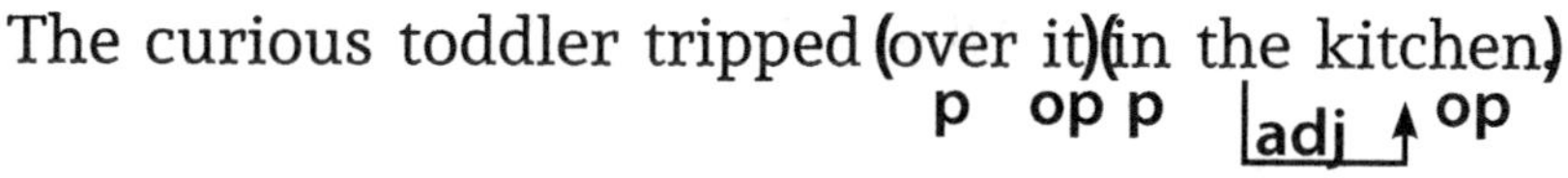

Part 1: Identify Phrases

a. (First, read the sentence aloud.) "The curious toddler tripped over it in the kitchen."

b. Chant: "The order of analysis is phrases, clauses, principal elements, modifiers."

c. "Are there any prepositional phrases?" (Choral response: "Yes, sir.")

d. "*Over it* is a prepositional phrase." (Place parentheses around the prepositional phrase.)

e. "*Over* is the preposition." (Place a lowercase *p* underneath the preposition.)

f. "*It* is the object of the preposition." (Place a lowercase *op* underneath the object of the preposition.)

g. "*In the kitchen* is a prepositional phrase." (Place parentheses around the prepositional phrase.)

h. "*In* is the preposition." (Place a lowercase *p* underneath the preposition.)

i. "*Kitchen* is the object of the preposition." (Place a lowercase *op* underneath the object of the preposition.)

j. "*The* is an adjective."[1] (Draw a straight line down from the adjective, then a horizontal line toward the word that it modifies, and then a straight line with an arrow pointing to the word it modifies. Write *adj* in lowercase letters in the elbow opposite the line with the arrow.)

Part 2: Identify Principal Elements and Modifiers

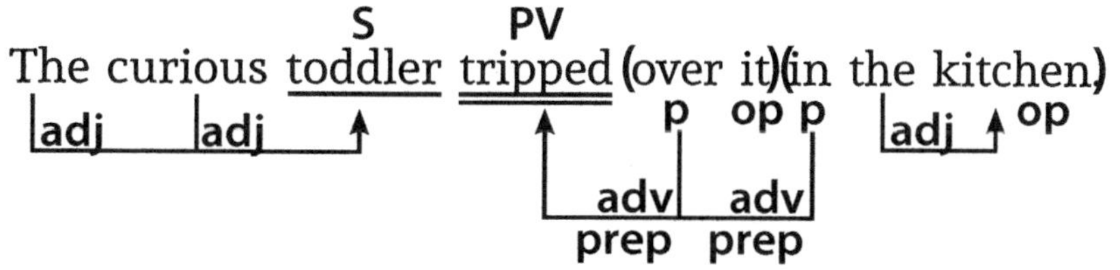

a. (Read the sentence aloud again.) "The curious toddler tripped over it in the kitchen."

b. "This is a sentence and it is declarative."

c. "This sentence is about *toddler*." (Underline the subject.) "So, *toddler* is the subject because it is what the sentence is about." (Place a capital letter *S* above the subject.)

d. "This sentence tells us that toddler *tripped*." (Double underline the predicate.) "So, *tripped* is the predicate because it is what the sentence tells us about *toddler*." (Place a capital letter *P* above the predicate.)

e. "It is a predicate verb because it shows action." (Place a capital letter *V* to the right of the letter *P* above the predicate.) "There is no linking verb because predicate verbs do not need linking verbs."

---

1. The words *article adjective* can be substituted in place of the word *adjective*.

f. "*In the kitchen* tells us *where* the toddler tripped." (Draw a straight line down from the letter *p* that's under the preposition, then a horizontal line toward the word that it modifies, and then a straight line with an arrow pointing to the word it modifies.) "So, *in the kitchen* is an adverbial element because it modifies a verb. It is an adverbial prepositional phrase." (Write ***adv*** in lowercase letters in the elbow opposite the line with the arrow. Write ***prep*** in lowercase letters directly below the ***adv***, underneath the modifier line.)

g. "*Over it* tells us *how* the toddler tripped." (Draw a straight line down from the letter *p* that's under the preposition, then a horizontal line toward the word that it modifies, and then a straight line with an arrow pointing to the word it modifies. This line connects to the other adverbial modifying line.) "So, *over it* is an adverbial element because it modifies a verb. It is an adverbial prepositional phrase." (Write ***adv*** in lowercase letters in the elbow opposite the line with the arrow. Write ***prep*** in lowercase letters directly below the ***adv***, underneath the modifier line.)

h. "*Curious* tells us *what kind* of toddler." (Draw a straight line down from the adjective, then a horizontal line toward the word that it modifies, and then a straight line with an arrow pointing to the word it modifies.) "So, *curious* is an adjective element because it modifies a noun. It is an adjective." (Write ***adj*** in lowercase letters in the elbow opposite the line with the arrow.)

i. "*The* is an adjective."[2] (Draw a straight line down from the adjective, then a horizontal line toward the word that it modifies and connect the line to the modifying line of the word *curious*. The two modifying lines are joined and point, with a straight line, toward the word they modify. Write *adj* in lowercase letters in the elbow opposite the line with the arrow.)

2. The words *article adjective* can be substituted in place of the word *adjective*.

Notes

Lessons to Learn
Prepositional Phrases—Adverbial

C

The order of the lesson is: **Review It**, **Practice It**, **Learn It**, and **Analyze It**.

Review It: Sing/chant and review definitions as a class. Have the students stand beside their desks while singing/chanting.

Review It

Reviewing is the backbone of learning new terms, so let's review some of the things you've learned:

Define a preposition.

List all of the prepositions that begin with the letter *t*.

What is a phrase?

What is the definition of object of the preposition?

Practice It: For this warm-up, see Well-Ordered Notes C.

Learn It: This part of the lesson can be an individual written exercise that is reviewed orally as a class when finished.

From the Sidelines: The answers provided in the teacher's edition are suggestions. Students may think of other possible prepositions for each sentence.

Learn It

1. Prepositions are connector words. They join the noun or pronoun that is the object of the preposition with another word in the sentence. Fill in the missing preposition in each of the following sentences to show the relationship between the object of the preposition and the verb.

Example: The raindrops dripped ___down___ the windowpane.

a. Several sailboats are anchored ___**in**___ the bay.

b. Peggy walked ___**under**___ an umbrella during the April showers.

c. Many children watched the rain ___**beneath**___ the shelter.

d. Suddenly Rex escaped ___**from**___ the house.

e. Heidi called ___**for**___ the naughty dog.

f. She slipped ___**in**___ a puddle.

g. Fortunately Theo grabbed Rex ______by______ the collar.

h. Theo dried Rex ______with______ an old beach towel.

2. Write a sentence about Rex and the rainy day, being sure to include a prepositional phrase in your sentence.

Rex ran out into the rain again!

____

Analyze It

Analyze the following sentences (*S* = subject; *PV* = predicate verb; *hv* = helping verb; *adv* = adverb; *adj* = adjective; *do* = direct object; *p* = preposition; *op* = object of the preposition; *prep* = prepositional phrase).

Analyze It: This is the essential part of the lesson. See Well-Ordered Notes C.

1. The curious toddler tripped (over it)(in the kitchen)

S: toddler; PV: tripped; adj, adj; p, op, p, adj, op; adv prep, adv prep

2. Unfortunately he spilled the water (on the floor)

S: he; PV: spilled; adv; adj, do; p, adj, op; adv prep

Lessons to Practice

Prepositional Phrases—Adverbial

C

1. Analyze the following sentences (*S* = subject; *PV* = predicate verb; *hv* = helping verb; *adv* = adverb; *adj* = adjective; *do* = direct object; *p* = preposition; *op* = object of the preposition; *prep* = prepositional phrase).

S PV
a. Yesterday Grandma Lola bought (peaches) (from the market)
adv do p adj op
adv prep

S hv PV
b. She is baking peach (pies) (in the kitchen) (for the boys.)
adj do p adj op p adj op
adv prep adv prep

S hv PV
c. Later Mom will sell the (pies) (at the bake sale) (for the team.)
adv adj do p adj op p adj op
adv prep adv prep

S hv PV
d. The basketball team is raising (money) (for new jerseys.)
adj adj do p adj op
adv prep

2. What is a *preposition*? **A preposition is a part of speech used to show the relationship between certain words in a sentence.**

3. Imagine the whole team is at the next game and they are all wearing their new jerseys. Write a sentence about it, being sure to use a prepositional phrase in it.

The team wore the new jerseys for the next game.

Notes

Review It: Sing/chant and review definitions as a class.

Review It

Answer the following review questions:

What is a preposition?

What is a phrase?

What is an object of the preposition?

Can you name the forty-seven prepositions you have learned in this chapter?

Learn It: Play Lightning, a review game that requires students to think quickly. Have students use some of the prepositions in a sentence.

Learn It

Play the review game Lightning by using some of the following prepositions in sentences. Your teacher will say a preposition, and a student has five seconds to think of an object of the preposition.

Example:

Teacher: "to"
Student: *"to the shore"*

aboard	about	above	across	after
against	along	among	around	at
before	behind	below	beneath	beside
between	beyond	by	down	during
except	for	from	inside	in
into	near	of	off	on
out	outside	over	past	since
through	throughout	to	toward	under
up	until	upon	with	within
without	underneath			

Write a sentence using one of the prepositional phrases from the Lightning game.

The fisherman dragged the boat *to the shore.*

1. Analyze the following sentences: (*S* = subject; *PV* = predicate verb; *hv* = helping verb; *adv* = adverb; *adj* = adjective; *do* = direct object; *p* = preposition; *op* = object of the preposition; *prep* = prepositional phrase).

    S PV
    a. Icicles slowly dripped (from the rooftop) outside.
    adv p adv adj op
    prep adv

    S hv PV
    b. The tiny snowflakes are dancing (around the pine tree) too.
    adj adj p adv adj adj op
    prep adv

    hv S PV
    c. Did Jack Frost paint (on the window) those icy designs?
    p adv adj op adj adj do
    prep

    S hv PV
    d. Now the winter winds are blowing the snow (into giant drifts.)
    adv adj adj adj do p adv adj op
    prep

2. On the lines provided, correct all of the following sentences by rewriting them with the proper capitalization and punctuation. Remember that the months of the year are proper nouns.

    a. red and white roses creep along the wooden fences in june

    Red and white roses creep along the wooden fences in June.

b. orange pumpkins grow rounder during colorful october

Orange pumpkins grow rounder during colorful October.

c. will may be robed in her flowered dress once more

W*ill *M*ay be robed in her flowered dress once more*?

d. holly and ivy are twisted into wreaths in december

***H*olly and ivy are twisted into wreaths in *D*ecember.**

3. List nine prepositions. **Answers will vary. See the preposition list on p. 79.**

What do you think of when you imagine a snowy winter day? Do you think of crunching snow? Or do you think of using the frosty air to blow clouds of smoke like a dragon? Elinor Wylie writes of a walk with a friend on a snowy day. What kinds of shoes do they imagine they wear to walk in the snow?

Velvet Shoes

by Elinor Wylie (1885–1928)

Let us walk in the white snow
In a soundless space;
With footsteps quiet and slow;
At a tranquil pace,
Under veils of white lace.

I shall go shod in silk,
And you in wool,
White as a white cow's milk,
More beautiful
Than the breast of a gull.

We shall walk through the still town
In a windless peace;
We shall step upon white down
Upon silver fleece,
Upon softer than these.

We shall walk in velvet shoes;
Wherever we go
Silence will fall like dews
On white silence below,
We shall walk in the snow.[1]

tranquil: peaceful
pace: speed at which something moves
shod: wearing shoes

down: soft feathers from the underside of a goose or duck
fleece: the soft wool of a sheep
velvet: a soft, thick, expensive fabric

1. Elinor Wylie, "Velvet Shoes," In *Favorite Poems Old and New*, ed. Helen Ferris (New York: Doubleday & Company, Inc., 1957), pp. 66–67.

Questions to Ponder

1. What does "I shall go shod in silk and you in wool" mean?
2. To what white things is the snow compared?
3. Which words in the poem describe the silence of the snowy scene?
4. To whom do you think the speaker is speaking in the poem?

Extras: Please note that the teacher's pages for this chapter include more material for extra practice, a quiz, and another Lessons to Enjoy section with discussion questions and activities. All this material, in reproducible form, is also included in the PDF that accompanies the textbook.

From the Sideline: For possible answers to these discussion questions, see p. a of the teacher's pages. For even more suggestions for discussion and for enrichment activities related to the poem, see p. b.

Lessons to Enjoy—Poem

Questions to Ponder

1. What does "I shall go shod in silk and you in wool" mean?

   The speaker of the poem imagines that walking in the snow will be like wearing shoes made of silk for her and shoes made of wool for her friend. Both images capture the whiteness, the softness, the quiet, and the beauty of the pristine, deep snow.

2. To what white things is the snow compared?

   The snow is compared to veils of white lace, white cow's milk, the breast of a gull, white down, and silver fleece. Not only are all of these things white, but they are also smooth, soft, and silky. For contrast, ask the students to think of white things that would not fit with these images, such as a blinding white light, a white cast over a broken bone, or a white marble statue. Point out that none of the images Wylie chooses to include in the poem indicate cold. The friends walking through the snow together are comfortable and warm. They are enjoying the walk—not rushing through a freezing night longing for the heat of a hearth fire. The white images have been selected carefully to convey a certain tone.

3. Which words in the poem describe the silence of the snowy scene?

   Some of the words that describe the silence are "a soundless space," "still town," "windless peace," "silence will fall like dews on white silence below." Rhythm, rhyme, and other sound effects are central in poetry, as they are in music, so it is unusual that a poem is so suggestive of silence. You can emphasize the quiet of the scene described by asking the students to read parts of the poem in a whisper.

4. To whom do you think the speaker is speaking in the poem?

   Answers will vary. It's unclear to whom the poet is speaking, but the language of the poem seems to indicate that the "I" and "you" in the poem are close friends. They are comfortable in the silence together. Encourage the students to imagine the friendship between these two people. Students may suggest that they love nature. It is clear in the poem that the two friends like to be together and don't need to be doing anything in particular. They are tuned in to the beauty around them, and it is enhanced by their being together.

Well-Ordered Notes—Poem

Read

- Read the poem slowly aloud to the students. Listen to a musical or choral version of the poem, such as Randall Thompson's "Velvet Shoes" sung by a descant choir (available at https://www.youtube.com/watch?v=mfkcL4P5ZNw).
- Ask the students to memorize their favorite stanza from the poem.

Retell

- Discuss the poem using the provided questions.
- Read the poem aloud slowly, removing all the prepositional phrases. Here is what remains when you take out the prepositional phrases, including all the prepositions, objects of prepositions, and adjectives modifying those objects:
  (Stanza 1) Let us walk.
  (Stanza 2) I shall go shod, and you.
  (Stanza 3) We shall walk. We shall step.
  (Stanza 4) We shall walk: wherever we go, silence will fall. We shall walk.
  Discuss the importance of prepositional phrases to the images and sounds of the poem, and ask the students to identify their favorite prepositional phrase.

Record

- Have the students paint a winter scene using watercolors. Once their paintings have dried, the students can copy the last stanza of the poem across the snowy picture or write a winter poem of their own, using velvet shoes as a theme.

Practice Sheet
Prepositional Phrases—Adverbial **ANSWERS**

Analyze the following sentences (*S* = subject; *PV* = predicate verb; *hv* = helping verb; *adv* = adverb; *adj* = adjective; *do* = direct object; *p* = preposition; *op* = object of the preposition; *prep* = prepositional phrase).

S PV
1. The little girls played (with the dollhouse) (during the rainy morning.)
adj adj p adj op p adj adj op
adv prep adv prep

S PV
2. Suddenly the sun shone brightly (through the window.)
adj adv p adj op
adv adv prep

S PV
3. Then a little brown bird sang (from the top branches.)
adj adj adj p adj adj op
adv adv prep

hv S PV
4. May we go (to the zoo) (after lunch?)
p adj op p op
adv prep adv prep

S hv PV
5. First they must put the (dolls) away (before the trip.)
adv adj do p adj op
adv
adv prep

hv S PV
6. Can Theo come (to the zoo) too?
p adj op
adv prep
adv

S hv PV
7. Mom will pack fruit snacks (for us)
adj do p op
adv prep

S PV
8. Peggy took (from the closet) the big backpack
p adj op adj adj do
adv prep

S PV
9. Lucy skipped (through the kitchen) (to the garage)
p adj op p adj op
adv prep adv prep

S PV
10. Theo carried the family camera (to the van)
adj adj do p adj op
adv prep

Quiz
Prepositional Phrases—Adverbial ANSWERS

1. Analyze the following sentences (*S* = subject; *PV* = predicate verb; *hv* = helping verb; *adv* = adverb; *adj* = adjective; *do* = direct object; *p* = preposition; *op* = object of the preposition; *prep* = prepositional phrase).

S hv hv PV
a. The girls will be harmonizing (in the choir)(at school) tomorrow.
adj p adj op p op
adv prep adv prep adv

S hv PV
b. We are singing (songs)(on the risers)(in the cafeteria)
do p adj op p adj op
adv prep adv prep

S hv PV
c. Uncle Ulysses will take (pictures)(with the big camera)
do p adj adj op
adv prep

S PV
d. Father invited the (neighbors)(for dessert)(after the school concert)
adj do p op p adj adj op
adv prep adv prep

2. What is a *preposition*?

A preposition is a part of speech used to show the relationship between certain words in a sentence.

3. List nine prepositions that *do not* begin with the letter *a*.

______________ ______________ ______________

______________ ______________ ______________

______________ ______________ ______________

Answers will vary. The following is a list of all of the prepositions from this chapter that do not begin with the letter *a*:

before	behind	below	beneath	beside
between	beyond	by	down	during
except	for	from	inside	in
into	near	of	off	on
out	outside	over	past	since
through	throughout	to	toward	under
up	until	upon	with	within
without	underneath			

Honesty is the best policy is a good motto to live by. This fable by Aesop speaks to the importance of telling the truth no matter what. In the tale, you will meet a Shepherd Boy, a Villager, a sheep, and a Wolf. Beware of crying "wolf" when attention is all that you are seeking.

The Shepherd Boy and the Wolf

by Aesop

dull: boring

A Shepherd Boy tended his Master's sheep near a dark forest not far from the village. In a short while, he found life in the pasture very dull. "I'm so bored," he thought. "I have nothing to do to amuse myself except for talking to my dog. The sheep are not interesting at all. They chew grass with a stupid look all day long."

One day as the Shepherd Boy sat watching the sheep and the quiet forest, he thought up a plan to have some fun. His Master had told him to call for help should a Wolf attack the flock, and the Villagers would drive it away. So now, though he had not seen anything that even looked like a Wolf, he ran toward the village shouting, "Help! Wolf! Help!"

Just as he expected, the Villagers heard the cry and dropped their work, running in great excitement to the pasture. But when they got there they found the Boy rolling on the ground. "I sure tricked you!" the Boy laughed. "Oh, that was a good joke!"

A few days later, the Shepherd Boy again shouted, "Wolf! Wolf!" The Villagers ran to help him, only to be laughed at again, "I got you twice!" the Boy laughed.

Then one evening as the sun was setting behind the forest, and the shadows of the forest were creeping over the pasture, a Wolf really did spring from the trees and fall upon the sheep. Its greedy teeth flashed in the gloom.

In terror, the Boy ran toward the village shouting, "Wolf! Help! Wolf!"

But though the Villagers heard the cry, they ignored it. "Wolf indeed!" they scoffed.

scoffed: mocked

"Please help!" shouted the Boy. "I'm telling the truth! Wolf!"

But the Villagers said, "He cannot fool us again."

The Wolf killed a great many of the sheep and then slipped silently into the forest.

Moral: Liars are not believed even when they speak the truth.[1]

Questions to Ponder

1. What did the Shepherd Boy lie about?
2. What does "to amuse myself" mean?
3. How many times were the Villagers fooled?
4. What happened at the end of the fable?
5. What does the expression "crying wolf" mean?

1. Aesop, "The Shepherd Boy and The Wolf," *Writing and Rhetoric Book 1: Fable*, by Paul Kortepeter (Camp Hill, PA: Classical Academic Press, 2013), pp. 93–94.

Lessons to Enjoy—Fable

Questions to Ponder

1. What did the Shepherd Boy lie about?

   He discovered that he could end his boredom and loneliness by calling the Villagers to help him defend the flock from a pretend Wolf attack. By raising a false alarm, he lies to the villagers, leading them to believe something untrue.

2. What does "to amuse myself" mean?

   To amuse oneself is to not need anyone else for entertainment, or to be engaged with an activity or thought. Your students are at an age when "I'm bored" or "What can I do?" are common refrains. The boy in the story was bored and amused himself for foolish reasons. Ask students to share clever ways in which they amuse themselves. You may want to have them consider particular situations that call for amusing oneself, such as having a lazy afternoon or waiting in the doctor's office, in a restaurant, for the rain to stop, etc.

3. How many times were the Villagers fooled?

   The Villagers were fooled twice before they ran out of patience and decided to ignore the boy.

4. What happened at the end of the fable?

   A Wolf really attacked but the Shepherd Boy got no help because no one would believe him. Unfortunately, the Wolf was the only winner in the end. The Villagers lost many sheep that day. Ask the students if they think this loss of the sheep was entirely the boy's fault. Do they also blame the Villagers for not coming to help? Or do they think the Villagers were right in ignoring the boy's third cry for help after he had lied to them?

5. What does the expression "crying wolf" mean?

   "Crying wolf" means to give a false alarm. Discuss with the students how this may happen in real life and why people may do it. What is the end result? For example, some children might pretend to be sick to avoid going to school. Their parents may fall for it once, but when it becomes apparent that they really are not sick, they have damaged their parents' trust in them. The next time they really don't feel well, they may find themselves in school anyway.

Well-Ordered Notes—Fable

Read

- ◇ Encourage the students' enjoyment of the fable by reading it aloud with dramatic expression for the Boy's and the Villagers' spoken parts.
- ◇ Have students sing/chant the definition of a fable (Fable, 1–14).

Retell

- ◇ Discuss the fable using the provided questions.
- ◇ Divide the class into three groups. Have each group perform its own version of the fable, adding creative details or dialogue. For example, they could give the wolf or the sheep some lines to say.

Record

- ◇ Have the students draw a scene from the fable and write captions for their drawings.

Fable Sentences

Prepositional Phrases—Adverbial ANSWERS

Analyze the following sentences (*S* = subject; *PV* = predicate verb; *hv* = helping verb; *adv* = adverb; *adj* = adjective; *do* = direct object; *p* = preposition; *op* = object of the preposition; *prep* = prepositional phrase).

```
     S        PV
1. A shepherd tended the (sheep) (near a dark forest)
   adj                   adj do   p    adj adj   op
                    adv prep
```
1. A shepherd tended the **sheep** (near a dark forest)

```
   S  hv       PV
2. He did not like the (work) (in the afternoon)
          adv       adj do    p   adj       op
                 adv prep
```
2. He did not like the **work** (in the afternoon)

```
                    S   PV
3. The mischievous boy thought (of a plan)
   adj adj                      p adj op
                 adv prep
```
3. The mischievous boy thought (of a plan)

mischievous: naughty

```
   S  PV
4. He cried (for help)
             p   op
   adv prep
```
4. He cried (for help)

```
                  S  hv      PV
5. The deceptive boy did not see the (Wolf) (during the day)
   adj adj               adv     adj do     p      adj op
                 adv prep
```
5. The deceptive boy did not see the **Wolf** (during the day)

deceptive: misleading

```
                           S        PV
6. Quickly the earnest Villagers hurried (to him)
   adv     adj adj                        p  op
                 adv prep
```
6. Quickly the earnest Villagers hurried (to him)

earnest: serious, sincere

S PV
7. The naughty boy laughed (at the people.)
adj adj ↑ p adj ↑ op
adv prep

S PV
8. Next the troublesome boy yelled (for help) again.
adj adj ↑ p op
adv adv prep adv

troublesome: annoying

S PV
9. The angry people ignored the cry.
adj adj ↑ adj ↑ do

S PV
10. Unfortunately the wolf devoured the sheep.
adj ↑ adj ↑ do
adv

From the Sideline: Regulate time. Use a timer to help students complete a task in a timely fashion. Sometimes a timer can be used for individual students to complete a task during independent work time. Don't let the slowest student dictate the pace of a class.

Chapter 4

Introductory Prepositional Phrases[A]

In the morning when you put on your shoes, do you put on one sock and one shoe and then put on the second sock and second shoe? Or do you put both socks on first before putting on your shoes? While it's obviously important that you not put a sock on over a shoe, the order in which you put on your socks and then your shoes isn't really all that important. It's up to you what order you do it in. Prepositional phrases are kind of like socks and shoes: When they behave like adverbs, as they often do, they can be put in a different order in a sentence. For instance, an author might put the prepositional phrase at the beginning of the sentence or at the end or even in the middle. *In this chapter*, we will continue our study of adverbial prepositional phrases. We might even say that we will continue *in this chapter* our study of adverbial prepositional phrases. We could also say that we will continue our study of adverbial prepositional phrases *in this chapter*. Do you get the idea?

[A]Ask two students to come to the front of the room and put on a pair of shoes. Have one student put on one sock first and then one shoe while the other student puts on both socks first and then both shoes. Connect this analogy to the placement of prepositional phrases, noting that a writer can place prepositional phrases in a number of positions within a sentence for emphasis without altering the basic meaning of the sentence.

Ideas to Understand[B]

An adverbial prepositional phrase behaves like an adverb even though the phrase is made up of several words. Most of the sentences we studied in the previous chapter included such phrases placed *after* the verb, a common position for the phrase because it functions as an adverb telling *where*, *when*, or *how* the verb does its action. In this chapter, you will learn that sometimes, for emphasis, a writer places a prepositional phrase at the beginning of the sentence. When it is in that position it is called an **introductory prepositional phrase** because it introduces the subject and the verb. A comma is often used after the introductory prep-

[B]Write on the board the passage from "The Wild Wood," chapter 3 in *The Wind in the Willows* by Kenneth Grahame (see p. 92). There is a more complete version of the chapter in The Curious Child's Literary Appendix.

ositional phrase to separate it from the principal elements. That way it receives more attention than it would if placed after the verb.

In the following excerpt from his book *The Wind in the Willows*, Kenneth Grahame uses two introductory adverbial prepositional phrases, "In the winter time" and "During the short day," to describe Rat's day in winter.

> In the winter time the Rat slept a great deal, retiring early and rising late. During his short day he sometimes scribbled poetry or did other small domestic jobs about the house; and, of course, there were always animals dropping in for a chat, and consequently there was a good deal of storytelling and comparing notes on the past summer and all its doings.[1]

By using prepositional phrases at the beginning of two of his sentences, Grahame emphasizes that these particular activities happened on Rat's winter days and not during the summer. When an adverbial prepositional phrase is placed at the beginning of a sentence, more attention is drawn to it than when it is placed after the verb. If an author wants to emphasize the *how*, *when*, or *where* of a verb, she may choose to use an introductory prepositional phrase. Whether placed at the start of the sentence or after the verb, neither position is more correct than the other for an adverbial prepositional phrase; the writer gets to choose.

Off the Shelf: The animals' adventures in *The Wind in the Willows* started out as bedtime stories that Kenneth Grahame told his young son. After Grahame put them together as a novel in 1908, one of its biggest fans was Theodore Roosevelt, who was the president of the United States at the time. A children's novel that a president can love—give it a try! You may fall in love with Mole, Rat, Toad, and Badger too.

From the Sideline: In this chapter, you will always use commas after introductory prepositional phrases to help students master the rules. You may want to point out that in this excerpt Grahame doesn't use commas after the phrases. You can use this to explain how experienced writers often make choices about the placement of punctuation. In this case, the phrases are so short that Grahame chooses to skip the commas.

[C]Play the appropriate CD tracks/audio files and have students sing/chant along. Remind students to commit the songs to memory by listening to these tracks/files at other times as well.

Terms to Remember[C]

Do you have the most common prepositions all memorized yet? When you have mastered the preposition list, identifying a prepositional phrase in a sentence will be as easy as . . . well, as putting on your socks and shoes!

Preposition *(1–16)*

A preposition *(a preposition)*
is a part of speech *(is a part of speech)*
used to show the relationship
between certain words in a sentence *(in a sentence)*. *(Repeat.)*

---

1. Kenneth Grahame "The Wild Wood," *The Wind in the Willows* (New York: The New American Library, Inc., 1969), pp. 56–57.

List of Prepositions *(1–17)*

Aboard, about, above, across, after, against, along, among, around
Preposition Words
Before, behind, below, beneath, beside, between, beyond, at, by
Preposition Words
Down, during, except, for, from, inside, in, into, near
Preposition Words
Of, off, on, out, outside, over, past, since, through
Preposition Words
Throughout, to, toward,
Under, up, until,
Upon, with, within,
Without, underneath
Preposition Words
Preposition Words
Preposition Words!

Object of the Preposition *(1–19)*

The object of the preposition
The object of the preposition
is the noun or pronoun
after the preposition. *(Repeat.)*

Sentences to Analyze [D]

Make sure that you review the order of analysis chant: "The order of analysis is phrases, clauses, principal elements, modifiers." Remember that when you analyze sentences you need to complete the steps in the following order:

Part 1: Identify Phrases (Clauses will be included later.)

Part 2: Identify Principal Elements and Modifiers

Keep in mind that wherever prepositional phrases are located in a sentence, parentheses should be placed around them before you analyze the sentence. That way it is easier to identify

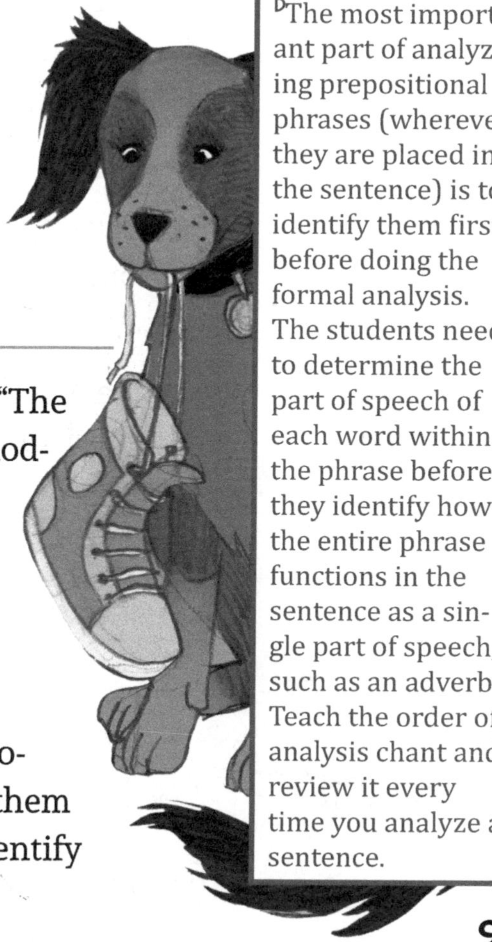

[D] The most important part of analyzing prepositional phrases (wherever they are placed in the sentence) is to identify them first before doing the formal analysis. The students need to determine the part of speech of each word within the phrase before they identify how the entire phrase functions in the sentence as a single part of speech, such as an adverb. Teach the order of analysis chant and review it every time you analyze a sentence.

what the sentence is about (subject) and what the subject is doing (predicate verb). As you learned in chapter 3, all the markings are first written beneath the phrase; then, you go on to analyze the principal elements of the sentence and the modifiers. As you neatly mark the sentence, say the analysis aloud.

Part 1: Identify Phrases

(In the morning) Winston paddled along.
p   adj   op

a. (First, read the sentence aloud.) "In the morning, Winston paddled along."

b. "The order of analysis is phrases, clauses, principal elements, modifiers."

c. "Are there any prepositional phrases?" (Since there is one in this sentence, you can answer yes.)

d. "*In the morning* is a prepositional phrase." (Since *in the morning* is a prepositional phrase, put parentheses around it.)

e. "*In* is the preposition." (Since *in* is a preposition, you can place a lowercase letter *p* underneath it.)

f. "*Morning* is the object of the preposition." (Since *morning* is connected to the preposition and is therefore the object of the preposition, you can place the lowercase letters *op* underneath it.)

g. "*The* is an adjective."[2] (Since *the* tells which morning, it is an adjective. You can draw a straight line down from the adjective, then a horizontal line toward the word it modifies, and then a straight line with an arrow pointing to *morning*. Write *adj* in lowercase letters in the elbow opposite the line with the arrow.)

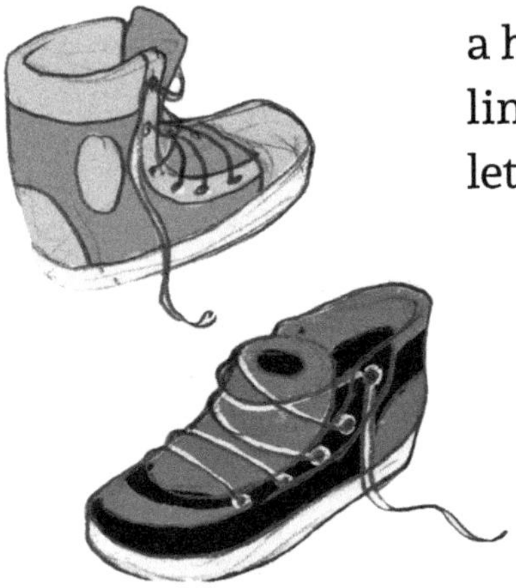

2. The words *article adjective* can be substituted in place of the word *adjective*.

Part 2: Identify Principal Elements and Modifiers

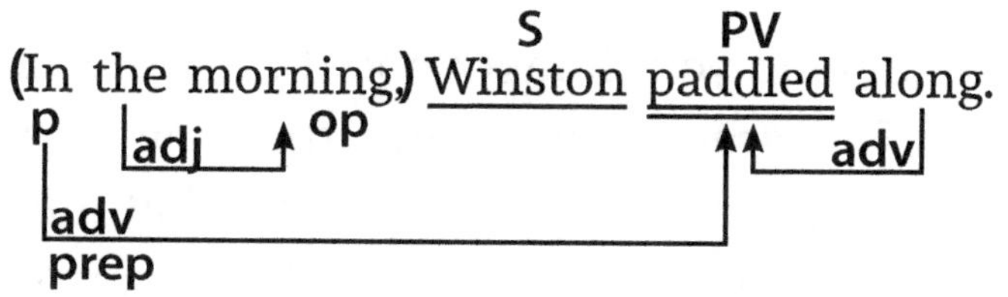

a. (Read the sentence again aloud.) "In the morning, Winston paddled along."

b. "This is a sentence and it is declarative."

c. "This sentence is about *Winston*. So, Winston is the subject because it is what the sentence is about." (Since *Winston* is the subject, underline the word and place a capital letter *S* above it.)

d. "This sentence tells us that Winston *paddled*. So, *paddled* is the predicate because it is what the sentence tells us about *Winston*." (Since *paddled* tells us something about Winston, double underline the predicate and place a capital letter *P* above it.)

e. "It is a predicate verb because it shows action. There is no linking verb because predicate verbs do not need linking verbs." (Since *paddled* shows action, place a capital letter *V* to the right of the letter *P* above the predicate.)

f. "*Along* tells us *where* Winston paddled. So, *along* is an adverbial element that modifies a verb. It is an adverb." (Since *along* is modifying where Winston is paddling, draw a straight line down from the adverb, then a horizontal line toward the word that it modifies, and then a straight line with an arrow pointing to the word it modifies. Place a lowercase *adv* in the elbow opposite the line with the arrow.)

g. "*In the morning* tells us *when* Winston paddled." (Since *in the morning* tells when Winston paddled, you can draw a straight line down from the letter *p* that's under the preposition, then a horizontal line toward the word that it modifies, and then a straight line with an arrow pointing to *paddled*.)

h. "So, *in the morning* is an adverbial element because it modifies a verb. It is an adverbial prepositional phrase." (Since the prepositional phrase is behaving like an adverb, write *adv* in lowercase letters in the elbow opposite the line with the arrow. Since the phrase

[E] For additional information about notation variations, please see p. a of the teacher's pages.

is a prepositional phrase, you can write *prep* in lowercase letters directly below the *adv*, underneath the modifier line.)[E]

In the previous chapter, you thought about prepositional phrases as apples and stems: The preposition is the little stem, and the noun or object of the preposition is the fruit. Now you see that the little stem can be attached to the branch in different places. When you are writing, you can choose where to put a prepositional phrase in your sentence for the best effect. *For greater emphasis*, the prepositional phrase comes at the beginning of the sentence. You can also put the prepositional phrase somewhere after the verb *in the more common position*. (Oh, look at those two sentences! What do you see?)

Notes

Chapter 4: Introductory Prepositional Phrases

[E]From p. 96. Marking notations:

a. **The flow of saying and writing the analysis:** When "in the morning, Winston paddled along" is said aloud, the modifying arrow is drawn to the verb and the lowercase letters *adv* are written in the opposite elbow of the opposing arrow. When "It is an adverbial prepositional phrase" is said, a lowercase *prep* is written underneath *adv*.

b. **Modifying line is drawn from the preposition:** Remember, the modifying line always comes from the lowercase *p* (preposition) no matter where the prepositional phrase is in the sentence. This reinforces that it is a prepositional phrase and not an object phrase. Therefore *do not* draw the line from the *op* (object of the preposition).

c. **Modifier lines are distinct and separate—before and after the verb:** If a sentence has more than one adverbial prepositional phrase before and one after the verb, then the modifier lines are distinct and separate. They are not to be joined under the verb, but they both have modifying lines pointing to the verb. For example, in the sentence "In the morning, Winston paddled along to the island," the modifier lines are not joined under the verb *paddled*.

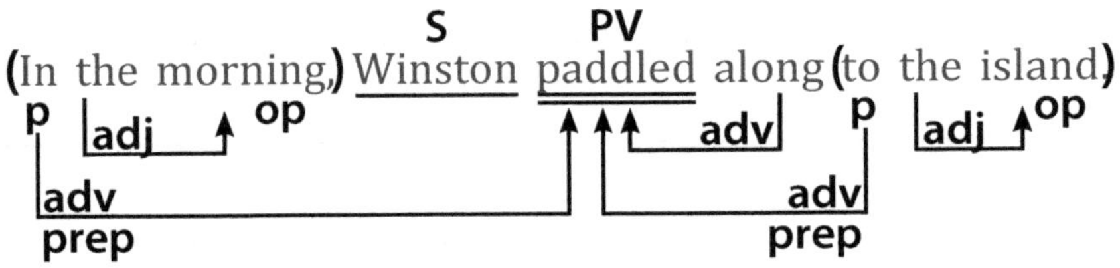

Notes

Well-Ordered Notes Introductory

Practice It

Play the game To the Board to have students practice using introductory prepositional phrases in sentences. Divide the students into two teams for this relay. Have one representative from each team stand at the board. Say one of the following introductory prepositional phrases (or come up with your own) to the students and then say "write." Each representative will construct a sentence using the phrase. The winner receives a point for his team for being the first to construct a sentence. Another point is rewarded for a neatly and correctly composed sentence with an introductory prepositional phrase (one or both of the students at the board can receive this). Insist on legible writing, and reinforce the proper usage of punctuation and capital letters. Just because it is a race doesn't mean that sloppy work is acceptable.

Variation: Give the students a topic, such as Valentine's Day or spring break, and ask them to write as many separate sentences about it as they can, using the introductory prepositional phrases provided.

Example:

Teacher: "Against the wall."
Student #1: "*Against the wall,* the team waited patiently."
Student #2: "*Against the wall,* the girls ate their lunches."

At a distance	During breakfast	On an island
Throughout the day	With a shovel	Across the field
Since yesterday	Between the two doors	

Analyze It

As a class, analyze the following sentences (*S* = subject; *PV* = predicate verb; *hv* = helping verb; *adv* = adverb; *adj* = adjective; *do* = direct object; *p* = preposition; *op* = object of the preposition; *prep* = prepositional phrase). Write the sentences on the board. Have the students analyze the sentences, reciting the analysis aloud using the following script. While the students recite, you will mark the sentence on the board.

S PV
1. (At the soccer game) Winston ordered a hamburger.
p adj adj op adj do
adv
prep

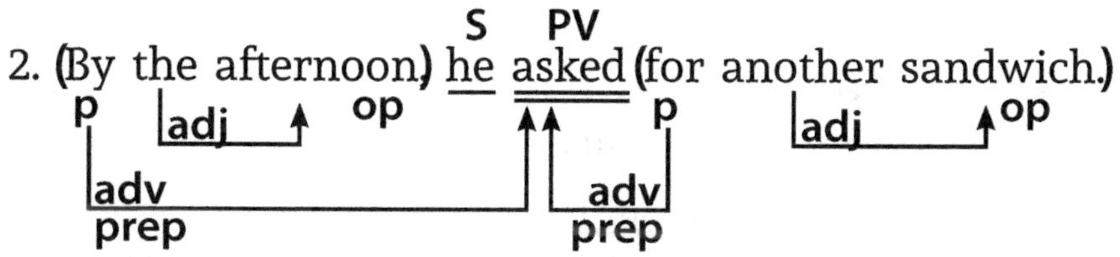

Part 1: Identify Phrases

a. (First, read the sentence aloud.) "At the soccer game, Winston ordered a hamburger."

b. Chant: "The order of analysis is phrases, clauses, principal elements, modifiers."

c. "Are there any prepositional phrases?" (Choral response: "Yes, sir.")

d. "*At the soccer game* is a prepositional phrase." (Place parentheses around the prepositional phrase.)

e. "*At* is the preposition." (Place a lowercase *p* underneath the preposition.)

f. "*Game* is the object of the preposition." (Place a lowercase *op* underneath the object of the preposition.)

g. "*Soccer* tells us *what kind* of game." (Draw a straight line down from the adjective, then a horizontal line toward the word that it modifies, and then a straight line with an arrow pointing to the word it modifies.) "So, *soccer* is an adjective element because it modifies a noun. It is an adjective." (Write *adj* in lowercase letters in the elbow opposite the line with the arrow.)

h. "*The* is an adjective."[1] (Draw a straight line down from the adjective, then a horizontal line toward the word that it modifies and connect the line to the modifying line of the word *soccer*. The two modifying lines are joined and point, with a straight line, toward the word they modify. Write *adj* in lowercase letters in the elbow opposite the line with the arrow.)

Part 2: Identify Principal Elements and Modifiers

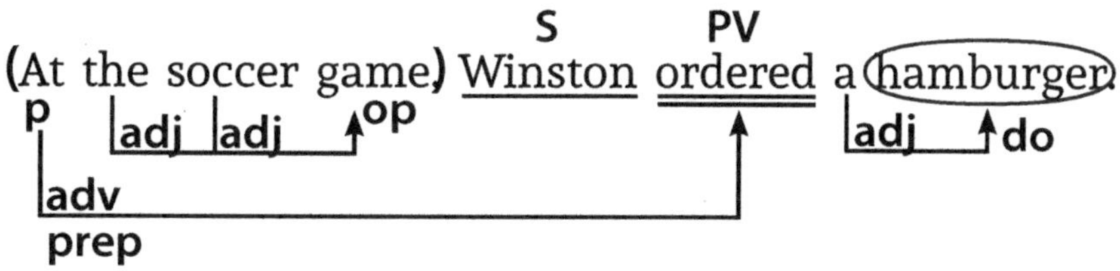

1. The words *article adjective* can be substituted in place of the word *adjective*.

a. (Read the sentence aloud again.) "At the soccer game, Winston ordered a hamburger."

b. "This is a sentence and it is declarative."

c. "This sentence is about *Winston*." (Underline the subject.) "So, *Winston* is the subject because it is what the sentence is about." (Place a capital letter *S* above the subject.)

d. "This sentence tells us that Winston *ordered*." (Double underline the predicate.) "So, *ordered* is the predicate because it is what the sentence tells us about *Winston*." (Place a capital letter *P* above the predicate.) "It is a predicate verb because it shows action." (Place a capital letter *V* to the right of the letter *P* above the predicate.) "There is no linking verb because predicate verbs do not need linking verbs."

e. "*Hamburger* tells us what Winston ordered." (Draw a circle around the word.) "So, *hamburger* is an objective element because it completes the meaning of the action verb. It is a direct object because it tells *what* Winston ordered." (Write *do* in lowercase letters beneath the direct object.)

f. "*A* is an adjective."[2] (Draw a straight line down from the adjective, then a horizontal line toward the word that it modifies, and then a straight line with an arrow pointing to the word it modifies. Write *adj* in lowercase letters in the elbow opposite the line with the arrow.)

g. "*At the soccer game* tells us *where* Winston ordered." (Draw a straight line down from the letter *p* that's under the preposition, then a horizontal line toward the word that it modifies, and then a straight line with an arrow pointing to the word it modifies.) "So, *at the soccer game* is an adverbial element because it modifies a verb. It is an adverbial prepositional phrase." (Write *adv* in lowercase letters in the elbow opposite the line with the arrow. Write *prep* in lowercase letters directly below the *adv*, underneath the modifier line.)

For the analysis of the second sentence, adjust the script accordingly.

2. The words *article adjective* can be substituted in place of the word *adjective*.

Notes

Introductory Lesson
Introductory Prepositional Phrases

The order of the lesson is: **Review It**, **Practice It**, **Learn It**, and **Analyze It**.

Review It: When reciting or singing the grammar definitions, the students should move around the room. The preposition song is a great song to march to as you review.

Review It

Did you know that in the English language there are more than 100 prepositions? Most of them are not used very often, so for now you have to memorize only the most common ones. Recite all forty-seven of them.

Practice It: For this warm-up, see Well-Ordered Notes Introductory.

Learn It: After the students complete the lesson in their books individually, review it together orally.

Learn It

You learned in *WOL1A* that a sentence is a group of words expressing a complete thought. You also know that to be complete, the sentence needs both a subject and a predicate, the principal elements. A group of words that looks like a sentence, starting with a capital letter and ending with a period, is not a sentence if it is missing either a subject or a predicate—or both. Then it is called a **fragment**. You should avoid fragments in your writing.

Determine if the following groups of words are sentences or fragments and on the lines provided write *sentence* or *fragment* as appropriate.

Example: ___fragment___ "Around the grayish-blue, rusty bike carrier." (This is a fragment since it does not have a subject and predicate.)

1. ___fragment___ On the old, yellow bicycle.
2. ___sentence___ Near the tall tower, the birds nested.
3. ___fragment___ Later after the girls' bike ride.
4. ___sentence___ Outside she cried.
5. ___fragment___ Throughout the ten miles of trails.
6. ___sentence___ Suddenly Lucy hiccuped.

Analyze It

Analyze the following sentences (*S* = subject; *PV* = predicate verb; *hv* = helping verb; *adv* = adverb; *adj* = adjective; *do* = direct object; *p* = preposition; *op* = object of the preposition; *prep* = prepositional phrase).

> **Analyze It:** This is the essential part of the lesson. See Well-Ordered Notes Introductory.

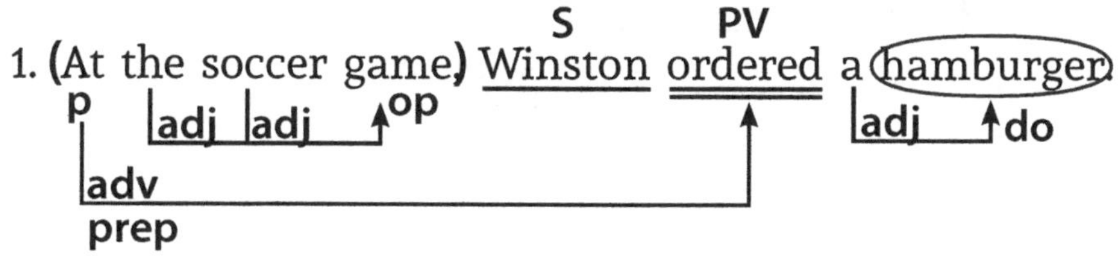

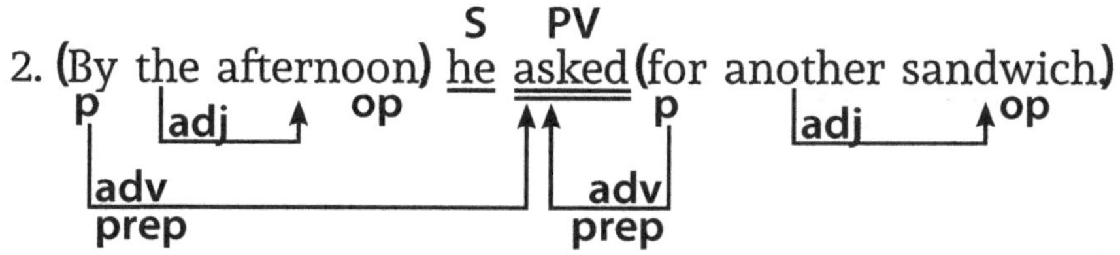

Introductory Practice

Introductory Prepositional Phrases

1. Analyze the following sentences (*S* = subject; *PV* = predicate verb; *hv* = helping verb; *adv* = adverb; *adj* = adjective; *do* = direct object; *p* = preposition; *op* = object of the preposition; *prep* = prepositional phrase).

S hv PV
a. (After the chores,) Dad might take all the neighbor (kids) (for ice cream.)
p adj op adj adj adj do p op
adv prep adv prep

S PV
b. (Along the wall,) the neighbors watched (for them.)
p adj op adj p op
adv prep adv prep

S PV
c. (Behind the garage,) the boys stored the (tools.)
p adj op adj adj do
adv prep

S PV
d. (Into the minivan,) Dad loaded five hungry (children.)
p adj op adj adj do
adv prep

2. What is a *preposition*?

A preposition is a part of speech used to show the relationship between certain words in a sentence.

3. Imagine that you are going for ice cream with your friends after doing chores. With that in mind, complete the phrase for each preposition listed, and then write a sentence that includes an introductory prepositional phrase.

Example: over __the railroad tracks__
Sentence: *Over the railroad tracks,* **the van wheels rumbled.**

a. at ________ **the ice cream parlor** ________

Sentence: **At the ice cream parlor, the kids ordered chocolate chip cookie dough ice cream in cones.**

b. between ________ **bites** ________

Sentence: **Between bites, they chattered about the hard work.**

Well-Ordered Notes A

Practice It

Play Around the Class. Write the following prepositions on five index cards: *at, after, before, during, throughout*. Have the students stand beside their desks. Have each student draw one card with a preposition written on it and use it to begin a sentence with an introductory prepositional phrase. (Have the student immediately return the card to you so that other students will have the same selection from which to choose.)

If a student is having a hard time thinking of an object of the preposition, provide her with one of the options listed below. When the student completes a sentence, she may be seated; if she cannot come up with a sentence in five seconds, she remains standing until you ask for her sentence.

> **From the Sideline:** This is a lively activity that should be quick. Remember to select students in a random popcorn fashion to encourage students to be ready.

Example:

A student selects the card labeled *during*.
Student: "*During* the tennis match, I lost my program."

tennis match	track meet	snowstorm
holiday parade	lunch	piano recital
basketball game	church potluck	flag ceremony
musical	band concert	school program

Analyze It

As a class, analyze the following sentences (*S* = subject; *PV* = predicate verb; *hv* = helping verb; *adv* = adverb; *adj* = adjective; *do* = direct object; *p* = preposition; *op* = object of the preposition; *prep* = prepositional phrase). Write the sentences on the board. Have the students analyze the sentences, reciting the analysis aloud using the following script. While the students recite, you will mark the sentence on the board.

S PV
1. (With axes,) the older boys split the wood (into pieces.)
p op adj adj adj do p op
adv prep adv prep

S PV
2. (Inside the family room,) the girls built a fire (in the fireplace.)
p adj adj op adj adj do p adj op
adv prep adv prep

(With axes,) the older boys split the wood (into pieces.)
p op p op

> **From the Sideline:** You'll notice that the question about conjunctions is not included in this script. From this point on, the conjunction question will appear only if there is, indeed, a conjunction in the sentence.

Part 1: Identify Phrases

a. (First, read the sentence aloud.) "With axes, the older boys split the wood into pieces."

b. Chant: "The order of analysis is phrases, clauses, principal elements, modifiers."

c. "Are there any prepositional phrases?" (Choral response: "Yes, sir.")

d. "*Into pieces* is a prepositional phrase." (Put parentheses around the prepositional phrase.)

e. "*Into* is the preposition." (Place a lowercase *p* underneath the preposition.)

f. "*Pieces* is the object of the preposition." (Place a lowercase *op* underneath the object of the preposition.)

g. "*With axes* is a prepositional phrase." (Put parentheses around the prepositional phrase.)

h. "*With* is the preposition." (Place a lowercase *p* underneath the preposition.)

i. "*Axes* is the object of the preposition." (Place a lowercase *op* underneath the object of the preposition.)

Part 2: Identify Principal Elements and Modifiers

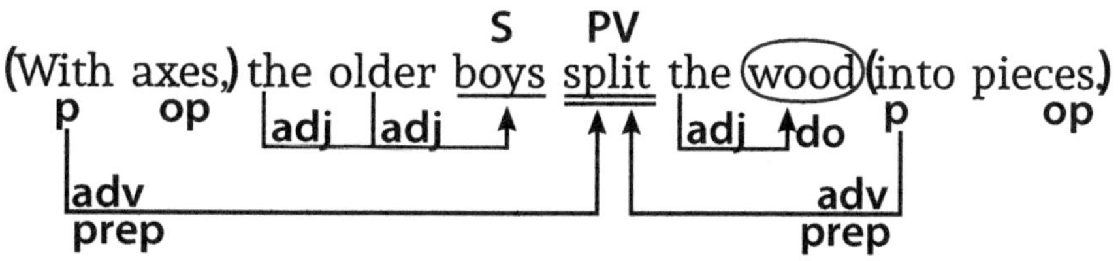

a. (Read the sentence aloud again.) "With axes, the older boys split the wood into pieces."

b. "This is a sentence and it is declarative."

c. "This sentence is about *boys*." (Underline the subject.) "So, *boys* is the subject because it is what the sentence is about." (Place a capital letter *S* above the subject.)

d. "This sentence tells us that boys *split*." (Double underline the predicate.) "So, *split* is the predicate because it is what the sentence tells us about *boys*." (Place a capital letter P above the predicate.) "It is a predicate verb because it shows action." (Place a capital letter V to the right of the letter P above the predicate.) "There is no linking verb because predicate verbs do not need linking verbs."

e. "*Wood* tells us what the boys split." (Draw a circle around the word.) "So, *wood* is an objective element because it completes the meaning of the action verb. It is a direct object because it tells *what* the boys split." (Write *do* in lowercase letters beneath the direct object.)

f. "*Into pieces* tells us *how* the boys split." (Draw a straight line down from the letter *p* that's under the preposition, then a horizontal line toward the word that it modifies, and then a straight line with an arrow pointing to the word it modifies.) "So, *into pieces* is an adverbial element because it modifies a verb. It is an adverbial prepositional phrase." (Write ***adv*** in lowercase letters in the elbow opposite the line with the arrow. Write ***prep*** in lowercase letters directly below the ***adv***, underneath the modifier line.)

g. "*The* is an adjective."[1] (Draw a straight line down from the adjective, then a horizontal line toward the word that it modifies, and then a straight line with an arrow pointing to the word it modifies. Write ***adj*** in lowercase letters in the elbow opposite the line with the arrow.)

h. "*Older* tells us *what kind* of boys." (Draw a straight line down from the adjective, then a horizontal line toward the word that it modifies. Write ***adj*** in lowercase letters in the elbow opposite the line with the arrow.) "So, *older* is an adjective element because it modifies a noun. It is an adjective." (Write ***adj*** in lowercase letters in the elbow opposite the line with the arrow.)

i. "*The* is an adjective."[2] (Draw a straight line down from the adjective, then a horizontal line toward the word that it modifies and connect the line to the modifying line of the word *older*. The two modifying lines are joined and point, with a straight line, toward the word they modify. Write ***adj*** in lowercase letters in the elbow opposite the line with the arrow.)

j. "*With axes* tells us *how* the boys split." (Draw a straight line down from the letter *p* that's under the preposition, then a horizontal line toward the word that it modifies, and then a straight line with an arrow pointing to the word it modifies. This line connects to the other adverbial modifying line.) "So, *with axes* is an adverbial element because it modifies a verb. It is an adverbial prepositional phrase." (Write ***adv*** in lowercase letters in the elbow opposite the line with the arrow. Write ***prep*** in lowercase letters directly below the ***adv***, underneath the modifier line.)

For the analysis of the second sentence, adjust the script accordingly.

1. The words *article adjective* can be substituted in place of the word *adjective*.
2. The words *article adjective* can be substituted in place of the word *adjective*.

Notes

Lessons to Learn
Introductory Prepositional Phrases

A

The order of the lesson is: **Review It**, **Practice It**, **Learn It**, and **Analyze It**.

Review It: Sing/chant and review definitions as a class.

Review It

Prepositions are little words, but they are very important words in our English language. Without them, sentences would fall apart.

What is a preposition? Name twenty prepositions.

What is an object of the preposition?

Give an example of a sentence with a prepositional phrase placed after the verb.

Give an example of a sentence with an introductory prepositional phrase.

Practice It: For this warm-up, see Well-Ordered Notes A.

Learn It: This lesson can be an oral or written exercise.

Learn It

Remember that a sentence is a group of words expressing a complete thought. It is a complete sentence only if it contains both a subject and a verb. Make the following fragments into complete sentences. As the writer, you get to choose whether the sentences have introductory prepositional phrases or not.

Example: "During lunch."
***During lunch,* the cousins planned the afternoon.**

1. underneath the clothes pile in the laundry room

   Underneath the clothes pile in the laundry room, two silly cousins hid.

2. throughout the long afternoon

   Throughout the long afternoon, the kids played games.

3. in the sunlight near the window

In the sunlight near the window, Stripes stretched out for a nap.

4. between two huge sock piles

Between two huge sock piles, Rex waited for another game.

Analyze It

Analyze the following sentences (*S* = subject; *PV* = predicate verb; *hv* = helping verb; *adv* = adverb; *adj* = adjective; *do* = direct object; *p* = preposition; *op* = object of the preposition; *prep* = prepositional phrase).

Analyze It: This is the essential part of the lesson. See Well-Ordered Notes A.

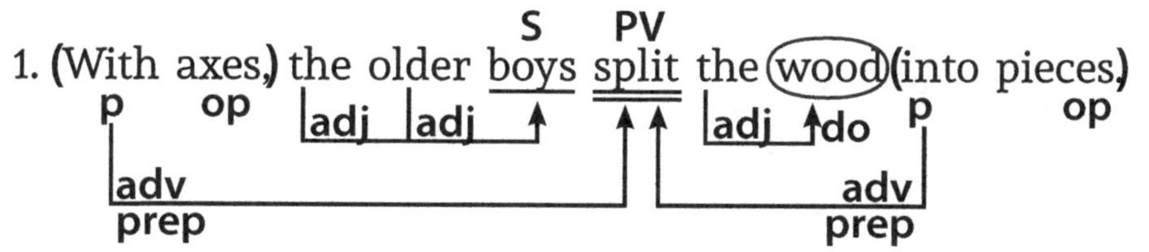

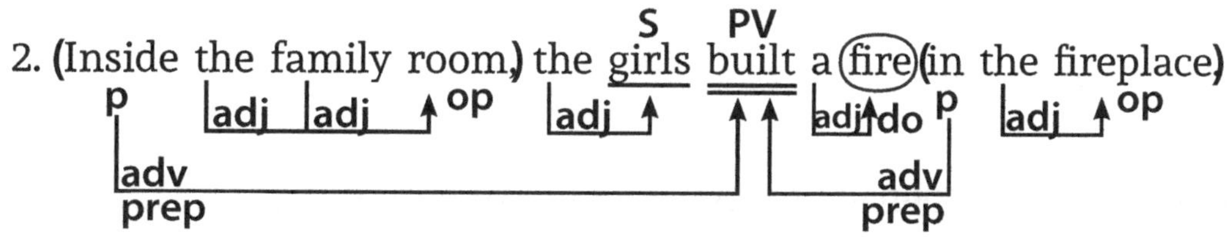

Lessons to Practice A
Introductory Prepositional Phrases

1. Analyze the following sentences (*S* = subject; *PV* = predicate verb; *hv* = helping verb; *adv* = adverb; *adj* = adjective; *do* = direct object; *p* = preposition; *op* = object of the preposition; *prep* = prepositional phrase).

   a. S PV
   (At school) the children devoured the birthday treat (before recess)
   p op adj adj adj do p op
   adv prep adv prep

   b. S PV
   (Near the playground) some children skipped (with jump ropes.)
   p adj op adj p adj op
   adv prep adv prep

   c. S PV
   (In the muddy fields) the two teams played soccer
   p adj adj op adj adj do
   adv prep

   d. S PV
   (After recess) the children had muddy shoes again.
   p op adj adj do
   adv prep adv

2. What is an object of the *preposition*?

   An object of the preposition is the noun or pronoun after the preposition.

3. Imagine that you are at a basketball game at school. With that in mind, complete the phrase for each preposition listed, and then write a sentence that includes the phrase.

   a. above **the basketball game**

   Sentence: **Above the basketball game, Fritz's balloon floated upward.**

   b. under **the bleachers**

   Sentence: **Under the bleachers, the boys searched for the lost mitten.**

Well-Ordered Notes B

Practice It

Play the game What Did You Do? Have the students stand in a circle or stand beside their desks. Ask the first student, "What did you do ______________?" (insert a prepositional phrase in the blank). The student will respond by beginning his answer with an introductory prepositional phrase and then finish the sentence. Next he will turn to a fellow student and ask, "What did you do ______________?" (insert a prepositional phrase in the blank) and so forth until every student answers a question. Write the following prepositional phrases on the board as options for the students to use. You should also encourage your students to think of their own phrases.

Example:

Teacher: "What did you do *aboard the train*?"
Student 1: "*Aboard the train,* I read the newspaper."

aboard the train	near the gym	beyond the fence
after the rain	down the tunnel	on Sunday
around the court	inside the rink	under the roof
in spring	during the movie	throughout the party

Analyze It

As a class, analyze the following sentences (*S* = subject; *PV* = predicate verb; *hv* = helping verb; *adv* = adverb; *adj* = adjective; *do* = direct object; *p* = preposition; *op* = object of the preposition; *prep* = prepositional phrase). Write the sentences on the board. Have the students analyze the sentences, reciting the analysis aloud using the following script. While the students recite, you will mark the sentence on the board.

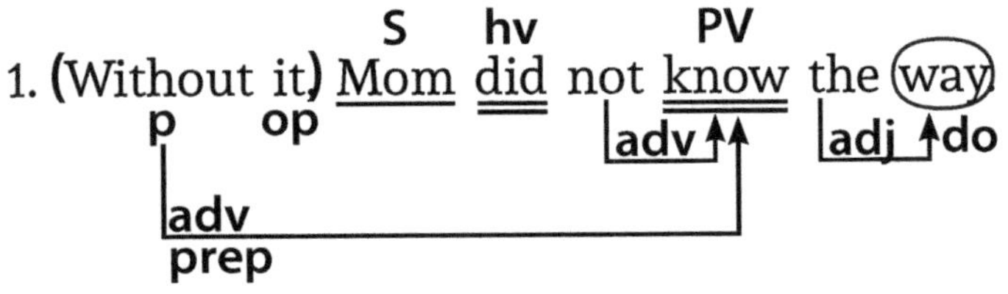

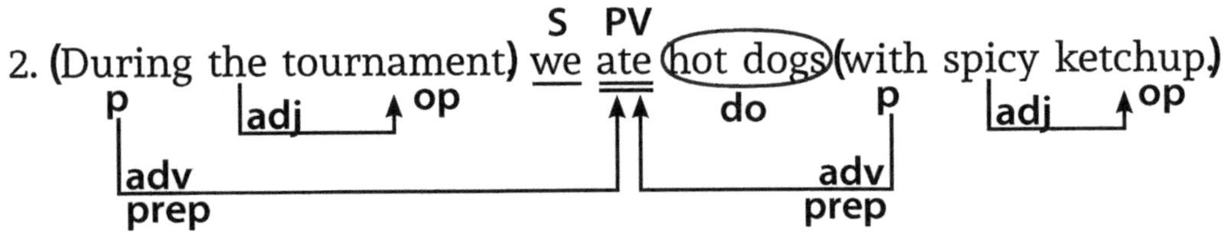

(Without it) Mom did not know the way.
p op

Part 1: Identify Phrases

a. (First, read the sentence aloud.) "Without it, Mom did not know the way."

b. Chant: "The order of analysis is phrases, clauses, principal elements, modifiers."

c. "Are there any prepositional phrases?" (Choral response: "Yes, sir.")

d. "*Without it* is a prepositional phrase." (Place parentheses around the prepositional phrase.)

e. "*Without* is the preposition." (Place a lowercase *p* underneath the preposition.)

f. "*It* is the object of the preposition." (Place a lowercase *op* underneath the object of the preposition.)

Part 2: Identify Principal Elements and Modifiers

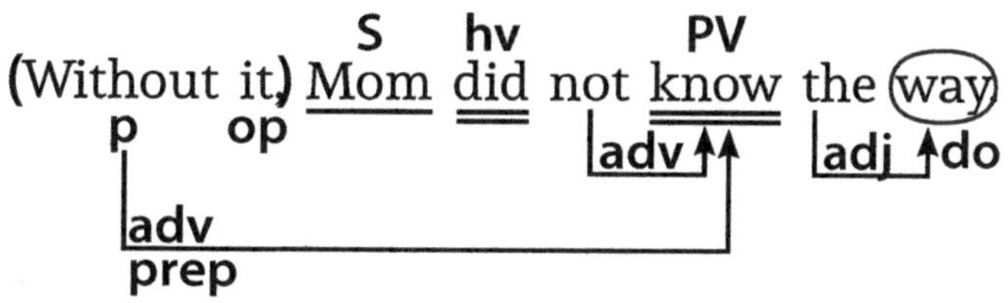

a. (Read the sentence aloud again.) "Without it, Mom did not know the way."

b. "This is a sentence and it is declarative."

c. "This sentence is about *Mom*." (Underline the subject.) "So, *Mom* is the subject because it is what the sentence is about." (Place a capital letter *S* above the subject.)

d. "This sentence tells us that Mom *did know*." (Double underline the helping verb and the predicate verb.) "So, *did know* is the predicate because it is what the sentence tells us about *Mom*." (Place a capital letter *P* above the action verb.) "It is a predicate verb because it shows action." (Place a capital letter *V* to the right of the letter *P*.) "There is no linking verb because predicate verbs do not need linking verbs. *Did* is the helping verb because it helps the verb." (Place a lowercase *hv* above the helping verb.)

e. "*Way* tells us what Mom did know." (Draw a circle around the word.) "So, *way* is an objective element because it completes the meaning of the action verb. It is a direct object because it tells *what* Mom did know." (Write *do* in lowercase letters beneath the direct object.)

f. "*The* is an adjective."[1] (Draw a straight line down from the adjective, then a horizontal line toward the word that it modifies, and then a straight line with an arrow pointing to the word it modifies. Write *adj* in lowercase letters in the elbow opposite the line with the arrow.)

1. The words *article adjective* can be substituted in place of the word *adjective*.

g. "*Not* tells us *how* Mom did know." (Draw a straight line down from the adverb, then a horizontal line toward the word that it modifies, and then a straight line with an arrow pointing to the word it modifies.) "So, *not* is an adverbial element because it modifies a verb. It is an adverb." (Write ***adv*** in lowercase letters in the elbow opposite the line with the arrow.)

h. "*Without it* tells us *how* Mom did know." (Draw a straight line down from the letter *p* that's under the preposition, then a horizontal line toward the word that it modifies, and then a straight line with an arrow pointing to the word it modifies.) "So, *without it* is an adverbial element because it modifies a verb. It is an adverbial prepositional phrase." (Write ***adv*** in lowercase letters in the elbow opposite the line with the arrow. Write ***prep*** in lowercase letters directly below the ***adv***, underneath the modifier line.)

For the analysis of the second sentence, adjust the script accordingly.

Notes

Lessons to Learn
Introductory Prepositional Phrases

B

The order of the lesson is: **Review It**, **Practice It**, **Learn It**, and **Analyze It**.

Review It: Sing/chant and review definitions as a class.

Review It

Practice makes perfect. Can you answer the following questions?

What is a preposition?

What is an object of the preposition?

What is a phrase?

List all of the forty-seven prepositions you have learned.

Practice It: For this warm-up, see Well-Ordered Notes B.

Learn It: This lesson can be an oral or written exercise. Ask the students to identify which introductory prepositional phrases answer *when* and which answer *where*.

Learn It

In the following sentences, use the words supplied in the word bank to fill in the missing subject or verb.

Example: In the breeze, the ___American flag___ waved softly.

Word Bank: scouts, collected, leader, pillow, unfolded, scolded

1. Before the campout, the scouts ___**collected**___ firewood.

2. During dinner, the ___**leader**___ assigned tents.

3. Near the fire, Theo neatly ___**unfolded**___ campstools.

4. Under the trees, five ___**scouts**___ roasted marshmallows.

5. Inside one tent, a ___**pillow**___ exploded into a cloud of feathers.

B Lessons to Learn
Introductory Prepositional Phrases

6. Outside that tent, the leader ____scolded____ the boys.

scolded

Analyze It

> **Analyze It**: This is the essential part of the lesson. See Well-Ordered Notes B.

Analyze the following sentences (*S* = subject; *PV* = predicate verb; *hv* = helping verb; *adv* = adverb; *adj* = adjective; *do* = direct object; *p* = preposition; *op* = object of the preposition; *prep* = prepositional phrase).

1. (Without it) Mom did not know the way.

   Without = p; it = op; Mom = S; did = hv; not = adv; know = PV; the = adj; way = do; (Without it) = adv prep

2. (During the tournament) we ate hot dogs (with spicy ketchup).

   During = p; the = adj; tournament = op; we = S; ate = PV; hot dogs = do; with = p; spicy = adj; ketchup = op; (During the tournament) = adv prep; (with spicy ketchup) = adv prep

Lessons to Practice B

Introductory Prepositional Phrases

1. Analyze the following sentences (*S* = subject; *PV* = predicate verb; *hv* = helping verb; *adv* = adverb; *adj* = adjective; *do* = direct object; *p* = preposition; *op* = object of the preposition; *prep* = prepositional phrase).

S PV
a. (From the north) the icy winds blew the cedar (trees) backward.
p adj op adj adj adj adj do
adv adv
prep

S PV
b. (During the storm) the cousins obediently stayed (inside the house)
p adj op adj adv p adj op
adv adv
prep prep

S PV
c. (Throughout the night) the snow flew (around the snow fort.)
p adj op adj p adj adj op
adv adv
prep prep

S PV
d. (From the window,) the children looked (at the fresh white carpet.)
p adj op adj p adj adj adj op
adv adv
prep prep

2. What is a *preposition*?

A preposition is a part of speech used to show the relationship between certain words in a sentence.

3. Imagine you are spending a snowy day with the cousins (Theo, Peggy, and Lucy) and Stripes. With that in mind, complete the phrase for each preposition listed, and then write a sentence that includes the phrase.

   a. beneath **the kitchen table**

      Sentence: **Beneath the kitchen table, Stripes quietly napped.**

   b. in **the basement**

      Sentence: **In the basement, the cousins played games.**

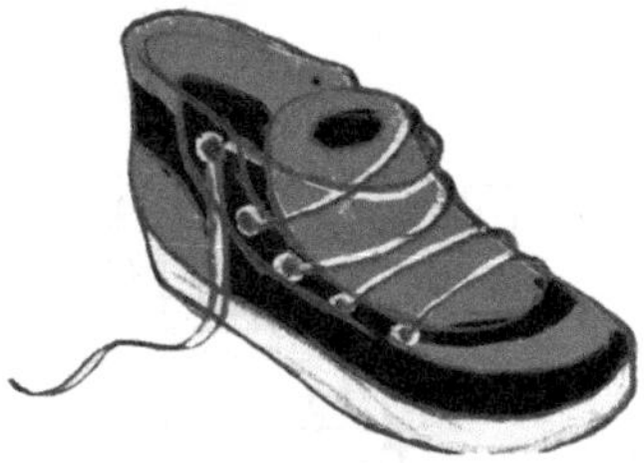

Well-Ordered Notes C

Practice It

Lead the class in the activity Add On. Divide the students into sets of partners and assign one of the following principal elements to each set. Have the groups add an introductory prepositional phrase to their assigned short sentence. Have one representative from each group share the pair's sentence with the class.

Variation: Write the following principal elements on index cards. Distribute the cards to each student. Have the students write their sentences on mini whiteboards and then share with a partner or small group. Have them erase their boards and pass their cards to another group.

Example: Waves dashed.
Against the rocks, the *waves dashed* relentlessly.

They laughed.	Squirrels chatter.	Gerbils drink.
Coyotes howl.	Balloon expands.	Worms wriggle.
Coach calls.	Rope twists.	He sketches.
Embers burn.	Wasps swarm.	Gardener digs.

Analyze It

As a class, analyze the following sentences (*S* = subject; *PV* = predicate verb; *hv* = helping verb; *adv* = adverb; *adj* = adjective; *do* = direct object; *p* = preposition; *op* = object of the preposition; *prep* = prepositional phrase). Write the sentences on the board. Have the students analyze the sentences, reciting the analysis aloud using the following script. While the students recite, you will mark the sentence on the board.

> **From the Sideline:** Please note that these sentences complement the fable for this chapter, which you can find in the teacher's edition and in the PDF material.

1. (In the barn,) the farmer had three horses.

S, PV
p, adj, op, adj, adj, do
adv prep

2. (Over the fence) the noisy neighbors talked (with the farmer.)

S, PV
p, adj, op, adj, adj, p, adj, op
adv prep, adv prep

Part 1: Identify Phrases

a. (First, read the sentence aloud.) "In the barn, the farmer had three horses."

b. "The order of analysis is phrases, clauses, principal elements, modifiers."

c. "Are there any prepositional phrases?" (Choral response: "Yes, sir.")

d. "*In the barn* is a prepositional phrase." (Place parentheses around the prepositional phrase.)

e. "*In* is the preposition." (Place a lowercase *p* underneath the preposition.)

f. "*Barn* is the object of the preposition." (Place a lowercase *op* underneath the object of the preposition.)

g. "*The* is an adjective."[1] (Draw a straight line down from the adjective, then a horizontal line toward the word that it modifies, and then a straight line with an arrow pointing to the word it modifies. Write *adj* in lowercase letters in the elbow opposite the line with the arrow.)

Part 2: Identify Principal Elements and Modifiers

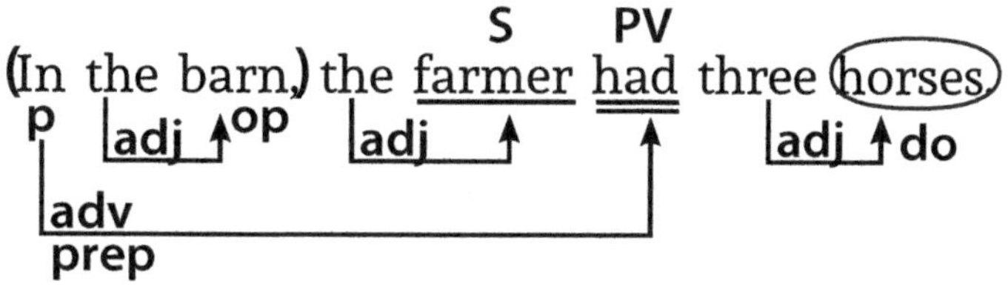

a. (Read the sentence aloud again.) "In the barn, the farmer had three horses."

b. "This is a sentence and it is declarative."

c. "This sentence is about *farmer*." (Underline the subject.) "So, *farmer* is the subject because it is what the sentence is about." (Place a capital letter *S* above the subject.)

d. "This sentence tells us that farmer *had*." (Double underline the predicate.) "So, *had* is the predicate because it is what the sentence tells us about *farmer*." (Place a capital letter *P* above the predicate.)

e. "It is a predicate verb because it shows action." (Place a capital letter *V* to the right of the letter *P* above the predicate.) "There is no linking verb because predicate verbs do not need linking verbs."

f. "*Horses* tells us what the farmer had." (Draw a circle around the word.) "So, *horses* is an objective element because it completes the meaning of the action verb. It is a direct object because it tells *what* the farmer had." (Write *do* in lowercase letters beneath the direct object.)

1. The words *article adjective* can be substituted in place of the word *adjective.*

g. "*Three* tells us *how many* horses." (Draw a straight line down from the adjective, then a horizontal line toward the word that it modifies. Write *adj* in lowercase letters in the elbow opposite the line with the arrow.) "So, *three* is an adjective element because it modifies a noun. It is an adjective." (Write *adj* in lowercase letters in the elbow opposite the line with the arrow.)

h. "*The* is an adjective."[2] (Draw a straight line down from the adjective, then a horizontal line toward the word that it modifies, and then a straight line with an arrow pointing to the word it modifies. Write *adj* in lowercase letters in the elbow opposite the line with the arrow.)

i. "*In the barn* tells us *where* the farmer had the horses." (Draw a straight line down from the letter *p* that's under the preposition, then a horizontal line toward the word that it modifies, and then a straight line with an arrow pointing to the word it modifies. This line connects to the other adverbial modifying line.) "So, *in the barn* is an adverbial element because it modifies a verb. It is an adverbial prepositional phrase." (Write *adv* in lowercase letters in the elbow opposite the line with the arrow. Write *prep* in lowercase letters directly below the *adv*, underneath the modifier line.)

For the analysis of the second sentence, adjust the script accordingly.

2. The words *article adjective* can be substituted in place of the word *adjective*.

Notes

Lessons to Learn
Introductory Prepositional Phrases

C

The order of the lesson is: **Review It**, **Practice It**, **Learn It**, and **Analyze It**.

Review It: Sing/chant and review definitions as a class. Have the students whisper or shout their singing/chanting.

Review It

Answer the following questions:

What do prepositions do in a sentence?

What are prepositions?

What is a phrase?

What is an object of the preposition?

Can you think of a sentence with a prepositional phrase following the verb?

Can you rearrange that sentence and make the prepositional phrase introductory?

Practice It: For this warm-up, see Well-Ordered Notes C.

Learn It: Write the sentences on the board and complete them together. Answers may vary. Ask the students how each phrase is related to each verb, either answering the question *where* or *when*.

Learn It

Keep in mind that introductory prepositional phrases are adverbial, so they tell *where* or *when* (and sometimes *how*) the action in the sentence is happening. Fill in the missing preposition in each of the following sentences.

Example: ____Beside____ the river, they collect rocks.

1. ____Near____ a cave, Dad found an arrowhead.

2. ____At____ the little waterfall, Mom took pictures.

3. ____Under____ a rock, Peggy found a crayfish.

4. ____Beneath____ the red cliffs, Theo saw a bumpy toad.

5. ____Within____ several pools, the tadpoles swam.

6. ____After____ lunch, the family drove to the beach.

Analyze It

Analyze the following sentences (*S* = subject; *PV* = predicate verb; *hv* = helping verb; *adv* = adverb; *adj* = adjective; *do* = direct object; *p* = preposition; *op* = object of the preposition; *prep* = prepositional phrase).

> **Analyze It:** This is the essential part of the lesson. See Well-Ordered Notes C.

1. (In the barn) the farmer had three horses.
   - In: p; the: adj → barn: op; (In the barn): adv prep → had
   - the: adj → farmer: S
   - had: PV
   - three: adj → horses: do

2. (Over the fence) the noisy neighbors talked (with the farmer.)
   - Over: p; the: adj → fence: op; (Over the fence): adv prep → talked
   - the: adj, noisy: adj → neighbors: S
   - talked: PV
   - with: p; the: adj → farmer: op; (with the farmer): adv prep → talked

Lessons to Practice

Introductory Prepositional Phrases

C

1. Analyze the following sentences (*S* = subject; *PV* = predicate verb; *hv* = helping verb; *adv* = adverb; *adj* = adjective; *do* = direct object; *p* = preposition; *op* = object of the preposition; *prep* = prepositional phrase).

a. (Beneath a full moon,) Grandpa stands (with Grandma) (near a garden wall.)

S: Grandpa; PV: stands
p adj adj op | p op | p adj adj op
adv prep | adv prep | adv prep

b. (Near the stone bench) Winston held a wooden sword (with a shield.)

S: Winston; PV: held
p adj adj op | adj adj do | p adj op
adv prep | adv prep

c. (Under the cabbage leaves,) a chubby baby lay (on a tiny blanket.)

S: baby; PV: lay
p adj adj op | adj adj | p adj adj op
adv prep | adv prep

d. (During the afternoon,) Fritz studied the old pictures (for hours.)

S: Fritz; PV: studied
p adj op | adj adj do | p op
adv prep | adv prep

2. What is an *object of the preposition*?

An object of the preposition is the noun or pronoun after the preposition.

3. Imagine Fritz finding a jellybean jar and knocking it over in the kitchen. With that in mind, complete the phrase for each preposition listed, and then write a sentence that includes the phrase.

   a. on ______ **the kitchen floor** ______

   Sentence: **On the kitchen floor, hundreds of jellybeans rolled.**

   b. with ______ **with a broom** ______

   Sentence: **With a broom, Fritz swept all the jellybeans into a dustpan.**

Lessons to Learn—Review
Introductory Prepositional Phrases

Review It: Sing/chant and review definitions as a class.

Review It

Answer the following review questions:

What is a preposition? What is an object of the preposition?

What is a phrase?

Can you list all forty-seven prepositions that you've learned?

Learn It: If, during the game of Lightning, a student can't come up with an answer in five seconds, pass him and circle around later to get his response.

Learn It

Play Lightning. Your teacher will say a preposition to a student and ask that student to construct a sentence. The sentence must include the preposition in a phrase placed where the teacher says, either at the beginning of the sentence or after the verb. The student has five seconds to supply a complete sentence that includes the correct form. Then the game moves on to the next student.

Example:

Teacher: "*Between*—introductory."
Student 1: "*Between* you and me, I think spring will be here soon."
Teacher: "*Since*—after the verb."
Student 2: "I have been here *since* Friday."

aboard	about	above	across	after
against	along	among	around	at
before	behind	below	beneath	beside
between	beyond	by	down	during
except	for	from	inside	in
into	near	of	off	on
out	outside	over	past	since
through	throughout	to	toward	under
up	until	upon	with	within
without	underneath			

On the lines provided, write your favorite sentence that was created during the game of Lightning.

Lessons to Practice—Review
Introductory Prepositional Phrases

1. Analyze the following sentences: (*S* = subject; *PV* = predicate verb; *hv* = helping verb; *adv* = adverb; *adj* = adjective; *do* = direct object; *p* = preposition; *op* = object of the preposition; *prep* = prepositional phrase).

S PV
a. (In the twilight,) the family watched (from the front window.)
p adj op adj p adj adj op
adv prep adv prep

S PV
b. (Above the wispy clouds,) two wild geese flew together (in the sky.)
p adj adj op adj adj adv p adj op
adv prep adv prep

S PV
c. (Outside the house,) Rex barked (at a neighbor.)
p adj op p adj op
adv prep adv prep

S PV
d. (Inside the house,) Grandfather read many familiar stories.
p adj op adj adj do
adv prep

2. What is a *preposition*?

A preposition is a part of speech used to show the relationship between certain words in a sentence.

3. Imagine Peggy and Lucy are listening to Grandpa read. With that in mind, complete the phrase for each preposition listed, and then write a sentence that includes the phrase.

   a. During **the stories**

      Sentence: **During the stories, Lucy snuggled on the coach.**

   b. After **the tales**

      Sentence: **After the tales, Grandpa carried Lucy up the stairs.**

Lessons to Enjoy—Poem
Introductory Prepositional Phrases

Elves, dwarves, and fairies are delightful imaginary creatures of the forest. In the play *A Midsummer Night's Dream*, William Shakespeare writes this song of a fairy. Another character asks the fairy where she is going, and this poem is her answer. Notice how introductory prepositional phrases are used to tell where she must go to serve her fairy queen.

dale: valley
brier: a tangle of prickly plants
pale: an area that is enclosed, as with a fence
sphere: revolution around the earth
orbs: orbits; a poetic name for the mushrooms called "fairy rings" because they grow in circles as if a fairy had danced there
cowslips: sweet-smelling yellow wildflowers
pensioners: royal attendants, known in Shakespeare's time for being tall and dressed in gold
favors: gifts, as in party favors
savors: sweet smells

Over Hill, Over Dale

by William Shakespeare (1564–1616)

Over hill, over dale,
Through bush, through brier,
Over park, over pale,
Through floor, through fire,
I do wander everywhere,
Swifter than the moon's sphere;
And I serve the fairy queen,
To dew her orbs upon the green.
The cowslips tall her pensioners be:
In their gold coats spots you see;
Those be rubies, fairy favors,
In those freckles live their savors:
I must go seek some dewdrops here
And hang a pearl in every cowslip's ear.[1]

1. William Shakespeare, Act II , Scene 1, "A Wood near Athens," from *A Midsummer Night's Dream* in *World Scope Family Library: Works of William Shakespeare*, ed. W.G. Clark and W.A. Wright (New York: The Universal Guide, Inc., 1950), p. 7.

Questions to Ponder

1. Where does the fairy wander?
2. In the poem, how many introductory prepositional phrases are placed before the first subject and verb?
3. How fast does the fairy travel?
4. What is the fairy's responsibility in the wood?
5. Who guards the fairy queen?

From the Sideline: For possible answers to these discussion questions, see p. a of the teacher's pages. For even more suggestions for discussion and for enrichment activities related to the poem, see p. b.

Extras: Please note that the teacher's pages for this chapter include more material for extra practice, a quiz, and another Lessons to Enjoy section with discussion questions and activities. All this material, in reproducible form, is also included in the PDF that accompanies the textbook.

Lessons to Enjoy—Poem

Questions to Ponder

1. Where does the fairy wander?

   The fairy wanders all around the fairy queen's territory as described in the first four lines. She travels over or through hills, valleys, the undergrowth, the open spaces, and the enclosed spaces.

2. In the poem, how many introductory prepositional phrases are placed before the first subject and verb?

   There are eight such introductory phrases. The first four lines contain two prepositional phrases each. All of these eight phrases come before the subject *I* and the verb *do wander*, so they are introductory. As adverbs, they all answer the question of *where* the fairy does wander. By piling up eight introductory prepositional phrases, Shakespeare emphasizes the vastness of the little fairy's wanderings.

3. How fast does the fairy travel?

   The fairy must move more quickly than the moon in order to complete her responsibilities.

4. What is the fairy's responsibility in the wood?

   In service to the fairy queen, this fairy has the jobs of spreading dew where the queen will dance and placing a dewdrop like a pearl earring on every cowslip flower. Point out to the student how the fairy seems very devoted to her work, attending to every detail.

5. Who guards the fairy queen?

   The queen's bodyguards are the sweet-smelling cowslip flowers, which are dressed in gold coats with ruby spots.

Well-Ordered Notes—Poem

Read

- Encourage the students' enjoyment of the poem by reading it aloud while they listen to a classical piece of music, such as "The Fairies Are Exquisite Dancers" by Claude Debussy (Debussy, *Préludes*, Book II, No. 4, *Les fées sont d'exquises danseuses*). Discuss the rich imagery in the poem.
- Ask the students to memorize the poem.

Retell

- Discuss the poem using the provided questions.
- Have the students orally "translate" the poem into modern prose.

Record

- Tell the students to write a description of a fairy that is busy over hill and dale.
- Have the students copy the poem into a copybook and draw a picture beside it of a fairy or a cowslip.

Practice Sheet

Introductory Prepositional Phrases

ANSWERS

Analyze the following sentences (*S* = subject; *PV* = predicate verb; *hv* = helping verb; *adv* = adverb; *adj* = adjective; *do* = direct object; *p* = preposition; *op* = object of the preposition; *prep* = prepositional phrase).

S hv PV
1. (Around the front yard) several robins were finding (worms).
p adj adj op adj do
adv prep

S PV
2. (In the afternoon) Mom then graciously had a tea (party) (for us.)
p adj op adv adv adj adj do p op
adv prep adv prep

S hv PV
3. (From the other room,) she could hear the (girls).
p adj adj op adj do
adv prep

S PV
4. (During the party) Grandma brought chocolate (cookies) over.
p adj op adj do
adv prep adv

S PV
5. (Underneath the table) the boys snuck slowly (toward them.)
p adj op adj adv p op
adv prep adv prep

S PV
6. (From the side) a hand reached (for the cookie.)
p adj op adj p adj op
adv prep adv prep

S PV
7. (By the teacups) another hand slowly stretched out.
p adj op adj adv adv
adv prep

S PV
8. (Above the table) the girls giggled (at the sneaky hands)
p adj op adj p adj adj op
adv prep adv prep

S PV
9. (Behind the door) Grandma watched the hungry boys.
p adj op adj adj do
adv prep

S PV
10. (In the kitchen) the boys later ate chocolate cookies too.
p adj op adj adv adj do
adv prep adv

Quiz

Introductory Prepositional Phrases — ANSWERS

1. Analyze the following sentences (*S* = subject; *PV* = predicate verb; *hv* = helping verb; *adv* = adverb; *adj* = adjective; *do* = direct object; *p* = preposition; *op* = object of the preposition; *prep* = prepositional phrase).

   a. (In the picture book,) the clay pot held an empty nest.

   S (pot) PV (held)
   p adj adj op adj adj do
   adv prep

   b. (Between the two rocks,) a poky snail inched along.

   S (snail) PV (inched)
   p adj adj op adj adj adv
   adv prep

   poky: very slow

   c. Several ducks dove (under the water)(for pond plants.)

   S (ducks) PV (dove)
   adj p adj op p adj op
   adv prep adv prep

   d. (Aboard the tiny lily pad,) three water spiders huddled together.

   S (spiders) PV (huddled)
   p adj adj op adj adj adv
   adv prep

2. What is a *preposition*?

   A preposition is a part of speech used to show the relationship between certain words in a sentence.

3. Imagine that you are looking at a book about pond life. With that in mind, complete the phrase for each preposition listed, and then write a sentence that includes the phrase.

   a. At **the pond**

      Sentence: **At the pond, many tadpoles swim around.**

   b. Near **the willow tree**

      Sentence: **Near the willow tree, ducks make nests.**

Have you ever had a really bad day? How about a really good day? Sometimes the main difference between a really good day and a really bad day is simply your own attitude, rather than the bad things or good things that you experienced. This Chinese fable tells of a farmer who has learned how to accept each day as it is, without judging it as either bad or good.

The Tale of the Chinese Farmer

Chinese Tale

prosperous: successful

Once there was a prosperous Farmer in China who owned a tall and strong Work Horse. During a lightning storm one night, the Horse broke out of his barn and ran away. The Farmer's Neighbors stopped by the Farmer's house to look at the broken barn door. "We are sorry for your bad day," the Neighbors said.

"How do you know it is a bad day?" the Farmer asked.

A few weeks later, the Horse returned to the Farmer's fields and it brought with it two beautiful wild horses. The Farmer's Neighbors stopped by the Farmer's house to cheer his good luck. "Three horses from one horse!" the Neighbors said. "This is a very good day."

"How do you know it is a good day?" the Farmer asked.

The next day, the Farmer's Son tried to catch one of the wild horses. The wild horse kicked him and broke the boy's leg. The Farmer's neighbors stopped by the Farmer's house to look at the poor boy's broken leg. "We're sorry for your bad day," the Neighbors said.

"How do you know it is a bad day?" the Farmer asked.

While the Farmer's Son was sick with pain and fever, a war broke out between two kings. Soldiers came to the Farmer's village and forced many young men and boys to join the army. The soldiers looked at the Farmer's Son, decided he was too sick to fight, and left him in bed. When the soldiers had left the village, the Farmer's Neighbors stopped by the Farmer's house to cheer his good luck. "Your Son is safe!" the Neighbors said. "This is a very good day."

"How do you know it is a good day?" the Farmer asked.

Moral: How you view good and bad events influences the way you deal with them.[1]

Questions to Ponder

1. How is this Chinese folktale both similar to and different from one of Aesop's fables?
2. What events do the Neighbors consider bad luck and which ones do they think are good luck?
3. What does "Three horses from one horse" mean?
4. Why does the Farmer keep asking "How do you know . . . ?" when the neighbors call a day either bad or good?

1. "The Tale of the Chinese Farmer," taken from *Writing & Rhetoric Book 1: Fable*, by Paul Kortepeter (Camp Hill, PA: Classical Academic Press, 2013), pp. 105–106.

Lessons to Enjoy—Fable

Questions to Ponder

1. How is this Chinese folktale both similar to and different from one of Aesop's fables?

   Unlike Aesop's fables, it features people, rather than talking animals. The situation it describes is more complex than that in most of Aesop's fables, and the outcome is less predictable. Like Aesop's fables, however, it draws a universal lesson from the specific actions and attitudes of its characters.

2. What events do the Neighbors consider bad luck and which ones do they think are good luck?

   The Neighbors think it's bad luck when the horse runs away, but good luck when it returns with two others. They think it's bad luck when one of the wild horses breaks the son's leg, but good luck when the broken leg and resulting fever keep the son from being drafted into the army.

3. What does "Three horses from one horse" mean?

   When the lost horse returns, it brings two wild horses with it. The neighbors see this as a mathematical equation: one plus two equals three. It's a net gain in economic terms. But the farmer does not think in such terms. He knows that gain might lead to loss and vice versa.

4. Why does the farmer keep asking "How do you know . . . ?" when the neighbors call a day either bad or good?

   The farmer wisely knows that one event leads to others. What looks like bad or good luck today may turn into the opposite tomorrow. One really cannot know for sure how a sequence of events will turn out. The farmer accepts each day just as it comes without judgment.

Well-Ordered Notes—Fable

Read

- To encourage the students to enjoy reading the fable, divide the class into parts (e.g., the Farmer, the Neighbors, even the Horse) and have them act the fable out.
- Have students sing/chant the definition of a fable (Fable, 1–14).

Retell

- Discuss the fable using the provided questions.
- Ask the students if they can think of other morals to be drawn from the tale. Examples: "Don't judge an event until all its consequences are clear"; or "A wise person does not jump to hasty conclusions." Ask the students to share their own experiences of bad or good events turning into the opposite.

Record

- Have students make a storyboard of this fable together as a class. Assign each student a sentence or two to illustrate on an index card. Have them write their sentence neatly under the illustration. Display the cards in the correct order blocked out on poster board.

Fable Sentences

Introductory Prepositional Phrases ANSWERS

Analyze the following sentences (*S* = subject; *PV* = predicate verb; *hv* = helping verb; *adv* = adverb; *adj* = adjective; *do* = direct object; *p* = preposition; *op* = object of the preposition; *prep* = prepositional phrase).

S PV
1. (In China,) a prosperous Farmer owned a strong (Horse.)
p op adj adj adj adj do
adv prep

S PV
2. (During a storm,) the Horse ran away (from the farm.)
p adj op adj adv p adj op
adv prep adv prep

S PV
3. (In the afternoon,) the Neighbors saw the broken barn (door.)
p adj op adj adj adj adj do
adv prep

S PV
4. (During bad days,) the friends grieved (for him.)
p adj op adj p op
adv prep adv prep

S PV
5. (In time,) the strong Horse returned (with two additional horses.)
p op adj adj p adj adj op
adv prep adv prep

S PV
6. (During good days,) the Neighbors cheered (for him.)
p adj op adj p op
adv prep adv prep

7. (In the morning,) the wild horse kicked the son.
S (horse), PV (kicked), do (son)
p In | adj the → op morning | adj the, adj wild → horse | adj the → do son
adv prep (In the morning) → kicked

8. (By evening,) the friends cried (for the son.)
S (friends), PV (cried)
p By, op evening | adj the → friends | p for, adj the → op son
adv prep (By evening) → cried | adv prep (for the son) → cried

9. (With mercy) the soldiers left the sick boy (at home.)
S (soldiers), PV (left), do (boy)
p With, op mercy | adj the → soldiers | adj the, adj sick → do boy | p at, op home
adv prep (With mercy) → left | adv prep (at home) → left

10. (In humility) the Farmer questioned all the comments.
S (Farmer), PV (questioned), do (comments)
p In, op humility | adj the → Farmer | adj all, adj the → do comments
adv prep (In humility) → questioned

From the Sideline: Designate teams. Divide the students into two groups to manage class size. This is helpful for line-up, choral response, or small groups. We name each group after the school colors, as in Gold Team and Blue Team.

Chapter 5

Compound Subjects[A]

Springtime is a great time to go biking with friends. It is a time when your feet and a pair of wheels determine where you can go and how fast you can get there. Sometimes you are slowly gliding along, and other times you feel like you're actually flying. An English sentence can be like a person on a bike. The subject of the sentence—the noun or pronoun—is the rider, and the predicate is the wheels.

There are many different kinds of bicycles: mountain bikes, racing bikes, BMX (bicycle motocross) bikes; bikes with gears, bikes with baskets, bikes with horns. A fun bike for good friends is a tandem bike, which is built for two or more riders. Can you imagine a sentence that is built for two subjects? Well, we don't call it a tandem sentence, but we do have a name for two subjects for one verb. Both subjects together are referred to as the **compound**■ **subject**. They are joined by a little word, such as *and*, which is called a conjunction. The subjects are the two bicycle riders, the conjunction is the bicycle frame that holds them together, and the predicate is the whole pedaling, wheeling mechanism that moves them along.

You see, English sentences can be either bicycles with one rider or bicycles with multiple riders. You can write a sentence about an individual (a singular subject) doing individual activities. Alternatively, you can write a sentence that is like a tandem bike with more than one rider. It has several individuals (a compound subject) doing together the activity expressed in the verb. Strap on your safety helmet. *You and your teacher* (compound subject!) are off for a ride.

[A]Bring in pictures of a bicycle and a tandem bicycle or actually bring a bicycle into class. You can use this visual to help students understand that multiple subjects—nouns or pronouns—can be joined with a conjunction to be a compound subject.

To the Source:

■ compound

The word *compound* comes from Latin *componere* meaning "to put together."

Ideas to Understand[B]

To the Source:

■ **conjunction**

In Latin *conjunction* is *conjunction*, which means "connection or joining together."

[B]Write the first four lines of the poem "The Walrus and the Carpenter" by Lewis Carroll on the board. The entire poem is available in The Curious Child's Literary Appendix.

When two or more subjects have the same predicate and are joined with a conjunction, they are called a compound subject. A conjunction acts like the glue in a sentence and does not express any distinct idea in itself; it serves to make a clearer connection between ideas. **Conjunctions**■ are one of the eight parts of speech. There are different kinds of conjunctions, and they can join words, phrases, or clauses. You'll learn more about them in *WOL Level 2*. In this chapter, we will focus on only two conjunctions—*and, or*—because they are the ones that most often glue nouns or pronouns together to form a compound subject.

In the middle of his nonsensical poem "The Walrus and the Carpenter" (you'll find the complete poem in The Curious Child's Literary Appendix), Lewis Carroll tells of two rather strange characters on a beach:

> The Walrus and the Carpenter
>   Walked on a mile or so,
> And then they rested on a rock
>   Conveniently low:
> And all the little Oysters stood
>   And waited in a row.
>
> 'The time has come,' the Walrus said,
>   'To talk of many things:
> Of shoes—and ships—and sealing wax—
>   Of cabbages—and kings—
> And why the sea is boiling hot—
>   And whether pigs have wings.'[1]

Carroll could have written "The Walrus walked on a mile or so" and "The Carpenter walked on a mile or so" as two separate sentences, but instead he combines two subjects, *Walrus* and *Carpenter*, into one sentence using the same verb—*walked*. He connects *Walrus* and *Carpenter* into a compound subject using the conjunction *and*. Notice that the third line quoted above uses the plural subject *they*. It is not a compound but simply a plural pronoun, so there is no conjunction.

---

1. Lewis Carroll, "The Walrus and the Carpenter," *Through the Looking-Glass* (New York: Random House, 1916), pp. 56–61.

When using a compound subject, you must make sure that the verb agrees with the subject. For most compound subjects joined with *and*, the rule is very simple: use the plural form of the verb.

> The Walrus and the Oysters **talk** of many things.
> The Oysters and the Walrus **talk** of many things.

For compound subjects connected with the conjunction *or*, the rule is a little more complicated. The part of the subject that is closer to the verb dictates the number of the verb (in other words, that's the part that decides whether the verb is singular or plural).

> The Walrus or the Oysters **talk** of many things.
> The Oysters or the Walrus **talks** of many things.

If the plural part of a compound subject with *or* is next to the verb, the verb takes a plural form: *the oysters **talk***. If the singular part of a compound subject with *or* is next to the verb, the verb takes a singular form: *the walrus **talks***.

If the sentence includes helping verbs, then the helping verb—rather than the main verb—follows the rules stated for agreeing in number with the subjects. The agreement of subjects and helping verbs will be explored more fully in later lessons, but here are a few examples of correct helping verb choices based on whether the conjunction in the compound subject is *and* or *or*:

1. The Walrus *and* the Oysters **are** talking of many things.
   Are the Walrus *and* the Oysters talking of many things?
2. The Walrus *or* the Oysters **are** talking of many things.
   Is the Walrus *or* the Oysters talking of many things?
3. The Oysters *or* the Walrus **is** talking of many things.
   Are the Oysters or the Walrus talking of many things?

From the Sideline: You might want to mention the exception to this rule. If the two words form a commonly understood unit and the two items are used as a single unit (such as *peanut butter and jelly* or *chips and salsa*), then the singular form of the verb is used. For example: Macaroni and cheese ***completes*** the dinner.

[c]Play the appropriate CD tracks/audio files and have students sing/chant along. Remind students to commit the songs to memory by listening to these tracks/files at other times as well.

Terms to Remember[c]

It is often said that once you learn how to ride a bike, you never forget. Well, once you memorize these grammar terms, you will know them for life.

Eight Parts of Speech *(1–1)*

The eight parts of speech are classes of words
with the same kind of meaning and use.
They are: nouns, verbs, adjectives, adverbs,
prepositions, pronouns, conjunctions, interjections.
These are the eight parts of speech,
classes of words with the same kind of meaning and use. *(Repeat.)*

Principal Elements *(1–3)*

Principal elements are the parts of the sentence
that are needed for the sentence to be completed.
Subject and predicate are those two parts.

Subject and Predicate *(1–4)*

A subject, a subject is a noun or a pronoun
and is what the sentence is about *(clap, clap)*.
A predicate, a predicate tells us something about the subject
like what it is doing or being *(clap, clap)*.

Nouns *(1–5)*

A noun is a part of speech.
It names a person, place, or thing.
A noun names a quality or an idea.
A noun is a part of speech.
It names a person, place, or thing.
A noun may be singular *(clap)* or plural *(clap clap clap)*. *(Repeat.)*

NEW! Conjunction *(1–20)*

A conjunction is a part of speech.
It joins elements of the same rank or name.

When two or more words are joined this way, they're called compounds. *(Repeat.)*

Sentences to Analyze[D]

Now that we are studying compound subjects, you need to be on the lookout for conjunctions in a sentence. When you find a conjunction, you will mark it with angle brackets (> <) on either side of the word: Walrus >and< Carpenter. We call the brackets "wings." Before you begin the rest of the analysis, make sure that you mark the conjunctions with wings. Then continue the analysis and mark the sentence using the questions below to help. Say the words in gray together.

S (Walrus), S (Carpenter), PV (walked)

The Walrus⟩and⟨the Carpenter walked together.

adj → Walrus; adj → Carpenter; adv → walked

a. (First, read the sentence aloud.) "The Walrus and the Carpenter walked together."

b. "Are there any conjunctions?" (Choral response: "Yes, sir.") (Since *and* is a conjunction, put wings before and after it.)

c. "The order of analysis is phrases, clauses, principal elements, modifiers."

d. "Are there any prepositional phrases?" (Choral response: "No, sir." Since there are none you can answer *no* and continue.)

e. "This is a sentence and it is declarative."

f. "This sentence is about *Walrus and Carpenter*. So, *Walrus and Carpenter* are the subjects because they are what the sentence is about." (Since *Walrus and Carpenter* are the subjects, underline them and place a capital letter *S* above each subject.)

g. "*And* is the conjunction."

h. "This sentence tells us that Walrus and Carpenter *walked*. So, *walked* is the predicate because it is what the sentence tells us about *Walrus and Carpenter*." (Since *walked* tells us something

[D]Write the sentence on the board. When teaching compounds, the key is identifying conjunctions first, even before phrases. Help the students mark conjunctions with angle brackets or "wings." You may pause to discuss possibilities of what the conjunction is joining, but to avoid confusion do not identify the compound as a subject until the appropriate moment in the analysis. After marking the wings, review the order of analysis chant. It should be reviewed every time you analyze a sentence. Model how to mark the sentence while the students chorally analyze the sentence, saying aloud the words in gray.

about Walrus and Carpenter, double underline the predicate and place a capital letter *P* above it.) "It is a predicate verb because it shows action. There is no linking verb because predicate verbs do not need linking verbs." (Since *walked* shows action, place a capital letter *V* to the right of the letter *P* above the predicate.)

i. "*Together* tells us *how* Walrus and Carpenter walked." (Since *together* tells *how* Walrus and Carpenter walked, draw a straight line down from the adverb, then a horizontal line toward the word it modifies, and then a straight line with an arrow pointing to the word it modifies. "So, *together* is an adverbial element because it modifies a verb. It is an adverb." (Write *adv* in lowercase letters in the elbow opposite the line with the arrow.)

j. "*The* is an adjective."[2] (Since *the* tells *which* carpenter, it an adjective. Draw a straight line down from the adjective, then a horizontal line toward the word it modifies, and then a straight line with an arrow pointing to *carpenter*. Write *adj* in lowercase letters in the elbow opposite the line with the arrow.)

k. "*The* is an adjective."[3] (Since *the* tells *which* walrus, it an adjective. Draw a straight line down from the adjective, then a horizontal line toward the word it modifies, and then a straight line with an arrow pointing to *walrus*. Write *adj* in lowercase letters in the elbow opposite the line with the arrow.)

Did you know that there are bicycles that are built for even more than two people? There are even bikes that can be used by five people! Just as there are bicycles that more than two people can ride, a compound subject can contain more than two subjects. The same grammar rules apply no matter how many subjects are contained in the compound.

If ever you have ridden a tandem bicycle, you know that the pedals work in unison, so the riders must move their feet together. They must lean into the turns together. Their tandem seats are connected together on the bicycle frame. So it is with the parts of a compound subject. They are connected together with a conjunction. Together they are what the sentence is about. One verb expresses the action that together they are doing.

---

2. The words *article adjective* can be substituted in place of the word *adjective*.
3. The words *article adjective* can be substituted in place of the word *adjective*.

Notes

Well-Ordered Notes Introductory

Practice It

Lead the students in the activity Up or Down. Have the students stand behind their desks. Read one of the following sentences and the two options for the missing verb. If the answer is the first option (e.g., ask), then the students put their thumbs up, but if the answer is the second option (e.g., asks), then they should put their thumbs down. Make sure all "thumb votes" are seen. Once the vote is cast, reread the sentence with the correct answer. If the students are correct, they remain standing; but if they are incorrect, they are seated. To keep everyone playing, have the students who are seated continue playing. They can earn the right to stand up by answering correctly for one of the sentences. This activity should be fast moving; don't let it drag.

Example:

Teacher: "Once again, Theo __________________ about rivers. (ask / asks)"
Students' thumbs should be pointing down.
Restate: "Theo asks about rivers."

1. The teacher and the student (read / reads) the next chapter.
2. (Do / Does) the Mississippi or the Missouri flow into the Gulf of Mexico?
3. Suddenly a quiet girl (raise / raises) her hand.
4. Two and three arms (wave / waves) in the air too.
5. The shy girl (answer / answers) the question correctly.

Analyze It

As a class, analyze the following sentences (*S* = subject; *PV* = predicate verb; *hv* = helping verb; *adv* = adverb; *adj* = adjective; *do* = direct object; *p* = preposition; *op* = object of the preposition; *prep* = prepositional phrase). Write the sentences on the board. Have the students analyze the sentences, reciting the analysis aloud using the following script. While the students recite, you will mark the sentence on the board.

1. You and I can surprise the cousins (with water balloons).
   (You = S; I = S; can = hv; surprise = PV; the = adj; cousins = do; with = p; water = adj; balloons = op; with water balloons = adv prep)

2. Did Uncle Ulysses or Theo put the balloons (in the crate)?
   (Did = hv; Uncle Ulysses = S; Theo = S; put = PV; the = adj; balloons = do; in = p; the = adj; crate = op; in the crate = adv prep)

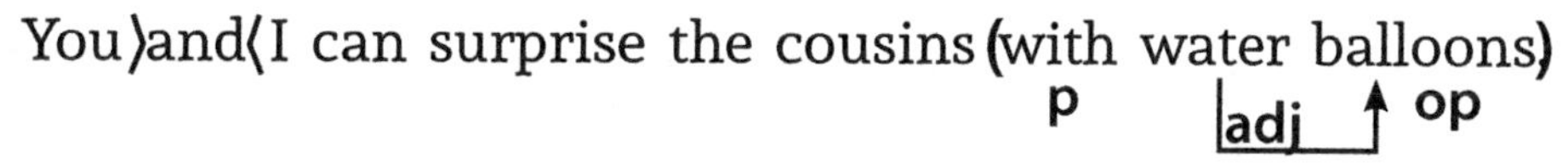

Part 1: Identify Phrases and Conjunctions

a. (First, read the sentence aloud.) "You and I can surprise the cousins with water balloons."

b. "Are there any prepositional phrases?" (Choral response: "Yes, sir.") (Mark the conjunction *and* with two angle brackets.)

c. "The order of analysis is phrases, clauses, principal elements, modifiers."

d. "Are there any prepositional phrases?" (Choral response: "Yes, sir.") "*With water balloons* is a prepositional phrase." (Place parentheses around the prepositional phrase.)

e. "*With* is the preposition." (Place a lowercase *p* underneath the preposition.)

f. "*Balloons* is the object of the preposition." (Place a lowercase *op* underneath the object of the preposition.)

g. "*Water* tells us *what kind* of balloons." (Draw a straight line down from the adjective, then a horizontal line toward the word that it modifies, and then a straight line with an arrow pointing to the word it modifies.) "So, *water* is an adjective element because it modifies a noun. It is an adjective." (Write *adj* in lowercase letters in the elbow opposite the line with the arrow.)

Part 2: Identify Principal Elements and Modifiers

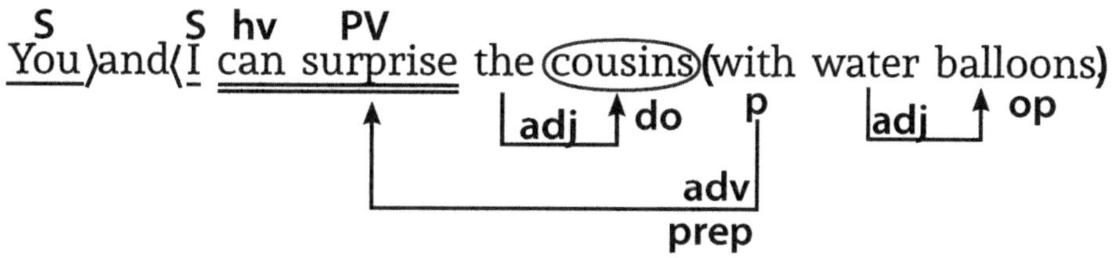

a. (Read the sentence aloud again.) "You and I can surprise the cousins with water balloons."

b. "This is a sentence and it is declarative."

c. "This sentence is about *you* and *I*." (Underline the subjects.) "So, *you* and *I* are the subjects because they are what the sentence is about." (Place a capital letter *S* above each subject.)

d. "*And* is the conjunction."

e. "This sentence tells us that you and I *can surprise*." (Double underline the helping verb and the predicate verb.) "So, *can surprise* is the predicate because it is what the sentence tells us about *you* and *I*." (Place a capital letter *P* above the action verb.) "It is a predicate verb because it shows action." (Place a capital letter *V* to the right of the letter *P*.) "There is no linking verb because predicate verbs do not need linking verbs. *Can* is the helping verb because it helps the verb." (Place a lowercase *hv* above the helping verb.)

f. "*Cousins* tells us whom you and I can surprise." (Draw a circle around the word.) "So, *cousins* is an objective element because it completes the meaning of the action verb. It is a direct object because it tells *whom* you and I can surprise." (Write *do* in lowercase letters beneath the direct object.)

g. "*The* is an adjective."[1] (Draw a straight line down from the adjective, then a horizontal line toward the word that it modifies, and then a straight line with an arrow pointing to the word it modifies. Write *adj* in lowercase letters in the elbow opposite the line with the arrow.)

h. "*With water balloons* tells us *how* you and I can surprise." (Draw a straight line down from the letter *p* that's under the preposition, then a horizontal line toward the word that it modifies, and then a straight line with an arrow pointing to the word it modifies.) "So, *with water balloons* is an adverbial element because it modifies a verb. It is an adverbial prepositional phrase." (Write *adv* in lowercase letters in the elbow opposite the line with the arrow. Write *prep* in lowercase letters directly below the *adv*, underneath the modifier line.)

For the analysis of the second sentence, adjust the script accordingly.

1. The words *article adjective* can be substituted in place of the word *adjective*.

Notes

Introductory Lesson
Compound Subjects

The order of the lesson is: **Review It**, **Practice It**, **Learn It**, and **Analyze It**.

Review It: Sing/chant and review definitions as a class.

Review It

You have learned a lot of grammar terms so far. Can you answer these questions without checking?

What are the eight parts of speech?

What are principal elements?

What are nouns?

What is a conjunction?

Practice It: For this warm-up, see Well-Ordered Notes Introductory.

Learn It: Write the sentences on the board with verbs omitted. After students complete them individually in their books, review as a class, filling in the blanks with sample answers.

Learn It

Remember that if the compound subject is joined by the word *and*, it is considered plural because there are two subjects. Since verbs must agree with their subjects, pay careful attention to both. Fill in the missing verbs in the sentences below.

Example: Lucy *and* Fritz usually ___climb___ on the jungle gym.

1. Theo and Winston ___**run**___ to the park.
2. Peggy and you ___**are**___ bringing the water bottles later.
3. Heidi and I ___**have**___ the soccer equipment.
4. Uncle Ulysses and the boys ___**are**___ coming to the game too.

Introductory Lesson
Compound Subjects

Analyze It

Analyze the following sentences (*S* = subject; *PV* = predicate verb; *hv* = helping verb; *adv* = adverb; *adj* = adjective; *do* = direct object; *p* = preposition; *op* = object of the preposition; *prep* = prepositional phrase).

> **Analyze It:** This is the essential part of the lesson. See Well-Ordered Notes Introductory.

1. You (S) and I (S) can (hv) surprise (PV) the (adj) cousins (do) (with (p) water (adj) balloons (op)) — prep, adv, modifies "surprise"

2. Did (hv) Uncle Ulysses (S) or Theo (S) put (PV) the (adj) balloons (do) (in (p) the (adj) crate (op))? — prep, adv, modifies "put"

Introductory Practice
Compound Subjects

1. Analyze the following sentences (*S* = subject; *PV* = predicate verb; *hv* = helping verb; *adv* = adverb; *adj* = adjective; *do* = direct object; *p* = preposition; *op* = object of the preposition; *prep* = prepositional phrase).

   a. S S PV
(On Tuesday,) Peggy and I went (with the family) (to the library.)
p op p adj op p adj op
adv prep — adv prep — adv prep

   b. hv S S PV
Did you and Dad get pirate books?
adj do

   c. S S hv hv hv PV
Theo and Lucy should not have been running (around the tables.)
adv — adv p adj op
prep

   d. S S PV
Afterward Dad and the group headed (to the market.)
adj p adj op
adv — adv prep

2. Complete the following sentences by adding a verb after the compound subject. You may also add a direct object, an adverb, or a prepositional phrase to construct each sentence.

   a. In the library, will Mr. Michaels and you **research together** ____________________?

   b. Yesterday Heidi and Peggy **checked out that book** ____________________.

c. Later Theo and two boys **drummed on the tables** ____________.

3. Imagine that you see Lucy at the library. With that in mind, write a sentence about it, being sure to include a compound subject.

The librarian and Lucy looked for books on the new shelves.

Well-Ordered Notes A

Practice It

Play Write What's Right. Divide the class into two or three teams. Have one representative from each team come to the board. Read one of the following sentences with the two verb options. Then say "Write what's right," which will signal the students to write the answer. The first student who writes the correct verb neatly and accurately gets the point. To maintain order during the game, subtract a point for the whole team if any team member says anything while the representative is writing.

> **Fewer than Five:** Rather than dividing the students into teams, have them all come to the board to play Write What's Right. The first student to choose and write the correct verb wins each round.

Example: ____________________ a fox or a rabbit fed before the hunt? (Is / Are)

1. The king and the queen (walk / walks) in the garden.
2. The squire and the knight (prepare / prepares) for the tournament.
3. The duchess or the duke (wait / waits) in the ballroom for the guests.
4. During dinner, the witty, clever jester (entertain / entertains) the entire court.

Analyze It

As a class, analyze the following sentences (*S* = subject; *PV* = predicate verb; *hv* = helping verb; *adv* = adverb; *adj* = adjective; *do* = direct object; *p* = preposition; *op* = object of the preposition; *prep* = prepositional phrase). Write the sentences on the board. Have the students analyze the sentences, reciting the analysis aloud using the following script. While the students recite, you will mark the sentence on the board.

1. Will (hv) the (adj) green (adj) knight (S) or the (adj) white (adj) knight (S) win (PV) the (adj) battle (do)?

2. (During (p) the (adj) tournament (op)) (adv prep) the (adj) queen (S) and the (adj) princess (S) return (PV).

Will the green knight⟩or⟨the white knight win the battle?

Part 1: Identify Phrases and Conjunctions

a. (First, read the sentence aloud.) "Will the green knight or the white knight win the battle?"

b. "Are there any conjunctions?" (Choral response: "Yes, sir.") (Mark the conjunction *or* with two angle brackets.)

c. "The order of analysis is phrases, clauses, principal elements, modifiers."

d. "Are there any prepositional phrases?" (Choral answer: "No, sir.")

Part 2: Identify Principal Elements and Modifiers

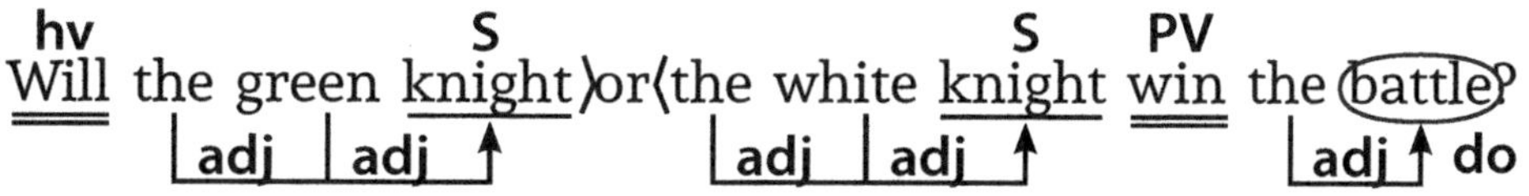

a. (Read the sentence aloud again.) "Will the green knight or the white knight win the battle?"

b. "This is a sentence and it is interrogative."

c. "This sentence is about *knight* and *knight*." (Underline the subject.) "So, *knight* and *knight* are the subjects because they are what the sentence is about." (Place a capital letter *S* above each subject.)

d. "*Or* is the conjunction."

e. "This sentence tells us that knight or knight *will win*." (Double underline the helping verb and the predicate verb. "So, *will win* is the predicate because it is what the sentence tells us about *knight* and *knight*." (Place a capital letter *P* above the action verb.) "It is a predicate verb because it shows action." (Place a capital letter *V* to the right of the letter *P*.) "There is no linking verb because predicate verbs do not need linking verbs. *Will* is a helping verb because it helps the verb." (Place a lowercase *hv* above the helping verb.)

f. "*Battle* tells us what the green knight and the white knight will win." (Draw a circle around the word.) "So, *battle* is an objective element because it completes the meaning of the action verb. It is a direct object because it tells *what* the green knight and the white knight will win." (Write *do* in lowercase letters beneath the direct object.)

g. "*The* is an adjective."[1] (Draw a straight line down from the adjective, then a horizontal line toward the word that it modifies, and then a straight line with an arrow pointing to the word it modifies. Write *adj* in lowercase letters in the elbow opposite the line with the arrow.)

1. The words *article adjective* can be substituted in place of the word *adjective*.

h. "*White* tells us *what kind* of knight." (Draw a straight line down from the adjective, then a horizontal line toward the word that it modifies, and then a straight line with an arrow pointing to the word it modifies. Write ***adj*** in lowercase letters in the elbow opposite the line with the arrow.) "So, *white* is an adjective element because it modifies a noun. It is an adjective."

i. "*The* is an adjective."[2] (Draw a straight line down from the adjective, then a horizontal line toward the word that it modifies, and then a straight line with an arrow pointing to the word it modifies. Write ***adj*** in lowercase letters in the elbow opposite the line with the arrow.)

j. "*Green* tells us *what kind* of knight." (Draw a straight line down from the adjective, then a horizontal line toward the word that it modifies, and then a straight line with an arrow pointing to the word it modifies. Write ***adj*** in lowercase letters in the elbow opposite the line with the arrow.) "So, *green* is an adjective element because it modifies a noun. It is an adjective."

k. "*The* is an adjective."[3] (Draw a straight line down from the adjective, then a horizontal line toward the word that it modifies and connect the line to the modifying line of the word *green*. The two modifying lines are joined and point, with a straight line, toward the word they modify. Write ***adj*** in lowercase letters in the elbow opposite the line with the arrow.)

For the analysis of the second sentence, adjust the script accordingly.

2. The words *article adjective* can be substituted in place of the word *adjective*.
3. The words *article adjective* can be substituted in place of the word *adjective*.

Notes

Lessons to Learn
Compound Subjects

A

The order of the lesson is: **Review It**, **Practice It**, **Learn It**, and **Analyze It**.

Review It: Sing/chant and review definitions as a class. Consider adding freshness by varying speed and volume or by asking individual students to paraphrase the meaning of a definition.

Review It

What is a conjunction?

Give an example of a sentence with the conjunction *and*.

Give an example of a sentence with the conjunction *or*.

Practice It: For this warm-up, see Well-Ordered Notes A.

Learn It: This part of the lesson can be completed individually and then volunteers can come to the board and write their sentences on the board.

Learn It

Remember, if a compound subject is joined by the word *or*, it can be either singular or plural depending on the subject that is closer to the verb. The verb must agree in number with the closer subject.

Example: Winston *or* the boys (is playing / are playing) basketball tonight.

The boys *or* Winston (is playing / are playing) basketball tonight.

Circle the correct verb that goes with the compound subject in each of the following sentences.

1. The neighbors or Grandpa Fred often (drives / drive) the kids.
2. Lucy or Theo (is coming / are coming) to the movies with us too.
3. Usually Fritz or the other boys (sits / sit) in the backseat.
4. Peggy or all the girls (is asking / are asking) for popcorn.
5. The aunts or just Grandma Lola (is meeting / are meeting) us there.

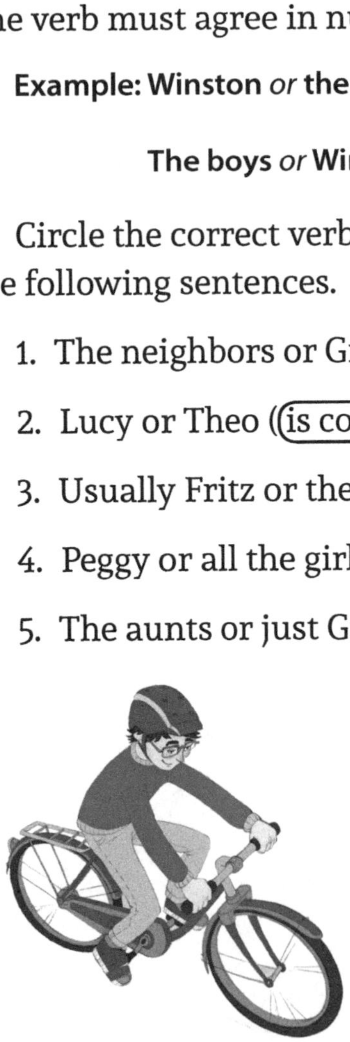

A Lessons to Learn
Compound Subjects

Analyze It

Analyze the following sentences (*S* = subject; *PV* = predicate verb; *hv* = helping verb; *adv* = adverb; *adj* = adjective; *do* = direct object; *p* = preposition; *op* = object of the preposition; *prep* = prepositional phrase).

> **Analyze It**: This is the essential part of the lesson. See Well-Ordered Notes A.

hv S S PV
1. Will the green knight or the white knight win the battle?
adj adj adj adj adj do

S S PV
2. (During the tournament) the queen and the princess return.
p adj op adj adj
adv
prep

Lessons to Practice

Compound Subjects

A

1. Analyze the following sentences (*S* = subject; *PV* = predicate verb; *hv* = helping verb; *adv* = adverb; *adj* = adjective; *do* = direct object; *p* = preposition; *op* = object of the preposition; *prep* = prepositional phrase).

   a. (Near the forest) the turtle and the rabbit have a race.

   S S PV
   p adj op adj adj adj do
   adv prep

   b. The sly fox and the brown hedgehog wait (for the turtle).

   S S PV
   adj adj adj adj p adj op
   adv prep

   c. Slowly the turtle crawls (along the path).

   S PV
   adj p adj op
   adv adv prep

   d. (At the end) does the turtle or the rabbit learn the lesson?

   hv S S PV
   p adj op adj adj adj do
   adv prep

2. Complete the following sentences by adding a verb after the compound subject. You may also add a direct object, an adverb, or a prepositional phrase to construct each sentence.

   a. Grandma and Grandpa are coming later today ____________________

   ____.

b. Will Mom or the girls **bring the cupcakes** ______________________________

______________________________?

c. Fritz and Lucy **were setting the table for dinner** ______________________________

______________________________.

3. Imagine there is a hedgehog at the race between the turtle and the rabbit. With that in mind, write a sentence about it, being sure to include a compound subject.

The hedgehog and the fox were cheering for the contestants. ______________________________

____

Well-Ordered Notes B

Practice It

Lead the class in the activity Write on White using mini whiteboards. Read aloud each of the following compound subjects and have the students write a corresponding verb on their boards and hold up their answers. As a teacher, you can quickly see if the selected verb agrees with the compound subject or not.

Variation: Have eight volunteers come to the board and have each take a turn writing a verb to match one of the compound subjects that you say aloud (i.e., each volunteer supplies one verb for one compound subject).

Example: Ice and snow **Ice and snow *melt*.**

1. Jack and Jill **fell**.
2. A caterpillar and a centipede **crawl**.
3. Lucy or Fritz **explores**.
4. Bees and butterflies **pollinate**.
5. A skylark or a sea gull **soars**.
6. Stripes and Rex **nap**.
7. You or I **come**.
8. Pollywogs and minnows **swim**.

pollywogs: tadpoles

Analyze It

As a class, analyze the following sentences (*S* = subject; *PV* = predicate verb; *hv* = helping verb; *adv* = adverb; *adj* = adjective; *do* = direct object; *p* = preposition; *op* = object of the preposition; *prep* = prepositional phrase). Write the sentences on the board. Have the students analyze the sentences, reciting the analysis aloud using the following script. While the students recite, you will mark the sentence on the board.

S S PV
1. The younger brother and the older sister raced (toward the red line.)
adj adj adj adj p adj adj op
adv
prep

hv S S PV
2. Will you or I award the winners?
adj do

The younger brother⟩and⟨the older sister raced (toward the red line)
p adj adj op

Part 1: Identify Phrases and Conjunctions

a. (First, read the sentence aloud.) "The younger brother and the older sister raced toward the red line."

b. "Are there any conjunctions?" (Choral response: "Yes, sir.") (Mark the conjunction *and* with two angle brackets.)

c. "The order of analysis is phrases, clauses, principal elements, modifiers."

d. "Are there any prepositional phrases?" (Choral response: "Yes, sir.") "*Toward the red line* is a prepositional phrase." (Place parentheses around the prepositional phrase.)

e. "*Toward* is the preposition." (Place a lowercase *p* underneath the preposition.)

f. "*Red line* is the object of the preposition." (Place a lowercase *op* underneath the object of the preposition.)

g. "*The* is an adjective."[1] (Draw a straight line down from the adjective, then a horizontal line toward the word that it modifies, and then a straight line with an arrow pointing to the word it modifies. Write *adj* in lowercase letters in the elbow opposite the line with the arrow.)

Part 2: Identify Principal Elements and Modifiers

S S PV
The younger brother⟩and⟨the older sister raced(toward the red line.)
adj adj adj adj p adj adj op
adv
prep

a. (Read the sentence aloud again.) "The younger brother and the older sister raced toward the red line."

b. "This is a sentence and it is declarative."

c. "This sentence is about *brother* and *sister*." (Underline the subjects.) "So, *brother* and *sister* are the subjects because they are what the sentence is about." (Place a capital letter *S* above each subject.)

d. "*And* is the conjunction."

e. "This sentence tells us that brother and sister *raced*." (Double underline the predicate.) "So, *raced* is the predicate because it is what the sentence tells us about *brother* and *sister*." (Place a capital letter *P* above the predicate.) "It is a predicate verb because it shows action." (Place a capital letter *V* to the right of the letter *P* above the predicate.) "There is no linking verb because predicate verbs do not need linking verbs."

1. The words *article adjective* can be substituted in place of the word *adjective*.

f. "*Toward the red line* tells us *where* brother and sister raced." (Draw a straight line down from the letter *p* that's under the preposition, then a horizontal line toward the word that it modifies, and then a straight line with an arrow pointing to the word it modifies.) "So, *toward the red line* is an adverbial element because it modifies a verb. It is an adverbial prepositional phrase." (Write ***adv*** in lowercase letters in the elbow opposite the line with the arrow. Write ***prep*** in lowercase letters directly below the ***adv***, underneath the modifier line.)

g. "*Older* tells us *what kind* of sister." (Draw a straight line down from the adjective, then a horizontal line toward the word that it modifies, and then a straight line with an arrow pointing to the word it modifies. Write ***adj*** in lowercase letters in the elbow opposite the line with the arrow.) "So, *older* is an adjective element because it modifies a noun. It is an adjective."

h. "*The* is an adjective."[2] (Draw a straight line down from the adjective, then a horizontal line toward the word that it modifies, and then a straight line with an arrow pointing to the word it modifies. Write ***adj*** in lowercase letters in the elbow opposite the line with the arrow.)

i. "*Younger* tells us *what kind* of brother." (Draw a straight line down from the adjective, then a horizontal line toward the word that it modifies, and then a straight line with an arrow pointing to the word it modifies. Write ***adj*** in lowercase letters in the elbow opposite the line with the arrow.) "So, *younger* is an adjective element because it modifies a noun. It is an adjective."

j. "*The* is an adjective."[3] (Connect the modifying line to ***brother*** and write ***adj*** in the elbow opposite the line with the arrow. Draw a straight line down from the adjective, then a horizontal line toward the word that it modifies and connect the line to the modifying line of the word ***brother***. The two modifying lines are joined and point, with a straight line, toward the word they modify. Write ***adj*** in lowercase letters in the elbow opposite the line with the arrow.)

For the analysis of the second sentence, adjust the script accordingly.

2. The words *article adjective* can be substituted in place of the word *adjective*.
3. The words *article adjective* can be substituted in place of the word *adjective*.

Notes

Lessons to Learn
Compound Subjects

B

The order of the lesson is: **Review It**, **Practice It**, **Learn It**, and **Analyze It**.

Review It: Sing/chant and review definitions as a class.

Review It

Can you answer the following questions by heart?

What are the eight parts of speech?

What are principal elements?

What are nouns?

What is a conjunction?

Practice It: For this warm-up, see Well-Ordered Notes B.

Learn It: This part of the lesson can be completed individually and then reviewed as a class as you or a student writes a possible answer for each sentence on the board.

Learn It

What happens to the predicate in a sentence when another subject is added? If the sentence has a compound subject that includes the conjunction *and*, then it is plural and the verb should agree with it. In the following sentences, add the conjunction *and* along with another subject to form a compound subject. Then, change the verb so it agrees with the compound subject. Write each new sentence on the lines provided.

Example: The robin sings in the morning.
The robin *and the blackbird sing* in the morning.

1. Stripes hides under the porch. **Stripes *and Lucy hide* under the porch together.**

2. Slowly Fritz brings the four buckets to the truck. **Slowly Fritz *and the boys bring* the four buckets to the truck.**

3. Heidi washes the car in the afternoon. **Heidi *and Peggy wash* the car in the afternoon.**

B Lessons to Learn
Compound Subjects

4. Dad surprises the kids with Popsicles. **Dad *and Mom surprise* the kids with Popsicles.**

Analyze It

> **Analyze It:** This is the essential part of the lesson. See Well-Ordered Notes B.

Analyze the following sentences (*S* = subject; *PV* = predicate verb; *hv* = helping verb; *adv* = adverb; *adj* = adjective; *do* = direct object; *p* = preposition; *op* = object of the preposition; *prep* = prepositional phrase).

1. The younger brother⟩and⟨the older sister raced (toward the red line.)

   S = brother, sister; **PV** = raced; **adj** = The, younger, the, older, the, red; **p** = toward; **op** = line; **adv** / **prep** = (toward the red line)

2. Will you⟩or⟨I award the winners?

   hv = Will; **S** = you, I; **PV** = award; **adj** = the; **do** = winners

Lessons to Practice B

Compound Subjects

1. Analyze the following sentences (*S* = subject; *PV* = predicate verb; *hv* = helping verb; *adv* = adverb; *adj* = adjective; *do* = direct object; *p* = preposition; *op* = object of the preposition; *prep* = prepositional phrase).

   a. The harsh winds and the icy rain pelted (against the window.)

   S: winds, rain; PV: pelted; adj: The, harsh, the, icy, the; p: against; op: window; adv prep: (against the window)

   b. Will Coach Stevens or Coach Howard cancel soccer practice tonight?

   hv: Will; S: Coach Stevens, Coach Howard; PV: cancel; adj: soccer; do: practice; adv: tonight

   c. Mom and the kids were hoping (for the phone call.)

   S: Mom, kids; hv: were; PV: hoping; adj: the, the, phone; p: for; op: call; adv prep: (for the phone call)

   d. Reluctantly Heidi and Fritz climbed (into the van)(for practice.)

   S: Heidi, Fritz; PV: climbed; adv: Reluctantly; p: into; adj: the; op: van; p: for; op: practice; adv prep: (into the van); adv prep: (for practice)

2. Add compound subjects to the sentences below.

   a. **Winston and Theo** race cars.

   b. **Mom and the boys** fly kites.

   c. **Fritz and Peggy** will climb trees.

   d. **Grandpa and the cousins** explore.

3. Imagine the soccer team is on the field in the rain. With that in mind, write a sentence about it, being sure to include a compound subject.

The coach and the soccer team practiced in the freezing rain for only one hour.

Well-Ordered Notes C

Practice It

Play the game To the Board. Divide the students into two teams for this relay. Have one representative from each team stand at the board and write. Say one of the following verbs to the students, and then say, "Write." Each representative is to construct a sentence using a subject compound and that verb. Tell students that verbs can be changed to fit the compound subject they use. The winner receives a point for his team for being first to construct a sentence. Another point is rewarded for a neatly and correctly composed sentence (either or both teams can receive this point). Insist on legible writing, and reinforce using correct punctuation and capital letters. Just because it is a race doesn't mean that sloppy work is acceptable.

> **Fewer than Five:** Adapt the relay by having each student write as many sentences as he can using compound subjects and the provided verbs. You can participate too. Whoever constructs the most correct, neatly written sentences wins.

Example: Teacher: "Chase."
Student 1: *Rex and Theo* chase after the Frisbee.
Student 2: *Fritz and Lucy* chase after Rex.

guide	throw	laugh
yawn	dunk	wonder
listen	squeak	

Analyze It

As a class, analyze the following sentences (*S* = subject; *PV* = predicate verb; *hv* = helping verb; *adv* = adverb; *adj* = adjective; *do* = direct object; *p* = preposition; *op* = object of the preposition; *prep* = prepositional phrase). Write the sentences on the board. Have the students analyze the sentences, reciting the analysis aloud using the following script. While the students recite, you will mark the sentence on the board.

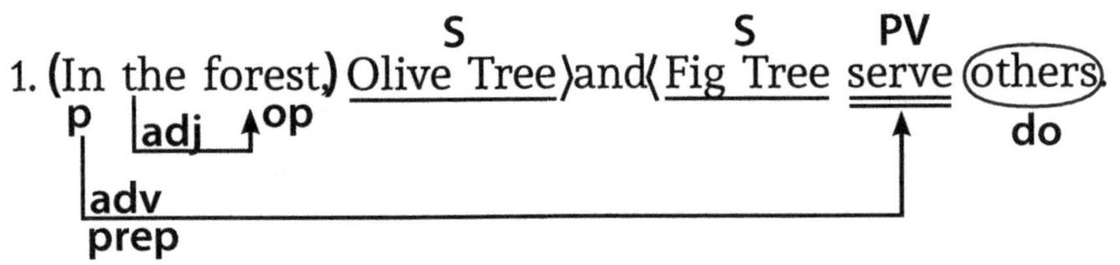

hv S S PV
2. Will Vine)or(Thornbush reign (over the trees)
p adj op
adv
prep

(In the forest) Olive Tree)and(Fig Tree serve others.
p adj op

Part 1: Identify Phrases and Conjunctions

a. (First, read the sentence aloud.) "In the forest, Olive Tree and Fig Tree serve others."

b. "Are there any conjunctions?" (Choral response: "Yes, sir.") (Mark the conjunction *and* with two angle brackets.)

c. "The order of analysis is phrases, clauses, principal elements, modifiers."

d. "Are there any prepositional phrases?" (Choral: "Yes, sir.") "*In the forest* is a prepositional phrase." (Place parentheses around the prepositional phrase.)

e. "*In* is the preposition." (Place a lowercase *p* underneath the preposition.)

f. "*Forest* is the object of the preposition." (Place a lowercase *op* underneath the object of the preposition.)

g. "*The* is an adjective."[1] (Draw a straight line down from the adjective, then a horizontal line toward the word that it modifies, and then a straight line with an arrow pointing to the word it modifies. Write *adj* in lowercase letters in the elbow opposite the line with the arrow.)

Part 2: Identify Principal Elements and Modifiers

S S PV
(In the forest,) Olive Tree)and(Fig Tree serve (others)
p adj op do
adv
prep

a. (Read the sentence aloud again.) "In the forest, Olive Tree and Fig Tree serve others."

b. "This is a sentence and it is declarative."

1. The words *article adjective* can be substituted in place of the word *adjective*.

c. "This sentence is about *Olive Tree* and *Fig Tree*." (Underline the subjects.) "So, *Olive Tree* and *Fig Tree* are the subjects because they are what the sentence is about." (Place a capital letter *S* above each subject.)

d. "*And* is the conjunction."

e. "This sentence tells us that Olive Tree and Fig Tree *serve*." (Double underline the predicate.) "So, *serve* is the predicate because it is what the sentence tells us about *Olive Tree* and *Fig Tree*." (Place a capital letter *P* above the predicate.) "It is a predicate verb because it shows action." (Place a capital letter *V* to the right of the letter *P* above the predicate.) "There is no linking verb because predicate verbs do not need linking verbs."

f. "*Others* tells us whom the Olive Tree and Fig Tree serve." (Draw a circle around the word.) "So, *others* is an objective element because it completes the meaning of the action verb. It is a direct object because it tells *whom* Olive Tree and Fig Tree serve." (Write *do* in lowercase letters beneath the direct object.)

g. "*In the forest* tells us *where* Olive Tree and Fig Tree serve." (Draw a straight line down from the letter *p* that's under the preposition, then a horizontal line toward the word that it modifies, and then a straight line with an arrow pointing to the word it modifies.) "So, *in the forest* is an adverbial element because it modifies a verb. It is an adverbial prepositional phrase." (Write *adv* in lowercase letters in the elbow opposite the line with the arrow. Write *prep* in lowercase letters directly below the *adv*, underneath the modifier line.)

For the analysis of the second sentence, adjust the script accordingly.

Notes

Lessons to Learn C
Compound Subjects

The order of the lesson is: **Review It**, **Practice It**, **Learn It**, and **Analyze It**.

Review It: Sing/chant and review definitions as a class. Consider adding freshness by varying speed and volume or by asking individual students to paraphrase the meaning of a definition.

Learn It: This part of the lesson can be completed individually and then reviewed as a class as you write possible answers on the board.

Review It

List the eight parts of speech on a sheet of paper. See if you can define from memory the seven parts of speech that you have learned. (You don't have to define an interjection yet. You'll learn that definition in *Well-Ordered Language Level 2*.)

Practice It: For this warm-up, see Well-Ordered Notes C.

Learn It

Subtract a subject and the conjunction from the following sentences and rewrite them on the lines provided. You might have to change the verb to make it agree with the subject.

Example: ***Winston and Theo play* basketball in the outside court.**
***Winston plays* basketball in the outside court.**

1. Peggy and Heidi eat potato chips on a bench nearby.

   Peggy eats potato chips on a bench nearby.

2. Does that water bottle or the thermos have a leak?

   Does that water bottle have a leak?

3. Lucy and Fritz watch silently at the park.

   Fritz watches silently at the park.

4. Will Dad or Mom come for the kids at noon?

   Will Mom come for the kids at noon?

C Lessons to Learn
Compound Subjects

Analyze It

Analyze the following sentences (*S* = subject; *PV* = predicate verb; *hv* = helping verb; *adv* = adverb; *adj* = adjective; *do* = direct object; *p* = preposition; *op* = object of the preposition; *prep* = prepositional phrase).

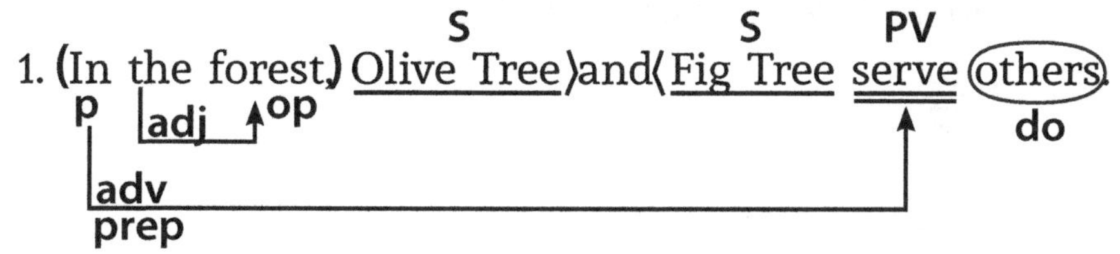

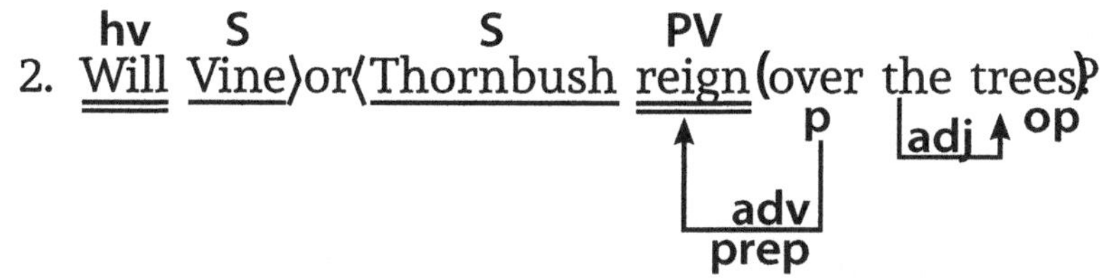

Analyze It: This is the essential part of the lesson. See Well-Ordered Notes C.

From the Sideline: Please note that these sentences complement the fable for this chapter. The names of the trees are proper nouns in the fable, so they are capitalized in these sentences as well. Note that "Olive Tree" is treated as a single proper noun and not a noun with an adjective. Likewise, "Fig Tree" is considered as a single word in the analysis.

Lessons to Practice C
Compound Subjects

1. Analyze the following sentences (*S* = subject; *PV* = predicate verb; *hv* = helping verb; *adv* = adverb; *adj* = adjective; *do* = direct object; *p* = preposition; *op* = object of the preposition; *prep* = prepositional phrase).

   a. S S PV
   Dad and the girls planned a trip (to the butterfly exhibit.)
   adj · adj · do · p · adj · adj · op · adv prep

   b. S S PV
   Peggy and Lucy love bright butterflies.
   adj · do

   c. PV S S PV
   Can Heidi or Fritz come along (on the trip)?
   adv · p · adj · op · adv prep

   d. S PV
   Later, (among the branches,) the girls saw beautiful butterflies.
   p · adj · op · adj · adj · do · adv prep · adv

2. Complete the following sentences by adding a verb after the compound subject. You may also add a direct object, an adverb, or a prepositional phrase to construct each sentence.

   a. The guitarist and drummer **played the song** ______________________.

   b. Lucy and Fritz **danced around the floor** ______________________.

c. Later, the lady singer and the piano player **sang a quiet song** ____.

3. Imagine Winston, Heidi, and Fritz are going to a concert with their parents. With that in mind, write a sentence about it, being sure to use a compound subject.

Dad and the kids listened to the solo.

Review It: Sing/chant and review definitions as a class.

Review It

Answer the following review questions:

What is a preposition?

What is an object of the preposition?

What is a phrase?

Can you list all of the forty-seven prepositions you've learned?

Learn It: Remember, Lightning is a review game that requires quickness. Give the students five seconds to answer.

Learn It

Play Lightning to form sentences with compound subjects. Your teacher will give a topic to the first student, who will say two nouns. The second student will construct a sentence using the two nouns (compound subject).

Example: Teacher: "Two rivers."
Student 1: "The Mississippi River and the Missouri River."
Student 2: "The Mississippi River and the Missouri River are major water highways."

Two pets people keep
Two players on a team
Two places your family visits
Two days of the week
Two toys you play with
Two books in your room
Two states bordering an ocean
Two months of the year
Two boys in your class
Two creatures in the forest
Two fruits you eat
Two games you play
Two foods you eat for lunch
Two people in your family
Two authors of books
Two people who sit near you
Two animals in a zoo
Two girls in your neighborhood
Two people you visit

1. Analyze the following sentences: (*S* = subject; *PV* = predicate verb; *hv* = helping verb; *adv* = adverb; *adj* = adjective; *do* = direct object; *p* = preposition; *op* = object of the preposition; *prep* = prepositional phrase).

    S S hv hv PV
    a. (On Monday) Mom)and(I will be working (at the food shelter.)
    p op p adj adj op
    adv prep adv prep

    S S PV
    b. Several men)and(women stood (in line) outside.
    p op
    adv adv prep adv

    hv S S PV
    c. Did she)or(you shovel the sidewalks (for the people)
    adj do p adj op
    adv prep

    S S PV
    d. Foolishly many children)and(toddlers raced about (at the shelter)
    adj adv p adj op
    adv adv prep

2. Complete the following sentences by adding a verb after the compound subject. You may also add a direct object, an adverb, or a prepositional phrase to construct each sentence.

    a. In science class, Heidi and Peggy **asked about birds** ______________________________

    ____.

b. Can a parrot or a toucan **talk** ______________________________

______________________________?

c. The teacher and the students **made parrot sounds** ______________________________

______________________________.

3. Imagine you are on a field trip at the zoo and you're standing in the bird room. With that in mind, write a sentence, being sure to use a compound subject.

A yellow canary and a green parrot flew around the bird room at the zoo.

____

Notes

Have you heard the saying "Be careful what you wish because you might get it"? Sometimes we are so sure we want something that we think we *must* have it no matter what. However, when we get it, we may end up regretting it. In this Hebrew fable, the forest trees decide they want a king to rule over them, so they ask an olive tree, a fig tree, a vine, and a thornbush each to be their leader. Which one will agree to be the leader, and will they be happy with their new king at the end?

The Trees Choose a King

Hebrew Fable

anoint: apply oil in a special ceremony

hold sway over: rule over

One day, the Trees went out to anoint a King for themselves. They said to the Olive Tree, "Be our King."

But the Olive Tree answered, "Should I give up my oil, by which both gods and men are honored, to hold sway over the Trees?"

Next, the Trees said to the Fig Tree, "Come and be our King."

But the Fig Tree replied, "Should I give up my fruit, so good and sweet, to hold sway over the Trees?"

Then the Trees said to the [Grape] Vine, "Come and be our King."

But the Vine answered, "Should I give up my wine, which cheers both gods and men, to hold sway over the Trees?"

Finally, the Trees said to the Thornbush, "Come and be our King."

The Thornbush said to the Trees, "If you really want to anoint me King over you, come and take refuge in my shade; but if not,

Cedars of Lebanon: in the ancient world, this vast forest of cedar trees in the country of Lebanon supplied wood for many structures, ships, and religious ceremonies in various cultures

then let fire come out of the Thornbush and consume the Cedars of Lebanon!"

Moral: May your mouth match the intentions of your heart.[1]

Extras: Please note that the teacher's pages for this chapter include more material for extra practice, a quiz, and another Lessons to Enjoy section with discussion questions and activities. All this material, in reproducible form, is also included in the PDF that accompanies the textbook.

Questions to Ponder

1. Why do you think the Trees wanted to anoint a King for themselves?
2. What Trees are named in the fable?
3. Can you tell in your own words what the Thornbush says to the Trees?

From the Sideline: For possible answers to these discussion questions, see p. a of the teacher's pages. For even more suggestions for discussion and for enrichment activities related to the poem, see p. b.

1. "The Trees Choose a King," taken from *Writing & Rhetoric Book 1: Fable* by Paul Kortepeter (Camp Hill, PA: Classical Academic Press, 2013), p. 115.

Lessons to Enjoy—Fable

Questions to Ponder

1. Why do you think the Trees wanted to anoint a King for themselves?

   Answers to this question will vary because no reason for the Trees' wish is stated clearly in the tale. Allow the students to use their imaginations in speculating why the Trees might want a King—perhaps for protection, for status in the eyes of others, or for someone to boss them around. Thinking about why people desire leaders will help the students understand the "intentions of your heart" part of the moral later in the discussion. You might ask them now if they think the Trees have good intentions or foolish ones.

2. What Trees are named in the fable?

   The Olive Tree, Fig Tree, Grape Vine, and Thornbush are named in the fable. You may also want to ask your students if they know what the Trees provide for the good of everyone. Help the students understand that the Trees already provide in special ways for the good of everyone without being King. The Olive Tree provides oil for cooking, for ointments, for medicine, and for religious ceremonies. The fruit of the Fig Tree is a sweet treat also used for medicine. The Grape Vine provides grapes and wine—and juice for modern children. In the tale, these three Trees nobly refuse to be King in order to continue providing for all. While the Thornbush provides shade (and can also be used medicinally), its value is more questionable than the other Trees. Its thorns are sharp and dangerous. As a bush, it grows low to the ground, so its shade is not easily accessible. Explain these characteristics of the Thornbush to help the students answer the rather difficult next question.

3. Can you tell in your own words what the Thornbush says to the Trees?

   The warning of the Thornbush can be expressed in other words like this: "If you want me for King, you must accept what I have to offer: thorns and sparse shade. But if you don't want what I have to offer and foolishly have asked me anyway, then I will burn down the whole forest." A more modern version is the maxim "Be careful: You might get what you ask for." This part of the discussion will help the students understand the "mouth" part of the moral. In short, one's words should carefully match the deepest longings of the heart—not the fleeting and illusory desires of the moment.

Well-Ordered Notes—Fable

Read

- Help the students enjoy the fable as you read it aloud by using different voices for the different trees.
- Have students sing/chant the definition of a fable (Fable, 1–14).

Retell

- Discuss the tale using the provided questions.

Record

- Rewrite the tale as a class using animals instead of trees.
- Make a class book using linoleum block prints for the illustrations (see below).

Linoleum Block Prints

The process of creating linoleum block prints involves etching an image of a tree on a linoleum plate and printing it on another surface.

1. Locate the following items in an art supply or craft store:
    a. Linoleum printing blocks
    b. Acrylic paint (easier to use) or printing ink (water-based or oil-based; more involved)
    c. Linoleum carving tools (found at art supply or hobby stores)
    d. Rollers (You can also use soft foam rollers.)
    e. Paint tray (You can also use sturdy paper plates or plastic lids.)
2. Draw tree designs on the linoleum block. (Sketch a rough draft first.)
3. Carefully cut the tree design into the linoleum. (Make sure an adult is present.)
4. Prepare the paint (or ink) and practice using small amounts. (Less is more!)
5. Roll the paint on the block.
6. Make the print.
    a. Gently place the paper on the block.
    b. With dry hands, gently push the paper flat.
    c. Carefully pull back the paper.
    d. Leave the paper to dry.

Fable Sentences
Compound Subjects

ANSWERS

Analyze the following sentences (*S* = subject; *PV* = predicate verb; *hv* = helping verb; *adv* = adverb; *adj* = adjective; *do* = direct object; *p* = preposition; *op* = object of the preposition; *prep* = prepositional phrase).

sovereign: having supreme authority or power

S S PV
1. The Trees)and(the Bushes looked (for a Sovereign King)
adj adj p adj adj op
adv prep

S S PV
2. Several Trees)and(some Bushes asked the Olive Tree.
adj adj adj do

hv S PV
3. Will you rule (over us)(in the forest)?
p op p adj op
adv prep adv prep

S PV
4. The Olive Tree questioned the reason.
adj adj do

S S PV
5. Next, several Bushes)and(some Trees asked the Fig Tree.
adj adj adj do
adv

hv S PV
6. Will you govern (over us)?
p op
adv prep

7. Then many Trees and a few Bushes asked the Grape Vine.

S (Trees), S (Bushes), PV (asked); adj (many), adj (a), adj (few), adj (the), do (Grape Vine); adv (Then)

8. (In curiosity) the Grape Vine wondered the point.

S (Grape Vine), PV (wondered); p (In), op (curiosity); adj (the), adj (the), do (point); adv prep (In curiosity)

9. Finally a few Trees and one Bush asked the Thornbush.

S (Trees), S (Bush), PV (asked); adj (a), adj (few), adj (one), adj (the), do (Thornbush); adv (Finally)

10. (In seriousness) the Thornbush warned them.

S (Thornbush), PV (warned); p (In), op (seriousness); adj (the), do (them); adv prep (In seriousness)

Practice Sheet
Compound Subjects

ANSWERS

Analyze the following sentences (*S* = subject; *PV* = predicate verb; *hv* = helping verb; *adv* = adverb; *adj* = adjective; *do* = direct object; *p* = preposition; *op* = object of the preposition; *prep* = prepositional phrase).

S S PV
1. Slowly ice and snow blanketed the yard (during the afternoon.)
adv adj do p adj op
adv prep

S S PV
2. Winston and Theo played chess again (in the library.)
do adv p adj op
adv prep

S S PV
3. A rook and two pawns fell (off the table.)
adj adj p adj op
adv prep

S S PV
4. (In the corner,) a toddler and another child squabbled (over a book.)
p adj op adj adj p adj op
adv prep adv prep

S S PV
5. Heidi and Peggy chose books (from the shelves.)
do p adj op
adv prep

S S PV
6. The bench and the book table had animal books (on them.)
adj adj adj adj do p op
adv prep

7. Did Fritz or Lucy grab the last puzzle?
(hv: Did; S: Fritz; S: Lucy; PV: grab; adj: the; adj: last; do: puzzle)

8. The librarian and the aide signaled (to us) (from the front desk)
(S: librarian; S: aide; PV: signaled; adj: The; adj: the; p: to; op: us; adv prep: to us; p: from; adj: the; adj: front; op: desk; adv prep: from the front desk)

9. Will Grandpa or Grandma meet us here (after library time?)
(hv: Will; S: Grandpa; S: Grandma; PV: meet; do: us; adv: here; p: after; adj: library; op: time; adv prep: after library time)

10. Mom and the girls will put the books (in the book bag) now.
(S: Mom; S: girls; hv: will; PV: put; adj: the; adj: the; do: books; p: in; adj: the; adj: book; op: bag; adv prep: in the book bag; adv: now)

Quiz
Compound Subjects

ANSWERS

1. Analyze the following sentences (*S* = subject; *PV* = predicate verb; *hv* = helping verb; *adv* = adverb; *adj* = adjective; *do* = direct object; *p* = preposition; *op* = object of the preposition; *prep* = prepositional phrase).

   a. (In the yard,) Fritz and Lucy lazily pick dandelions.

   S S PV; p adj op; adv; do; adv prep

   b. Mom and Aunt Gabby were planting spring flowers (in the front flowerboxes.)

   S S hv PV; adj do p adj adj op; adv prep

   c. (Beyond the fence,) the neighbor boys and Winston are mowing the tall grass.

   S S hv PV; p adj op adj adj; adj adj do; adv prep

   d. Did Theo or you rake the grass piles (with that metal rake?)

   hv S S PV; adj adj do p adj adj op; adv prep

2. Complete the sentences below by adding a verb after the compound subject. You may also add a direct object, an adverb, or a prepositional phrase to construct each sentence.

   a. Rex and Stripes **were chasing after butterflies** ________.

   b. Cardinals and robins **built nests** ________.

c. Is he or she **bird watching with Peggy later** ______________________________?

3. Imagine the Winston, Theo, and Peggy are outside doing chores. With that in mind, write a sentence about it, being sure to use a compound subject.

Winston and Theo worked very hard in the yard.

The American poet Eugene Field captures the imaginative journey of three children fishing in the stars with their boat, a wooden shoe. At the end of the poem, he tells who these three fishermen are. Pay attention and don't slumber off.

Wynken, Blynken, and Nod

by Eugene Field (1850–1895)

Wynken, Blynken, and Nod one night
Sailed off in a wooden shoe,—
Sailed on a river of crystal light
Into a sea of dew.
"Where are you going and what do you wish?"
The old moon asked the three.
"We have come to fish for the herring fish
That lives in this beautiful sea—
Nets of silver and gold have we,"
Said Wynken,
Blynken,
And Nod.

The old moon laughed and sang a song,
As they rocked in the wooden shoe;
And the wind that sped them all night long
Ruffled the waves of dew.
The little stars were the herring fish
That lived in the beautiful sea—
"Now cast your nets wherever you wish,
Never afeard are we!"
So cried the stars to the fisherman three,
Wynken,
Blynken,
And Nod.

afeard: afraid

All night long their nets they threw
To the stars in the twinkling foam,—
Then down from the skies came the wooden shoe,
Bringing the fishermen home:
'Twas all so pretty a sail, it seemed
As if it could not be;
And some folk thought 'twas a dream they'd dreamed
Of sailing that beautiful sea;
But I shall name you the fishermen three:
Wynken,
Blynken,
And Nod.

Wynken and Blynken are two little eyes,
And Nod is a little head,
And the wooden shoe that sailed the skies
Is a wee one's trundle-bed;
So shut your eyes while mother sings
Of wonderful sights that be,
And you shall see the beautiful things
As you rock in the misty sea
Where the old shoe rocked the fishermen three:—
Wynken,
Blynken,
And Nod.[1]

trundle-bed: a low bed that, when not in use, can be pushed under a larger bed

misty: foggy, as in a layer of fog over the water

Questions to Ponder

1. What is this poem about?
2. Who is speaking (or singing) the poem?
3. What does "We have come to fish for the herring fish" mean?
4. Who are Wynken, Blynken, and Nod?

1. Eugene Field, "Wynken, Blynken, and Nod," in *Favorite Poems Old and New*, ed. Helen Ferris (New York: Doubleday & Company, Inc., 1957), pp. 55–56.

Lessons to Enjoy—Poem

Questions to Ponder

1. What is this poem about?

   The poem is literally about three characters who sail in a wooden shoe through the night sky fishing for stars. The last stanza reveals that the poem is about a child falling asleep in a little wooden bed and dreaming of beautiful things.

2. Who is speaking (or singing) the poem?

   This poem is a good illustration of how a reader should be careful not to assume the poet is the speaker of a poem. The poet may be using his own voice to describe a mother lulling her sleepy-eyed child to sweet dreams. On the other hand, the line "while mother sings" in the last stanza could reveal that the voice is feminine. Mothers often refer to themselves as "Mother" or "Mommy" when speaking to their very small children. Allow your students to entertain different interpretations.

3. What does "We have come to fish for the herring fish" mean?

   The fish are the stars, so the child's slumber is like fishing for them all night in the misty sea of the sky. The casting of nets in the twinkling foam is an image of peaceful dreaming.

4. Who are Wynken, Blynken, and Nod?

   They represent the child's sleepy eyes and nodding head. Ask the students to describe how they imagine them as characters. Are they elves? Do they look something like Snow White's dwarves? Perhaps your students are steeped in modern cartoons and will envision Wynken and Blynken as round eyes with arms and legs. Allow the students to use their imaginations but make sure they stay true to the peaceful, calming imagery of the poem.

Well-Ordered Notes—Poem

Read

- Read the poem to the students or play the folk song "Winkin', Blinkin', and Nod" by Carly Simon and Lucy Simon (available at https://www.youtube.com/watch?v=ZgmKcbLJVxg) while the students read along silently.
- Ask the students to memorize a favorite stanza from the poem.

Retell

- Discuss the poem using the provided questions.
- Write on the board these two sentences taken from the poem: "Wynken and Blynken are two little eyes" and "Wynken, Blynken, and Nod one night sailed off in a wooden shoe." Have students compare them and discuss the compound subjects in both sentences. Point out how three subjects are still considered a compound subject, and note the commas between the list of three proper nouns.

Record

- Have the students write about an adventure in a wooden shoe.
- Give the students black paper and colored chalk to illustrate the poem. Remind them that Wynken, Blynken, and Nod call the stars "herring fish."

[A]Throughout the chapter we use the term *compound verb* to mean multiple verbs that are joined with a conjunction and that together function as a single verb for a single subject. Some grammarians use the term *compound verb* (or *compound predicate*) differently from the way we define it. For example, some use it for a compound word that is a verb (e.g., babysit), for verbs paired with helping verbs (e.g., had been taken), and for other verbs comprised of multiple words but not including a conjunction.

From the Sidelines: Teach concretely. Use concrete illustrations and examples from what is known to bridge a path to the unknown. Let the known explain the unknown.

Chapter 6

Compound Verbs[A]

When you think of a thunderstorm, flashes of lightning and booms of thunder are probably the first things that come to your mind. Did you know that lightning and thunder actually happen at the same time? A bolt of lightning, which is more than 40,000 degrees Fahrenheit, heats the air around it, causing the air to expand quickly. Thunder is the result of the rapid expanding and contracting of the atmosphere that is caused by the bolt of lightning. The two events happen at the same time, but light travels faster than sound (in other words, you see the lightning before you hear the thunder).

From the Sidelines: Share with your students an interesting way to figure out the distance of a storm from your location. Count the number of seconds after a lightning flash is seen until you hear the boom of thunder. Count "one Mississippi, two Mississippi, three Mississippi." For every five seconds counted, the storm is one mile away. Divide the number of seconds you count by five to determine the number of miles the storm is away.

In an English sentence, when one thing (a subject) does two or more actions (has two verbs), those actions are called a **compound verb**.[A] Sometimes writers use many subjects with only one verb (a compound subject), and sometimes writers use one subject with many verbs (a compound verb). Either way, the compound elements are joined together with conjunctions. A compound verb gives you the power to describe vividly with multiple action words that midnight storm that once woke you up with a jolt: "The terrible tempest *flashed and rumbled*."

[B]Write excerpt from chapter one, "How the Whale Got His Throat" from *Just So Stories* by Rudyard Kipling on the board (see p. 150).

Ideas to Understand[B]

When two or more verbs are joined with a conjunction and have the same subject, they are called a compound verb. In Rudyard Kipling's story "How the Whale Got His Throat," two verbs—*swam* and *swam*—are joined with a conjunction, *and*. Together they form a compound verb:

Off the Shelf: Kipling's Whale is swimming and swimming to a precise location on the globe that is indicated by "latitude" and "longitude." Have you ever noticed the parallel lines on a globe, including the equator, that are drawn horizontally? They are lines of latitude. The vertical lines that are drawn between the North and South Poles are called longitude. Can you find latitude 50 North, longitude 40 West on a globe? That's where the Whale swam and swam.

> So the Whale swam and swam to latitude Fifty North, longitude Forty West, as fast as he could swim and *on* a raft, *in* the middle of the sea, *with* nothing to wear except a pair of blue canvas breeches, a pair of suspenders (you must particularly remember the suspenders, Best Beloved), *and* a jack-knife, he found one single, solitary shipwrecked Mariner, trailing his toes in the water.[1]

Kipling doubles his verbs and uses a long sentence to demonstrate the great distance the Whale swam. He didn't just swim; he *swam **and** swam*. Kipling's compound verb is unusual because it is the same word repeated twice. Compound verbs are often two different verbs or even more than two verbs. In the sentence "The whales swam, dove, and fished," the subject is *whales*, and three verbs—*swam*, *dove*, and *fished*—connected by a conjunction form the compound verb.

Just as in any other sentence, subjects and compound verbs must agree in number. A whale swims and swims, but whales swim and swim. The singular subject *whale* agrees with singular verbs, *swims* and *swims*. The plural subject *whales* agrees with plural verbs, *swim* and *swim*.

The verbs in a compound verb also can be separated by more than just a conjunction. Sometimes a direct object or even a prepositional phrase can separate the verbs. Take a look at the following examples:

With a ***conjunction***:

The whale *swims* >and< *spurts* water.

With a ***direct object*** and ***conjunction***:

The whale *spurts* water >and< *splashes* the dolphins.

With a ***direct object***, ***conjunction***, and ***prepositional phrase***:

The whale *spurts* water into the air >and< *splashes* the dolphins nearby.

A compound verb can include helping verbs too. If the compound verb includes only one helping verb, there is an implied helping verb for the second verb. For instance, consider the following sentence: "The whale is swimming and spurting water." The helping verb *is* assists both verbs to complete their meaning. The author is really saying that the whale *is swimming* >and< *is spurting* water, but the helping verb does not need to be repeated.

1. Rudyard Kipling, "How the Whale Got His Throat," *Just So Stories* (New York: Doubleday, CO, 1952), p. 9.

Terms to Remember[C]

Since there are only a couple of definitions to practice for this chapter, now is a good time to add an important concept to memorize. Do you already know what **synonyms**, **antonyms**, and **homonyms** are? In this chapter, knowing synonyms will come in handy for a few of the lessons. Remember, a synonym is a word that means almost the same thing as another word. For example, a synonym for *ocean* is *sea*.

[C]Play the appropriate CD tracks/audio files and have students sing/chant along. Remind students to commit the songs to memory by listening to these tracks/files at other times as well.

Verbs and Helping Verbs *(1–6)*

A verb is a part of speech. *(echo)*
A verb shows action or a state of being. *(echo)*
A verb is a part of speech. *(echo)*
A verb shows action or a state of being. *(echo)*
A helping verb helps another verb to express its meaning.
A helping verb stands near the verb.
It is called an auxiliary.
Am, is, are, was, were, be, being, been, has, have, had, do, does, did, may, might, must, should, could, would, shall, will, and *can*.
A helping verb stands near the verb and is called an auxiliary.
A helping verb stands near the verb. It is called an auxiliary.

Conjunction *(1–20)*

A conjunction is a part of speech.
It joins elements of the same rank or name.
When two or more words are joined this way, they're called compounds. *(Repeat.)*

NEW! Synonyms, Antonyms, and Homonyms *(1–21)*

Synonyms, antonyms, and homonyms
Synonyms are words that mean almost the same thing.
Antonyms are words that have the opposite meaning.
Homonyms are words that sound the same, but have different meaning and sometimes spelling—words that sound the same, but do not mean the same thing.
Synonyms, antonyms, and homonyms
Synonyms: little and small

Antonyms: short and tall
Homonyms: threw the ball, walk through the mall
Synonyms, antonyms, and homonyms
Synonyms, antonyms, and homonyms.

[D] As with compound subjects, analyzing compound verbs requires identifying conjunctions first. Help the students mark conjunctions with angle brackets or "wings" (> <). Then continue with the analysis as usual. Be sure to review the order of analysis chant. See p. a in the teacher's pages for a note about marking notations.

Sentences to Analyze[D]

As you learned in chapter 5, when you are studying sentences that contain compounds, you need to be on the lookout for conjunctions. Conjunctions are marked with two angle brackets, or "wings," on either side of the word: swam >and< splashed. Before you begin your complete analysis of a sentence, make sure that you mark the conjunctions with wings. The questions that have been added to your analysis script are there to help you analyze the sentence.

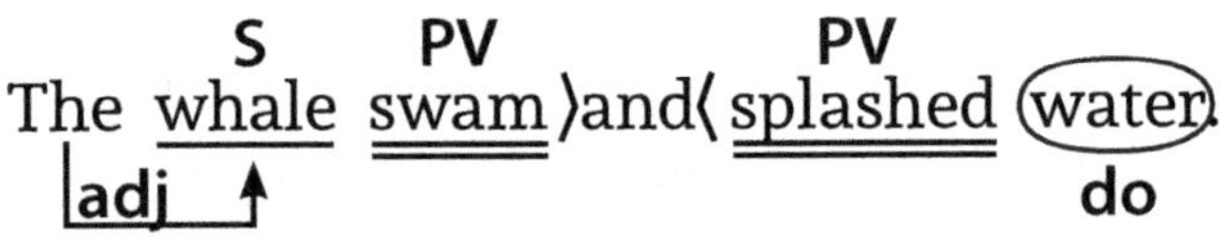

a. (First, read the sentence aloud.) "The whale swam and splashed water."

b. "Are there any conjunctions? (Choral response: "Yes, sir.") (Since *and* is a conjunction, put wings before and after it.)

c. "The order of analysis is phrases, clauses, principal elements, modifiers."

d. "Are there any prepositional phrases?" (Since there are none, you can answer *no* and continue.)

e. "This is a sentence, and it is declarative."

f. "This sentence is about *whale*. So, *whale* is the subject because it is what the sentence is about." (Since *whale* is the subject, underline it and place a capital letter *S* above it.)

g. "This sentence tells us that whale *swam* and *splashed*. So, *swam* and *splashed* are the predicates because they are what the sentence tells us about *whale*." (Since *swam* and *splashed* tell something about whale, double underline the predicates and place a capital letter *P* above each of them.) "They are predicate verbs because they show action. There is no linking verb because predicate verbs do not need linking verbs." (Since *swam* and *splashed* both show action, place a capital letter *V* to the right of the letter *P* above each predicate.)

h. "*And* is the conjunction."

i. "*Water* tells us what whale swam and splashed." (Since *water* tells *what* whale swam and splashed, draw a circle around it.) "So, *water* is an objective element because it completes the meaning of an action verb. It is a direct object because it tells *what* whale swam and splashed." (Write *do* in lowercase letters beneath the direct object.)

j. "*The* is an adjective."[2] (Since *the* is an adjective, draw a straight line down from the adjective, then a horizontal line toward the word that it modifies, and then a straight line with an arrow pointing to the word it modifies. Write *adj* in lowercase letters in the elbow opposite the line with the arrow.) **E**

[E]See p. a of the following teacher's pages for this note.

Do you remember our vivid sentence about the thunderstorm? "The terrible tempest *flashed and rumbled*." Using a compound verb made the scene described in the sentence easier to imagine. Now let's take that same sentence and apply some of the other things you are learning in this chapter. Let's choose different verbs and add direct objects and prepositional phrases: "The terrible tempest *shook* my bedroom in the middle of the night *and rattled* the trophies on my shelf." Adding a helping verb to a compound verb can make the action exciting and immediate, like this: "The thunderstorm *is terrifying* Rex *and keeping* me awake!" The words that you choose as a writer and where you place them in the sentence help you express your ideas in lively ways.

2. The words *article adjective* can be substituted in place of the word *adjective*.

Chapter 6: Compound Verbs

[E]From p. 153. Marking notations: When marking adverbial elements in a sentence with a compound verb, draw the modifier line to the closest verb.

a. **Adverb:** If a sentence has an adverb for its adverbial element, the modifier line must be drawn to the closest verb. For example, in the sentence "Suddenly the whale swam and splashed water," the modifier line connects *suddenly* and *swam*.

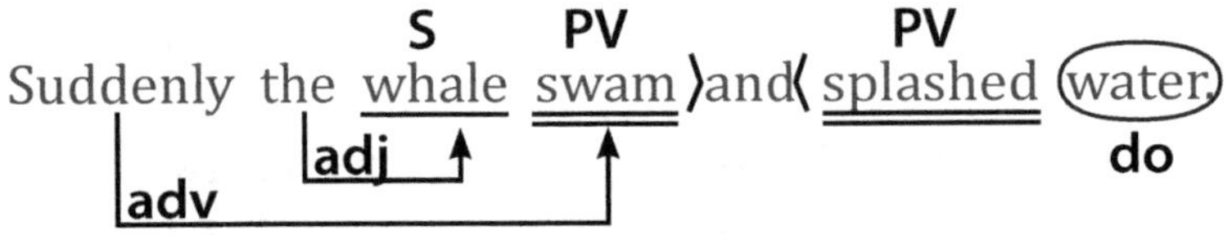

b. **Adverbial prepositional phrase:** If a sentence has an adverbial prepositional phrase for its adverbial element, the modifier lines must be drawn to the closest verb. For example, in the sentence "The whale swam and splashed water in the afternoon," the modifier line connects *in the afternoon* and *splashed*.

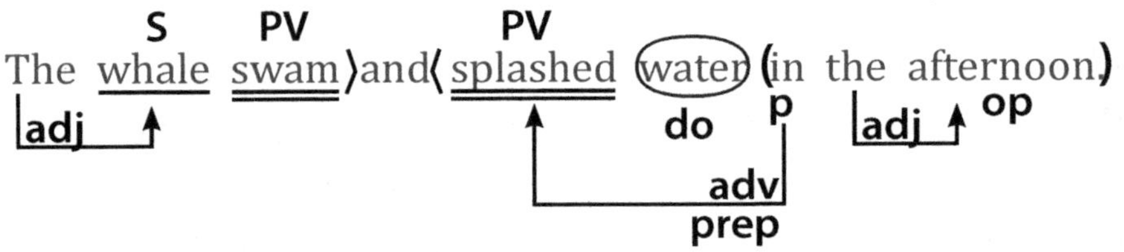

c. **Adverb with an adverbial prepositional phrase:** If a sentence has both an adverb and an adverbial prepositional phrase, the modifier lines must be drawn to the closest verb without connecting or intersecting. For example, in the sentence "Suddenly the whale swam and splashed water in the afternoon," a modifier line connects *in the afternoon* and *splashed* and another modifier line connects *suddenly* and *swam*.

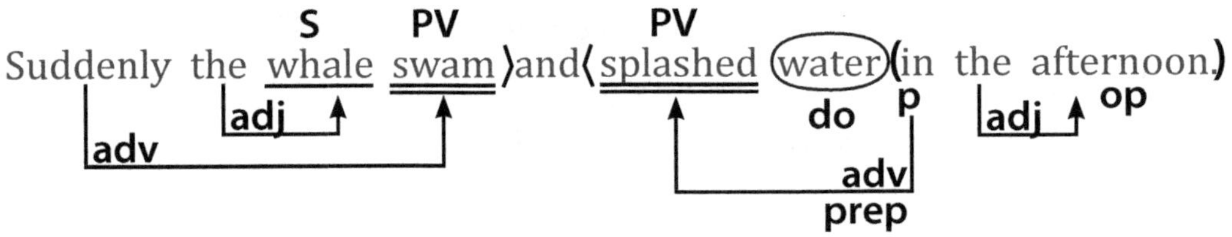

Notes

Well-Ordered Notes Introductory

Practice It

Play a game of Charades using the following synonyms for the verb *walk*. First, write the list on the board and discuss the subtle variations in meaning. Then, have the students draw an index card from a deck on which you've already written the synonyms, one per card. Each student takes a turn pantomiming the synonym while the other students guess which verb is being acted out.

From the Sidelines: Sing the Synonyms, Antonyms, and Homonyms song (1–21) to reinforce the definition of a synonym.

limp	dawdle (walk slowly while being pleasantly absentminded)
stomp	dart (walk speedily toward an object)
stride (walk confidently with long steps)	hike
march	sashay (walk like a model on a runway, swinging the hips, extending a bent arm)
patrol (walk alertly, scanning the scene)	tramp (walk with a heavy, loud step)
stroll (walk leisurely for recreation)	saunter (walk leisurely with no particular destination)
trudge (walk laboriously or wearily)	pace (walk back and forth slowly)
trip	toddle (walk unsteadily)
waddle	mosey (walk slowly, wasting time, perhaps with a shuffle)

Analyze It

As a class, analyze the following sentences (*S* = subject; *PV* = predicate verb; *hv* = helping verb; *adv* = adverb; *adj* = adjective; *do* = direct object; *p* = preposition; *op* = object of the preposition; *prep* = prepositional phrase). Write the sentences on the board. Have the students analyze the sentences, reciting the analysis aloud using the following script. While the students recite, you will mark the sentence on the board.

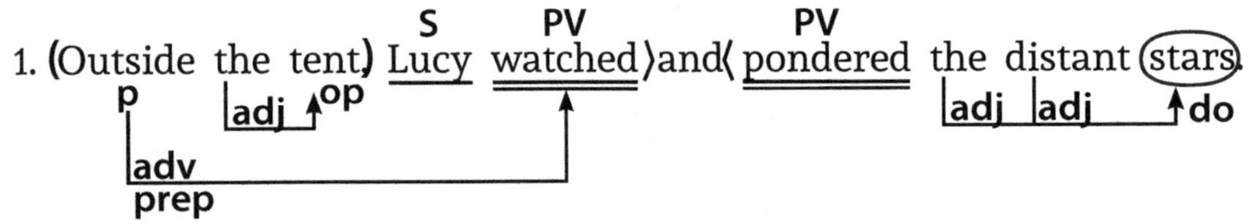

S PV PV

2. (Under the night sky) Theo stretched ⟩and⟨ yawned loudly.

p adj adj op adv

adv prep

(Outside the tent) Lucy watched and pondered the distant stars.

p adj op

Part 1: Identify Phrases and Conjunctions

a. (First, read the sentence aloud.) "Outside the tent, Lucy watched and pondered the distant stars."

b. "Are there any conjunctions?" (Choral response: "Yes, sir.") (Mark the conjunction *and* with two angle brackets.)

c. "The order of analysis is phrases, clauses, principal elements, modifiers."

d. "Are there any prepositional phrases?" (Choral response: "Yes, sir.") "*Outside the tent* is a prepositional phrase." (Place parentheses around the prepositional phrase.)

e. "*Outside* is the preposition." (Place a lowercase *p* underneath the preposition.)

f. "*Tent* is the object of the preposition." (Place a lowercase *op* underneath the object of the preposition.)

g. "*The* is an adjective."[1] (Draw a straight line down from the adjective, then a horizontal line toward the word that it modifies, and then a straight line with an arrow pointing to the word it modifies. Write *adj* in lowercase letters in the elbow opposite the line with the arrow.)

Part 2: Identify Principal Elements and Modifiers

S PV PV

(Outside the tent) Lucy watched ⟩and⟨ pondered the distant (stars)

p adj op adj adj do

adv prep

a. (Read the sentence aloud again.) "Outside the tent, Lucy watched and pondered the distant stars."

b. "This is a sentence and it is declarative."

1. The words *article adjective* can be substituted in place of the word *adjective*.

c. "This sentence is about *Lucy*." (Underline the subject.) "So, *Lucy* is the subject because it is what the sentence is about." (Place a capital letter *S* above the subject.)

d. "This sentence tells us that Lucy *watched* and *pondered*." (Double underline the predicates.) "So, *watched* and *pondered* are the predicates because they are what the sentence tells us about *Lucy*." (Place a capital letter *P* above each predicate.) "They are predicate verbs because they show action." (Place a capital letter *V* to the right of the letter *P* above each predicate.) "There is no linking verb because predicate verbs do not need linking verbs."

e. "*And* is the conjunction."

f. "*Stars* tells us what Lucy watched and pondered." (Draw a circle around the word.) "So, *stars* is an objective element because it completes the meaning of the action verb. It is a direct object because it tells *what* Lucy watched and pondered." (Write *do* in lowercase letters beneath the direct object.)

g. "*Distant* tells us *what kind* of stars." (Draw a straight line down from the adjective, then a horizontal line toward the word that it modifies, and then a straight line with an arrow pointing to the word it modifies. Write *adj* in lowercase letters in the elbow opposite the line with the arrow.) "So, *distant* is an adjective element because it modifies a noun. It is an adjective."

h. "*The* is an adjective."[2] (Draw a straight line down from the adjective, then a horizontal line toward the word that it modifies, and then a straight line with an arrow pointing to the word it modifies. Write *adj* in lowercase letters in the elbow opposite the line with the arrow.)

i. "*Outside* tells us *where* Lucy watched and pondered." (Draw a straight line down from the adverb, then a horizontal line toward the word that it modifies, and then a straight line with an arrow pointing to the word it modifies. Draw the modifier lines to the nearest verb, not to both. Write *adv* in lowercase letters in the elbow opposite the line with the arrow.) "So, *outside* is an adverbial element because it modifies a verb. It is an adverb."

For the analysis of the second sentence, adjust the script accordingly.

2. The words *article adjective* can be substituted in place of the word *adjective*.

Notes

Introductory Lesson
Compound Verbs

The order of the lesson is: **Review It**, **Practice It**, **Learn It**, and **Analyze It**.

Review It: Sing/chant and review definitions as a class.

Review It

What is a verb? Can you think of five verbs? Can you add helping verbs to the verbs? Can you add another verb to each of your original five verbs? What is a synonym? Can you think of a synonym for *jump*?

Practice It: For this warm-up, see Well-Ordered Notes Introductory.

Learn It: This part of the lesson can be done as an oral or written exercise.

Learn It

How does a sentence change when another verb is added to it? Using the following sentences, construct new sentences by adding a conjunction (*and*, *or*) and another verb to form compound verbs.

Example: The new season came ___*and changed*___ the prairie.

1. The spring birds chirped ___**and called**___ to one another.

2. Joyously the flowers grew ___**and bloomed**___.

3. On April 6, a storm drenched ___**and froze**___ the ground.

4. In the garden, the crocus flowers wilted ___**and died**___.

Analyze It

Analyze the following sentences (*S* = subject; *PV* = predicate verb; *hv* = helping verb; *adv* = adverb; *adj* = adjective; *do* = direct object; *p* = preposition; *op* = object of the preposition; *prep* = prepositional phrase).

> **Analyze It:** This is the essential part of the lesson. See Well-Ordered Notes Introductory.

1. (Outside the tent) Lucy watched ⟩and⟨ pondered the distant stars.
   - Outside = p; the = adj; tent = op; (Outside the tent) = adv prep, modifying watched
   - Lucy = S; watched = PV; pondered = PV
   - the = adj; distant = adj; stars = do

2. (Under the night sky) Theo stretched ⟩and⟨ yawned loudly.
   - Under = p; the = adj; night = adj; sky = op; (Under the night sky) = adv prep, modifying stretched
   - Theo = S; stretched = PV; yawned = PV
   - loudly = adv, modifying yawned

Introductory Practice
Compound Verbs

1. Analyze the following sentences (*S* = subject; *PV* = predicate verb; *hv* = helping verb; *adv* = adverb; *adj* = adjective; *do* = direct object; *p* = preposition; *op* = object of the preposition; *prep* = prepositional phrase).

   a. Four girls wrapped)and(stacked the birthday gifts.
   S: girls; PV: wrapped; PV: stacked; adj: Four; adj: the; adj: birthday; do: gifts

   b. The older boys swept)and(cleaned the den (for the party.)
   S: boys; PV: swept; PV: cleaned; adj: The; adj: older; adj: the; do: den; p: for; adj: the; op: party; adv prep: for the party

   c. Aunt Gabby baked)and(decorated a birthday cake (for them.)
   S: Aunt Gabby; PV: baked; PV: decorated; adj: a; adj: birthday; do: cake; p: for; op: them; adv prep: for them

   d. Suddenly Mom)and(Dad surprised us (with ice cream.)
   S: Mom; S: Dad; PV: surprised; adv: Suddenly; do: us; p: with; op: ice cream; adv prep: with ice cream

2. Imagine how different people and animals *walk*. With that in mind, write the following sentences using synonyms for the word *walk*.

   a. Write a sentence about a *girl walking*.

   The carefree girl skipped back to the car.

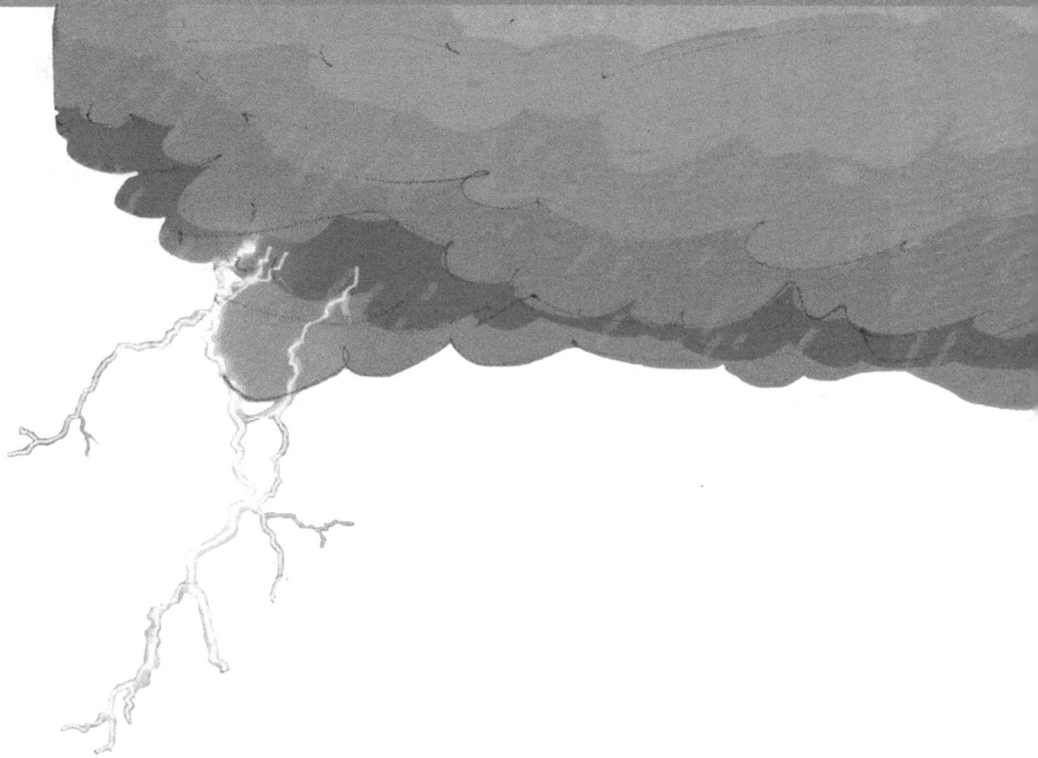

b. Write a sentence about a *poodle walking.*

The little poodle is racing about.

c. Write a sentence about a *scientist walking.*

The thoughtful scientist wandered toward the door.

Well-Ordered Notes A

Practice It

Have students play the game What Can You Do? Students should stand in a circle or beside their desks. Ask the first student, "What can you do?" He will respond by answering the question using a compound verb and then acting out both actions. Next that student turns to a fellow student and asks, "What can you do?" and so forth until every student answers the question. Write the following verbs on the board as options for the students to use, but also encourage students to think of their own verbs.

Example:

Teacher: "What can you do?"
Student 1: "I can hop and jump."

bark	bounce	buzz
chirp	dash	fall
gallop	giggle	groan
hiccup	hike	hiss
hop	hum	jog
jump	leap	march
purr	shout	sneeze
step	stretch	wave
whine	whistle	zip

Analyze It

As a class, analyze the following sentences (*S* = subject; *PV* = predicate verb; *hv* = helping verb; *adv* = adverb; *adj* = adjective; *do* = direct object; *p* = preposition; *op* = object of the preposition; *prep* = prepositional phrase). Write the sentences on the board. Have the students analyze the sentences, reciting the analysis aloud using the following script. While the students recite, you will mark the sentence on the board.

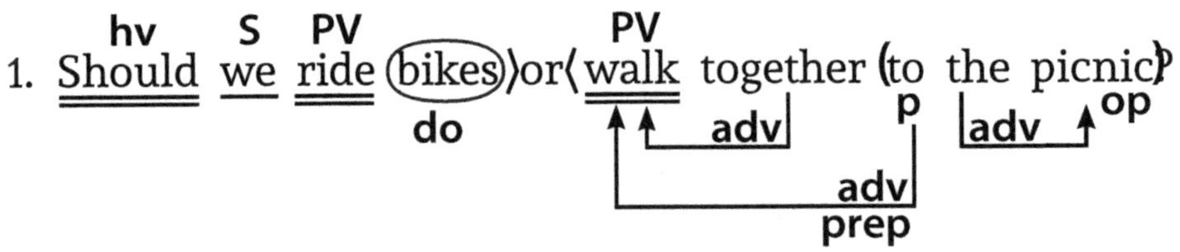

S PV PV

2. Afterward the cousins played (games) and romped outside.

adj do adv

adv

Should we ride bikes ⟩or⟨ walk together (to the picnic)

p adj op

Part 1: Identify Phrases and Conjunctions

a. (First, read the sentence aloud.) "Should we ride bikes or walk together to the picnic?"

b. "Are there any conjunctions?" (Choral response: "Yes, sir.") (Mark the conjunction *or* with two angle brackets.)

c. "The order of analysis is phrases, clauses, principal elements, modifiers."

d. "Are there any prepositional phrases?" (Choral answer: "Yes, sir.") "*To the picnic* is a prepositional phrase." (Place parentheses around the prepositional phrase.) "*To* is the preposition." (Place a lowercase *p* underneath the preposition.) "*Picnic* is the object of the preposition." (Place a lowercase *op* underneath the object of the preposition.)

e. "*The* is an adjective."[1] (Draw a straight line down from the adjective, then a horizontal line toward the word that it modifies, and then a straight line with an arrow pointing to the word it modifies. Write *adj* in lowercase letters in the elbow opposite the line with the arrow.)

Part 2: Identify Principal Elements and Modifiers

hv S PV PV

Should we ride (bikes) ⟩or⟨ walk together (to the picnic)

do adv p adj op

adv prep

a. (Read the sentence aloud again.) "Should we ride bikes or walk together to the picnic?"

b. "This is a sentence and it is interrogative."

c. "This sentence is about *we*." (Underline the subject.) "So, *we* is the subject because it is what the sentence is about." (Place a capital letter *S* above the subject.)

d. "This sentence tells us that we *should ride* or *walk*." (Double underline the helping verb and the predicate verb.) "So, *should ride* or *walk* are the predicates because they are what the sentence tells

1. The words *article adjective* can be substituted in place of the word *adjective*.

us about *we*." (Place the capital letter *P* above each of the action verbs.) "They are predicate verbs because they show action." (Place a capital letter *V* to the right of the letter *P* above each of the action verbs.) "There is no linking verb because predicate verbs do not need linking verbs. "*Should* is a helping verb because it helps the verb." (Place a lowercase ***hv*** above the helping verb.)

e. "*Or* is the conjunction."

f. "*To the picnic* tells us *where* we ride or walk." (Draw a straight line down from the letter *p* that's under the preposition, then a horizontal line toward the word that it modifies, and then a straight line with an arrow pointing to the word it modifies.) "So, *to the picnic* is an adverbial element because it modifies a verb. It is an adverbial prepositional phrase." (Write ***adv*** in lowercase letters in the elbow opposite the line with the arrow. Write ***prep*** in lowercase letters directly below the ***adv***, underneath the modifier line.)

g. "*Together* tells us *how* we walk and ride." (Draw the modifier lines to the nearest verb, not to both. Draw a straight line down from the adverb, then a horizontal line toward the word that it modifies, and then a straight line with an arrow pointing to the word it modifies.) "So, *together* is an adverbial element because it modifies a verb. It is an adverb." (Write ***adv*** in lowercase letters in the elbow opposite the line with the arrow.)

h. "*Bikes* tells us what we should ride." (Draw a circle around the word.) "So, *bikes* is an objective element because it completes the meaning of the action verb. It is a direct object because it tells *what* we should ride." (Write ***do*** in lowercase letters beneath the direct object.)

For the analysis of the second sentence, adjust the script accordingly.

Notes

Lessons to Learn
Compound Verbs

A

The order of the lesson is: **Review It**, **Practice It**, **Learn It**, and **Analyze It**.

To the Source:

■ **review**

Review is from the Latin word *revidere*, from *re-* "again" + *videre* "to see," hence "to see again." The sense of the word is the "process of going over something again."

Review It: Sing/chant and review definitions as a class. Consider adding freshness by varying speed and volume or by asking individual students to paraphrase the meaning of a definition.

Learn It: This part of the lesson can be oral or written.

Review It

To *review*■ something means you are to look back on or keep thinking about something. Review the following grammar terms.

Verbs

Helping verbs

Compound verbs

Conjunctions

Synonym

Antonyms

Homonyms

Practice It: For this warm-up, see Well-Ordered Notes A.

Learn It

Using the following sentences, construct new sentences by adding a conjunction (*and*, *or*) and another verb to form compound verbs.

Example: Earlier Mom drove <u>and listened to</u> the kids before the game.

1. Does the team often practice ______ or drill ______ in the sleet?

2. Both girls shivered ______ and shook ______ in the cold during the soccer game.

3. The white snow fell ______ and covered ______ the field.

4. Heidi dribbled **and passed** the ball down the field.

5. Suddenly the parents shouted **and cheered** for another goal.

Analyze It

Analyze the following sentences (*S* = subject; *PV* = predicate verb; *hv* = helping verb; *adv* = adverb; *adj* = adjective; *do* = direct object; *p* = preposition; *op* = object of the preposition; *prep* = prepositional phrase).

> **Analyze It:** This is the essential part of the lesson. See Well-Ordered Notes A.

1. Should we ride bikes or walk together (to the picnic).

   hv Should; **S** we; **PV** ride; **do** bikes; **PV** walk; **adv** together; **p** to; **adj** the; **op** picnic; **adv prep** (to the picnic)

2. Afterward the cousins played games and romped outside.

   adv Afterward; **adj** the; **S** cousins; **PV** played; **do** games; **PV** romped; **adv** outside

Lessons to Practice

Compound Verbs

A

1. Analyze the following sentences (*S* = subject; *PV* = predicate verb; *hv* = helping verb; *adv* = adverb; *adj* = adjective; *do* = direct object; *p* = preposition; *op* = object of the preposition; *prep* = prepositional phrase).

   a. Winston (S) sorted (PV) and counted (PV) the (adj) stamps (do).

   b. He (S) should (hv) have (hv) kept (PV) and cherished (PV) the (adj) rare (adj) stamp (adj) book (do).

   c. Grandpa Fred (S) carefully (adv) cut (PV) and sealed (PV) each (adj) envelope (do) (for (p) him (op)) (adv prep).

   d. (After (p) lunch (op)) (adv prep) Fritz (S) came (PV) and watched (PV) the (adj) two (adj) stamp (adj) collectors (do).

2. Imagine how different people *talk*. With that in mind, write the following sentences using synonyms for the word *talk*.

   a. Write a sentence about a *librarian talking*.

   The young librarian whispered to the noisy girls.

b. Write a sentence about a *coach talking*.

Their coach drawled directions to the team.

c. Write a sentence about a *grumpy old man talking*.

The grumpy old man grumbled about the rain.

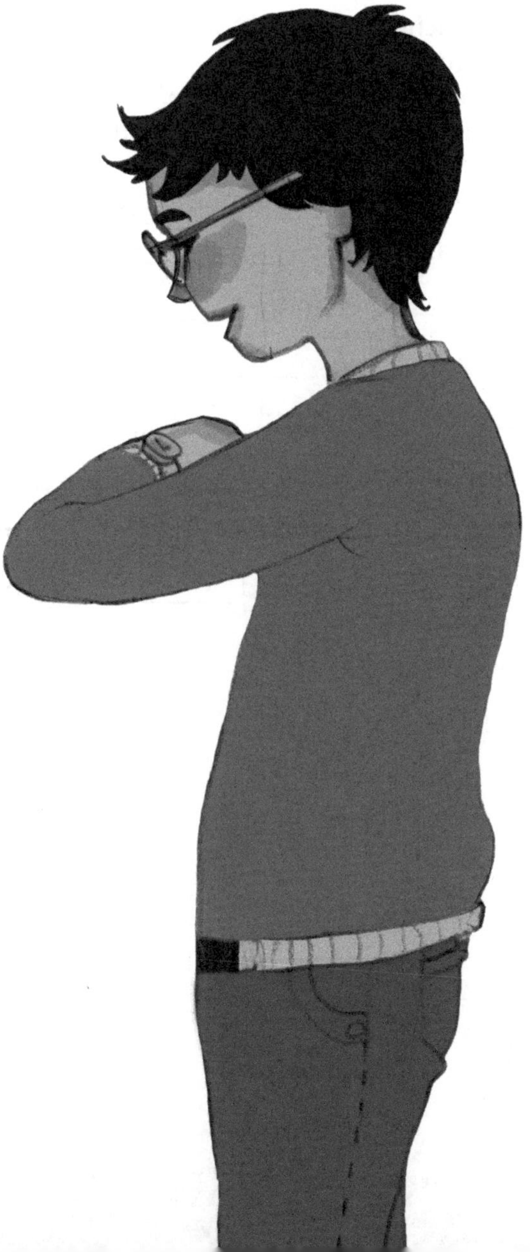

Well-Ordered Notes B

Practice It

Play Lightning, a review game that requires students to think on their feet. Have each student stand beside her desk and be seated after she has provided a second verb to make a compound verb. Using the following sentences, say the principal elements, including the blank (Bobolinks sing and ______________) and ask what else the subject does (nest). The student has five seconds to give a compound verb. If she correctly supplies a verb, she may sit down; if not, she is to wait until you return to her. This activity is to be fast moving and light. Note: You can use this activity as a fun alternative to saying "Be seated." After each student gives an answer, he can be seated. Slowly the class is all seated and ready for the rest of the lesson.

Fewer than Five: The student can stand to complete the first compound verb, sit for the next, stand, sit, and so on. No changing position, though, unless successfully giving the compound verb.

Example:

Teacher: "Bobolinks sing and ___________."
Student: *"Nest."*
Teacher: "Restate, please."
Student: "Bobolinks sing and *nest*."

bobolinks: common North American songbirds

1. Bubbles float and ___**pop**___.
2. Lizards dart and ___**crawl**___.
3. Snakes slither and ___**glide**___.
4. Frogs hop and ___**croak**___.
5. Rabbits nibbled and ___**sniffed**___.
6. Ducks waddle and ___**quack**___.
7. Raccoons scamper and ___**run**___.
8. Squirrels chatter and ___**climb**___.

Analyze It

As a class, analyze the following sentences (*S* = subject; *PV* = predicate verb; *hv* = helping verb; *adv* = adverb; *adj* = adjective; *do* = direct object; *p* = preposition; *op* = object of the preposition; *prep* = prepositional phrase). Write the sentences on the board. Have the students analyze the sentences, reciting the analysis aloud using the following script. While the students recite, you will mark the sentence on the board.

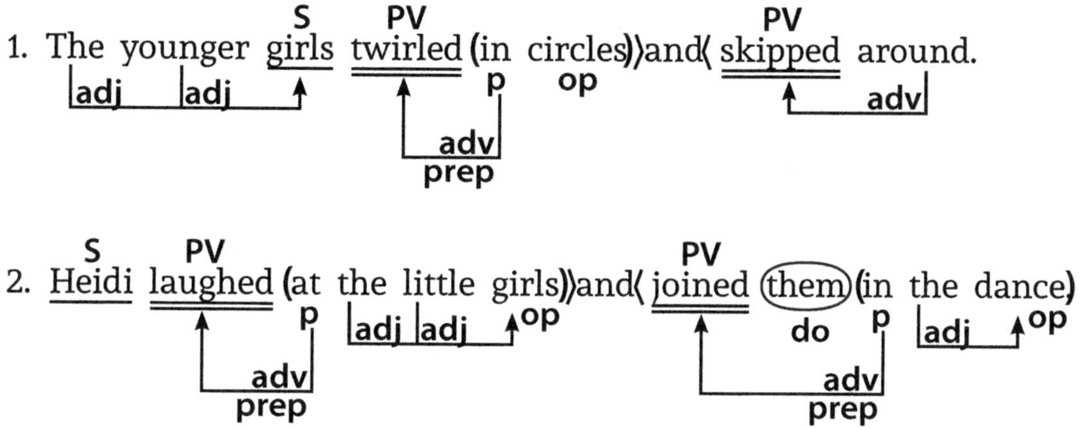

The younger girls twirled (in circles)⟩and⟨ skipped around.
p op

Part 1: Identify Phrases and Conjunctions

a. (First, read the sentence aloud.) "The younger girls twirled in circles and skipped around."

b. "Are there any conjunctions?" (Choral response: "Yes, sir.") (Mark the conjunction *and* with two angle brackets.)

c. "The order of analysis is phrases, clauses, principal elements, modifiers."

d. "Are there any prepositional phrases?" (Choral answer: "Yes, sir.") "*In circles* is a prepositional phrase." (Place parentheses around the prepositional phrase.)

e. "*In* is the preposition." (Place a lowercase *p* underneath the preposition.)

f. "*Circles* is the object of the preposition." (Place a lowercase *op* underneath the object of the preposition.)

Part 2: Identify Principal Elements and Modifiers

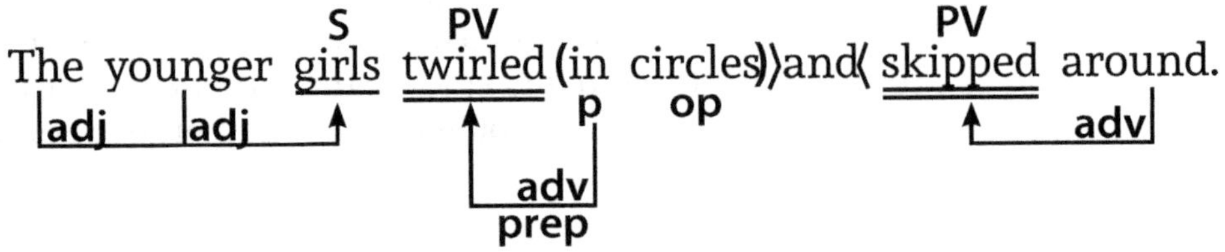

a. (Read the sentence aloud again.) "The younger girls twirled in circles and skipped around."

b. "This is a sentence and it is declarative."

c. "This sentence is about *girls*." (Underline the subject.) "So, *girls* is the subject because it is what the sentence is about." (Place a capital letter *S* above the subject.)

d. "This sentence tells us that girls *twirled* and *skipped*." (Double underline the predicates.) "So, *twirled* and *skipped* are the predicates because they are what the sentence tells us about *girls*." (Place a capital letter *P* above each predicate.) "They are predicate verbs because they show action." (Place a capital letter *V* to the right of the letter *P* above each predicate.) "There is no linking verb because predicate verbs do not need linking verbs."

e. "*And* is the conjunction."

f. "*Around* tells us *where* the girls skipped." (Draw a straight line down from the adverb, then a horizontal line toward the word that it modifies, and then a straight line with an arrow pointing to the word it modifies. Write *adv* in lowercase letters in the elbow opposite the line with the arrow.) "So, *around* is an adverbial element because it modifies a verb. It is an adverb."

g. "*In circles* tells us *how* the girls twirled." (Draw a straight line down from the letter *p* that's under the preposition, then a horizontal line toward the word that it modifies, and then a straight line with an arrow pointing to the word it modifies.) "So, *in circles* is an adverbial element because it modifies a verb. It is an adverbial prepositional phrase." (Write *adv* in lowercase letters in the elbow opposite the line with the arrow. Write *prep* in lowercase letters directly below the *adv*, underneath the modifier line.)

h. "*Younger* tells us *what kind* of girls." (Draw a straight line down from the adjective, then a horizontal line toward the word that it modifies, and then a straight line with an arrow pointing to the word it modifies. Write *adj* in lowercase letters in the elbow opposite the line with the arrow.) "So, *younger* is an adjective element because it modifies a noun. It is an adjective."

i. "*The* is an adjective."[1] (Draw a straight line down from the adjective, then a horizontal line toward the word that it modifies, and then a straight line with an arrow pointing to the word it modifies. Write *adj* in lowercase letters in the elbow opposite the line with the arrow.)

For the analysis of the second sentence, adjust the script accordingly.

1. The words *article adjective* can be substituted in place of the word *adjective*.

Notes

Lessons to Learn
Compound Verbs

B

The order of the lesson is: **Review It**, **Practice It**, **Learn It**, and **Analyze It**.

Review It: Sing/chant and review definitions as a class.

Review It

Recitation (repeating something aloud) is a part of good learning. You will remember for your whole life these important definitions you're learning in the Well-Ordered Language series. See how well you can answer the following questions from memory: What is a verb? Can you name the twenty-three helping verbs? What is a conjunction? What is a synonym? What is an antonym? What is a homonym?

Practice It: For this warm-up, see Well-Ordered Notes B.

Learn It: Write the sentences on the board. Organize the students into teams of three. To the following sentences, have the students add first adjective(s), then adverb(s), and finally a prepositional phrase(s). (Answers may vary.)

Learn It

As you work in teams of three students, your teacher will guide you to add words to the following sentences to construct more descriptive sentences.

Example: "The tadpole swims."
Teacher: "Add another verb."
Student 1: "The tadpole swims *and dives*."
Teacher: "Add an adjective."
Student 2: "The *frisky* tadpole swims and dives."
Teacher: "Add a prepositional phrase."
Student 3: "The frisky tadpole swims and dives *in the shallow pool*."

1. The monkeys reached.

   ***Suddenly* the *silly* monkeys reached *for the bananas*.**

2. The chimpanzees ran.

   The *curious* chimpanzees *quickly* ran *after the monkeys*.

3. Are those apes dancing?

Are those *two* apes *really* dancing *under that tree*?

____

____

4. That zookeeper laughed.

That *old* zookeeper laughed *aloud at the animals*.

____

____

5. Write your favorite newly constructed sentence below.

____

____

Analyze It

> **Analyze It:** This is the essential part of the lesson. See Well-Ordered Notes B.

Analyze the following sentences (*S* = subject; *PV* = predicate verb; *hv* = helping verb; *adv* = adverb; *adj* = adjective; *do* = direct object; *p* = preposition; *op* = object of the preposition; *prep* = prepositional phrase).

1. The younger girls twirled (in circles) and skipped around.
   - The (adj) younger (adj) girls (S) twirled (PV) (in (p) circles (op)) — adv prep modifying twirled; and skipped (PV) around (adv).

2. Heidi laughed (at the little girls) and joined them (in the dance).
   - Heidi (S) laughed (PV) (at (p) the (adj) little (adj) girls (op)) — adv prep modifying laughed; and joined (PV) them (do) (in (p) the (adj) dance (op)) — adv prep modifying joined.

Lessons to Practice

Compound Verbs

B

1. Analyze the following sentences (*S* = subject; *PV* = predicate verb; *hv* = helping verb; *adv* = adverb; *adj* = adjective; *do* = direct object; *p* = preposition; *op* = object of the preposition; *prep* = prepositional phrase).

   a. Coach Howard talked (to the team) and encouraged them (before warm-ups.)

   S: Coach Howard; PV: talked; PV: encouraged; p: to; adj: the; op: team; adv prep: to the team; do: them; p: before; op: warm-ups; adv prep: before warm-ups

   b. (For hours,) the team dribbled and passed the basketball.

   p: For; op: hours; adv prep: For hours; adj: the; S: team; PV: dribbled; PV: passed; adj: the; do: basketball

   c. Patiently he taught the boys and drilled them (on new plays.)

   adv: Patiently; S: he; PV: taught; adj: the; do: boys; PV: drilled; do: them; p: on; adj: new; op: plays; adv prep: on new plays

   d. Did Theo help or cripple the team (during the practice?)

   hv: Did; S: Theo; PV: help; PV: cripple; adj: the; do: team; p: during; adj: the; op: practice; adv prep: during the practice

2. Imagine how different people *hold* things. With that in mind, write the following sentences using synonyms for the word *hold*.

   a. Write a sentence about a *waitress holding* something.

   A waitress tightly clung to the wobbly tray.

b. Write a sentence about a *musician holding* something.

The musician cradled his violin on his shoulder.

c. Write a sentence about a *football player holding* something.

The football player grabbed the ball.

Well-Ordered Notes C

Practice It

Lead the class in the activity Add On. As a class, see how large you can build a sentence by adding elements to it. Use the following sentences to provide the principal elements. Then have each student add some element to the sentence, beginning with a compound verb.

Example:

Teacher: "Winston coughs."
Student 1: "Winston *sneezes and* coughs."
Student 2: "*Continually* Winston sneezes and coughs."
Student 3: "Continually Winston sneezes and coughs *into a tissue*."

Variation: Divide the students into groups of three or four and assign one of the following sentences to them. Have the groups create a compound verb in their assigned short sentence. Have one representative from each group share the group's sentence with the class.

1. Fritz climbs.
   Fritz *stretches and* climbs. *Repeatedly* Fritz stretches and climbs.
   Repeatedly Fritz stretches and climbs *in the tree.*

2. The boy shoots.
   The boy *jumps and* shoots. The boy jumps and shoots *again.*
   On the basketball court, the boy jumps and shoots again.

3. Will Heidi score?
   Will Heidi *dribble and* score? Will Heidi *frequently* dribble and score?
   Will Heidi frequently dribble and score *during the game*?

4. Rex whimpers.
   Rex *whines and* whimpers. Rex whines and whimpers *repeatedly.*
   On the porch Rex whines and whimpers repeatedly.

Analyze It

As a class, analyze the following sentences (*S* = subject; *PV* = predicate verb; *hv* = helping verb; *adv* = adverb; *adj* = adjective; *do* = direct object; *p* = preposition; *op* = object of the preposition; *prep* = prepositional phrase). Write the sentences on the board. Have the students analyze the sentences, reciting the analysis aloud using the following script. While the students recite, you will mark the sentence on the board.

S PV PV
1. The grasshopper played)and(danced (throughout the summer months.)
adj p adj adj op
adv
prep

S PV PV
2. The ant busily worked)and(gathered (food) (for winter)
adj adv do p op
adv
prep

The grasshopper played)and(danced (throughout the summer months)
p adj adj op

Part 1: Identify Phrases and Conjunctions

a. (First, read the sentence aloud.) "The grasshopper played and danced throughout the summer months."

b. "Are there any conjunctions?" (Choral response: "Yes, sir.") (Mark the conjunction *and* with two angle brackets.)

c. "The order of analysis is phrases, clauses, principal elements, modifiers."

d. "Are there any prepositional phrases?" (Choral answer: "Yes, sir.") "*Throughout the summer months* is a prepositional phrase." (Place parentheses around the prepositional phrase.)

e. "*Throughout* is the preposition." (Place a lowercase *p* underneath the preposition.)

f. "*Months* is the object of the preposition." (Place a lowercase *op* underneath the object of the preposition.)

g. "*Summer* tells us *what kind* of months." (Draw a straight line down from the adjective, then a horizontal line toward the word that it modifies, and then a straight line with an arrow pointing to the word it modifies. Write *adj* in lowercase letters in the elbow opposite the line with the arrow.)

h. "*The* is an adjective."[1] (Draw a straight line down from the adjective, then a horizontal line toward the word that it modifies, and then a straight line with an arrow pointing to the word it modifies. Write *adj* in lowercase letters in the elbow opposite the line with the arrow.)

Part 2: Identify Principal Elements and Modifiers

S PV PV
The grasshopper played)and(danced (throughout the summer months)
adj p adj adj op
adv
prep

1. The words *article adjective* can be substituted in place of the word *adjective*.

a. (Read the sentence aloud again.) "The grasshopper played and danced throughout the summer months."

b. "This is a sentence and it is declarative."

c. "This sentence is about *grasshopper*." (Underline the subject.) "So, *grasshopper* is the subject because it is what the sentence is about." (Place a capital letter *S* above the subject.)

d. "This sentence tells us that grasshopper *played* and *danced*." (Double underline the predicates.) "So, *played* and *danced* are the predicates because they are what the sentence tells us about *grasshopper*." (Place a capital letter *P* above each predicates.) "They are predicate verbs because they show action." (Place a capital letter *V* to the right of the letter *P* above each predicate.) "There is no linking verb because predicate verbs do not need linking verbs."

e. "*And* is the conjunction."

f. "*Throughout the summer months* tells us *when* the grasshoppers played and danced." (Draw a straight line down from the letter *p* that's under the preposition, then a horizontal line toward the word that it modifies, and then a straight line with an arrow pointing to the word it modifies.) "So, *throughout the summer months* is an adverbial element because it modifies a verb. It is an adverbial prepositional phrase." (Write *adv* in lowercase letters in the elbow opposite the line with the arrow. Write *prep* in lowercase letters directly below the *adv*, underneath the modifier line.)

g. "*The* is an adjective."[2] (Draw a straight line down from the adjective, then a horizontal line toward the word that it modifies, and then a straight line with an arrow pointing to the word it modifies. Write *adj* in lowercase letters in the elbow opposite the line with the arrow.)

For the analysis of the second sentence, adjust the script accordingly.

2. The words *article adjective* can be substituted in place of the word *adjective*.

Notes

Lessons to Learn
Compound Verbs

C

The order of the lesson is: **Review It**, **Practice It**, **Learn It**, and **Analyze It**.

Review It: Sing/chant and review definitions as a class. Consider adding freshness by varying speed and volume or by asking individual students to paraphrase the meaning of a definition.

Review It

You have learned a great deal about verbs. Let's review some of it.

Can you think of ten verbs?

Can you think of ten helping verbs?

Can you make compound verbs by adding another verb to each of the verbs you came up with?

What is a synonym for *happy*? What is an antonym for *happy*?

Practice It: For this warm-up, see Well-Ordered Notes C.

Learn It: This part of the lesson can be oral or written. (Answers may vary.)

Learn It

Fill in compound verbs to complete the following sentences.

Example: We will ___wash and dry___ the clothes for the trip to Wyoming.

1. The cowboys ___**guided and steered**___ the cattle to the barn.

2. Grandpa ___**shouted and called**___ the children to dinner.

3. The cattle were ___**mooing and bellowing**___.

4. Fritz ___**ran and chased**___ the ranch dog.

C Lessons to Learn
Compound Verbs

Analyze It

Analyze the following sentences (*S* = subject; *PV* = predicate verb; *hv* = helping verb; *adv* = adverb; *adj* = adjective; *do* = direct object; *p* = preposition; *op* = object of the preposition; *prep* = prepositional phrase).

> **Analyze It:** This is the essential part of the lesson. See Well-Ordered Notes C.

1. The grasshopper played)and(danced (throughout the summer months)

   S: grasshopper; PV: played; PV: danced; adj: The; p: throughout; adj: the; adj: summer; op: months; adv prep: (throughout the summer months) → danced

2. The ant busily worked)and(gathered (food) (for winter)

   S: ant; PV: worked; PV: gathered; adj: The; adv: busily → worked; do: food; p: for; op: winter; adv prep: (for winter) → gathered

> **From the Sideline:** Please note that these sentences complement the fable for this chapter.

Lessons to Practice

Compound Verbs

C

1. Analyze the following sentences (*S* = subject; *PV* = predicate verb; *hv* = helping verb; *adv* = adverb; *adj* = adjective; *do* = direct object; *p* = preposition; *op* = object of the preposition; *prep* = prepositional phrase).

   a. S PV PV
   (In the bushes) Lucy made a fort and played alone.
   p adj op adj do adv
   adv prep

   b. S PV PV
   Suddenly she cried loudly and ran (to the house.)
   adv adv p adj op
   adv prep

   c. S PV PV
   Later (during the appointment) she itched and scratched the red bumps.
   p adj op adj adj do
   adv prep
   adv

   d. S PV PV
   Anxiously Mom sat and waited (with Lucy)(for the doctor.)
   adv p op p adj op
   adv prep adv prep

2. Imagine how different people and animals run. With that in mind, write the following sentences, being sure to use synonyms for the word *run*.

   a. Write a sentence about *kindergartners running*, but use a synonym for *run*.

   The two kindergärtners were sprinting on the playground.

b. Write a sentence about a *dog running*, but use another synonym for *run*.

The brown dog was chasing the motor scooter.

c. Write a sentence about a *gymnast running*, but use another synonym for *run*.

The strong gymnast sprinted toward the vault.

Review It: Sing/chant and review definitions as a class.

Review It

Answer the following questions:

What is a verb?

Can you list twenty-three helping verbs?

What is conjunction?

What is a synonym?

What is an antonym?

What are homonyms?

Learn It: Before class, write a number of vivid action verbs on cards and place them in a verb jar. Have each child select a card and read it quietly. Each student should then create a compound verb and construct a sentence that uses both verbs. Have the students share their sentences with the whole class.

Learn It

Putting words together to make sentences requires a lot of thought, and constructing good sentences requires careful selection of words. For this exercise, you'll use one of the following verbs or choose a card from the "verb jar." Think of a second verb, join the verbs with a conjunction, and construct a sentence using the compound verb you create. See how many sentences you can construct with compound verbs in this way. Can you think of a few with compound subjects too?

Example: *tickles*

Student: (adds verb) ***scratches***

Student (rephrase): "Grandpa ***tickles*** **and** ***scratches*** **Rex under his ear."**

flops	gardens	tramps	sprints	throws
blows	swims	cracks	scrubs	hides
drops	circles	cries	wrestles	limps
slides	crouches	lifts	scurries	hammers

1. Analyze the following sentences: (*S* = subject; *PV* = predicate verb; *hv* = helping verb; *adv* = adverb; *adj* = adjective; *do* = direct object; *p* = preposition; *op* = object of the preposition; *prep* = prepositional phrase).

   a. Theo (S) held (PV) the (adj) cardboard (adj) box (do) and peeked (PV) (at (p) the (adj) little (adj) creature (op)) — adv prep

   b. (Inside (p) the (adj) box (op)) — adv prep — a (adj) tiny (adj) rabbit (S) huddled (PV) and slept (PV) (under (p) the (adj) blanket (op)) — adv prep

   c. (Underneath (p) the (adj) steps (op)) — adv prep — two (adj) chipmunks (S) burrow (PV) tunnels (do) and store (PV) nuts (do)

   d. The (adj) furry (adj) squirrel (S) climbed (PV) trees (do) and chattered (PV) loudly (adv) (at (p) them (op)) — adv prep

2. Imagine how different people *throw* things. With that in mind, write the following sentences, being sure to use synonyms for the word *throw*.

   a. Write a sentence about a *bride throwing* something, but use a synonym for throw.

   The bride tossed her bouquet.

b. Write a sentence about a *garbage man throwing* something, but use another synonym for throw.

Earlier the garbage man launched the heavy chair into his truck.

c. Write a sentence about a *baseball player throwing* a ball, but use another synonym for throw.

The baseball player pitched the ball slowly.

Notes

Lessons to Enjoy—Poem
Compound Verbs

Christina Rossetti was a nineteenth-century English poet who grew up in London and probably spent her holidays at the beach. Her poem "I Dug and Dug Amongst the Snow" contrasts digging in snow with digging in sand. Why do you think she may have written this poem?

I Dug and Dug Amongst the Snow

by Christina Rossetti (1830–1894)

I dug and dug amongst the snow,
And thought the flowers would never grow;
I dug and dug amongst the sand,
And still no green thing came to hand.

Melt, O snow! the warm winds blow
To thaw the flowers and melt the snow;
But all the winds from every land
Will rear no blossom from the sand.[1]

Extras: Please note that the teacher's pages for this chapter include more material for extra practice, a quiz, and another Lessons to Enjoy section with discussion questions and activities. All this material, in reproducible form, is also included in the PDF that accompanies the textbook.

Questions to Ponder

1. What did the poet think about the flowers in winter?
2. What does it mean that "no green thing came to hand"?
3. Is the poem hopeful or sad?

From the Sideline: For possible answers to these discussion questions, see p. a of the teacher's pages. For even more suggestions for discussion and for enrichment activities related to the poem, see p. b.

1. Christina Rossetti, "I Dug and Dug Amongst the Snow" from *Illustrated Poems and Songs for Young People*, ed. Mrs. Lucy Sale Barker (London: George Routledge and Sons, 1885), p. 242. Available at: https://books.google.com/books?id=c4ubK21PVw4C.

Notes

Lessons to Enjoy—Poem

Questions to Ponder

1. What did the poet think about the flowers in winter?

   The poet fears that the flowers will never grow. It can be hard to believe in the midst of winter that spring will come again. But in the lines "Melt, O snow! The warm winds blow / To thaw the flowers and melt the snow," the poet expresses hope.

2. What does it mean that "no green thing came to hand"?

   It means that the speaker finds no plants or anything growing in the sand. While the flowers are dormant beneath the snow awaiting spring and warmth, there is no potential for blossoms in the sand no matter the season or temperature.

3. Is the poem hopeful or sad?

   This is an open-ended question with no correct answer. Both emotions are expressed in the poem: hope that the flowers will come eventually from beneath the snow; sadness that there will never be blossoms growing from the sand. Each student will be drawn to one or the other individually. Perhaps the point is that the act of digging in nature frees a person to delve deeper into thoughts and feelings. In any case, the sounds and images in the poem capture the experience cleverly and beautifully.

Well-Ordered Notes—Poem

Read

- Read the poem to the students while they look at Mary Cassatt's pictures "Picking Flowers in a Field" (1875) and "Children Playing on the Beach" (1884).
- Have the students memorize the poem.

Retell

- Discuss the poem using the provided questions.
- Ask your students to identify the compound verbs and conjunctions in the poem. They will probably quickly find *dug and dug* in the first and third lines, but will they notice that *and thought* is part of the first compound verb? The subject *I* has a three-part compound verb: *dug and dug and thought*. In lines five and six, *blow and melt* are also a compound verb.

From the Sidelines: Note: *To thaw the flowers* is an infinitive phrase functioning as an adverb. In Level 4 of the Well-Ordered Language series, students will learn about infinitive phrases.

Record

- Have the students copy the poem neatly into a copybook.
- Help students make origami tulips using the following directions.

Make Your Own Origami Tulip! (Part 1)

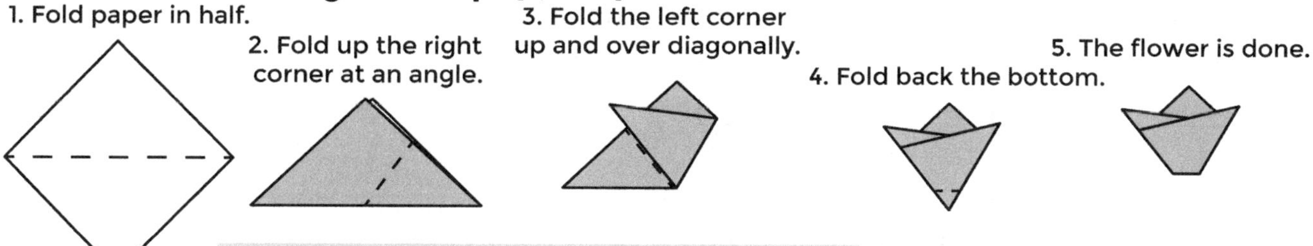

Important: Be sure to use a square sheet of paper.

Make Your Own Origami Tulip! (Part 2) **Important:** Be sure to use a square sheet of paper.

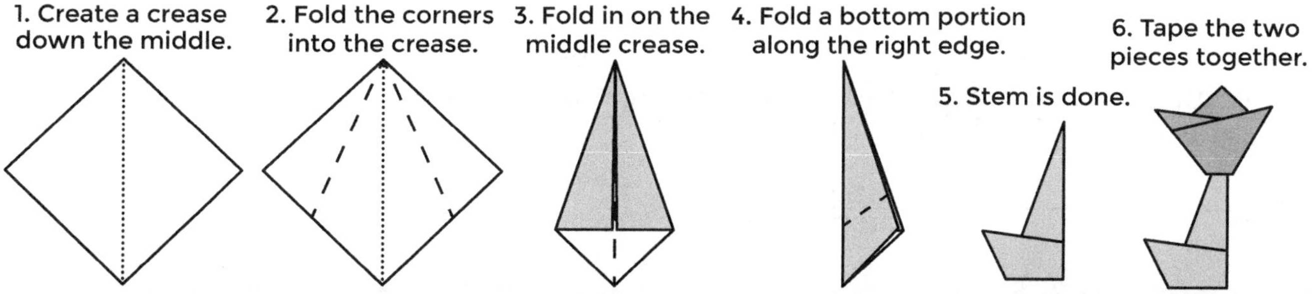

Practice Sheet
Compound Verbs

ANSWERS

Analyze the following sentences (*S* = subject; *PV* = predicate verb; *hv* = helping verb; *adv* = adverb; *adj* = adjective; *do* = direct object; *p* = preposition; *op* = object of the preposition; *prep* = prepositional phrase).

S S PV PV
1. Dad)and(the kids stand)and(wait patiently (for the beach trolley)
adj adv p adj adj op
adv prep

S hv PV PV
2. Theo is eagerly chattering)and(laughing (with the cousins)
adv p adj op
adv prep

S PV PV
3. The waves roll)and(crash (on the sandy beach.)
adj p adj adj op
adv prep

S PV PV
4. (On the sea) boats sailed)and(glided (across the water.)
p adj op p adj op
adv prep adv prep

S PV PV
5. Rapidly a kayak swerved)and(dipped (over the waves.)
adj p adj op
adv adv prep

S PV PV
6. (In the sun) Theo filled (pails)(with sand))and(made (towers).
p adj op do p op do
adv prep adv prep

S S PV PV
7. Peggy ⟩and⟨ Lucy dug the (moat) ⟩and⟨ built the several (turrets).
adj do adj adj do

turrets: small towers

S hv PV PV
8. The others were skipping (rocks) ⟩and⟨ strolling (along the beach.)
adj do p adj op
adv prep

S PV PV
9. (Above them,) seagulls cawed ⟩and⟨ swooped gracefully.
p op adv
adv prep

S hv PV PV
10. They were circling ⟩and⟨ hunting (for tiny sand crabs.)
p adj adj op
adv prep

Quiz
Compound Verbs
ANSWERS

1. Analyze the following sentences (*S* = subject; *PV* = predicate verb; *hv* = helping verb; *adv* = adverb; *adj* = adjective; *do* = direct object; *p* = preposition; *op* = object of the preposition; *prep* = prepositional phrase).

   a. S PV PV
   (In the afternoon,) the family cleared ⟩and⟨ organized the campsite.
   p adj op adj adj do
   adv prep

   b. S PV PV
   Winston carried wood ⟩and⟨ helped (with the fire.)
   do p adj op
   adv prep

   c. S PV PV
   The smoke drifted upward ⟩and⟨ moved (toward the river.)
   adj adv p adj op
   adv prep

   d. S PV PV
   Later Dad caught ⟩and⟨ fried fish (in the iron skillet) (on the coals.)
   adv do p adj adj op p adj op
   adv prep adv prep

2. Imagine how different people and animals eat food. With that in mind, write the following sentences, being sure to use synonyms for the word *eat*.

   a. Write a sentence about a *football player eating*.

   The hungry football player gobbled his burger.

b. Write a sentence about a *giraffe eating*.

The elegant giraffe tenderly plucked a leaf and munched it.

c. Write a sentence about a *mouse eating*.

The small mouse gnawed the sunflower seed.

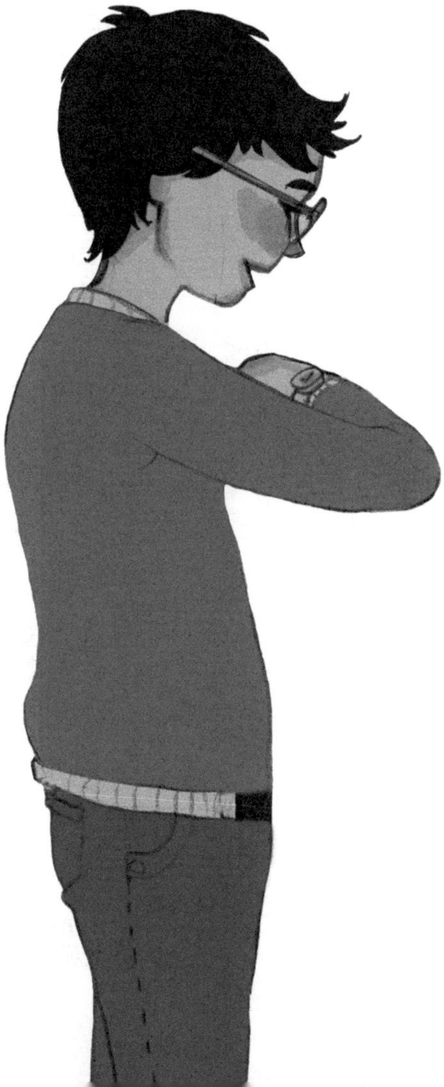

Lessons to Enjoy—Fable
Compound Verbs

Have your parents ever told you that you can't play until your work is completed? In this fable, a grasshopper plays before the work is done. See what happens to such a fellow who neglects his chores.

The Ant and the Grasshopper

by Aesop

One bright day in late autumn, a family of Ants was bustling about in the warm sunshine, drying out the grain they had stored up during the summer, when a starving Grasshopper, his fiddle under his arm, came up and humbly begged for a bite to eat.

"What!" cried the Ants in surprise. "Haven't you stored anything away for the winter? What in the world were you doing all last summer?"

"I didn't have time to store up any food," whined the Grasshopper. "I was so busy making sweet music that before I knew it the summer was gone."

disgust: annoyance and anger toward something that is not good or fair

The Ants shrugged their shoulders in disgust. "Making music, were you?" they cried. "Very well, now dance!" And they turned their backs on the Grasshopper and went on with their work.

Moral: There's a time for work and a time for play.[1]

1. Aesop, "The Ant and the Grasshopper," taken from *Writing & Rhetoric Book 1: Fable* by Paul Kortepeter (Camp Hill, PA: Classical Academic Press, 2013), pp. 134-135.

Questions to Ponder

1. What happens before the tale begins “one bright day in late autumn”?
2. What does “Making music, were you . . . now dance” mean?
3. What is the lesson the Grasshopper learned?

Lessons to Enjoy—Fable

Questions to Ponder

1. What happens before the tale begins "one bright day in late autumn"?

   The family of Ants has worked hard all summer preparing for winter so they will not starve. The Grasshopper has spent his summer playing music on his fiddle. "Making sweet music" occupied all his time and he has not prepared for winter.

2. What does "Making music, were you . . . now dance" mean?

   It means that making music all summer was not a productive activity. Instead of providing him something practical, such as food, the Grasshopper's fiddling can only yield something equally useless—dancing. Yet the Grasshopper seems to think of himself as an artist. He calls his music "sweet," suggesting it has a purpose beyond merely having fun. In sarcastically telling the Grasshopper to dance, the Ants recognize no tangible value in his music.

3. What is the lesson the Grasshopper learned?

   The Grasshopper learns the hard way that he should have finished his work before he turned to enjoying himself. His music would seem even sweeter if he knew he would have enough food for a comfortable winter. It is an important lesson that children also must learn in school and at home.

Well-Ordered Notes—Fable

Read

- Read the fable aloud to the students.
- Have students sing/chant the definition of a fable (Fable, 1–14).

Retell

- Discuss the fable using the provided questions.
- Have the students work together in small groups to make stick puppets of the ants and a grasshopper and then act out the fable. **Variation:** Have them act out a version of the tale in which the Ants learn a lesson. For example, an alternative ending might include the Ants paying the grasshopper in food to entertain them while they work.

Record

- Have the students copy this fable neatly into a copybook.
- Have students make ants around the page as a border, using an eraser from a pencil to dip in black ink or paint and a black pen to add legs and antennae.

Fable Sentences

Compound Verbs

ANSWERS

Analyze the following sentences (*S* = subject; *PV* = predicate verb; *hv* = helping verb; *adv* = adverb; *adj* = adjective; *do* = direct object; *p* = preposition; *op* = object of the preposition; *prep* = prepositional phrase).

S hv PV PV
1. (During the summer) the Ants were bustling about) and (drying grain.
p adj op adj adv do
adv prep

S PV PV
2. The foolish Grasshopper played the fiddle) and (waltzed around.
adj adj adj do adv

S PV PV
3. (In the late autumn,) the Ants continually gathered) and (stored food.
p adj adj op adj adv do
adv prep

S PV PV
4. The hungry Grasshopper came) and (humbly begged the Ants (for food.)
adj adj adv adj do p op
adv prep

S PV PV
5. The prudent Ants questioned) and (admonished the Grasshopper.
adj adj adj do

prudent: wise, careful about the future
admonished: scolded

S hv PV
6. Sadly, the Grasshopper did not have wisdom.
adj adv do
adv

7. (In disgust) the Ants said (nothing).
S: Ants; PV: said; p: In; op: disgust; adj: the; do: nothing; adv prep: In disgust

8. The Grasshopper begged again ⟩and⟨ pleaded (for help).
S: Grasshopper; PV: begged; PV: pleaded; adj: The; adv: again; p: for; op: help; adv prep: for help

9. Wisely the Ants went ⟩and⟨ continued the (work).
S: Ants; PV: went; PV: continued; adv: Wisely; adj: the; adj: the; do: work

10. The sad Grasshopper learned a serious (lesson).
S: Grasshopper; PV: learned; adj: The; adj: sad; adj: a; adj: serious; do: lesson

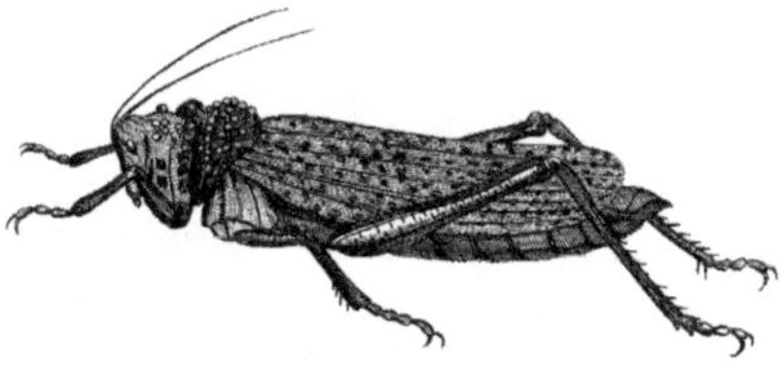

From the Sidelines: Teach chorally. Have the students recite definitions or responses chorally. Do not allow dull or disrespectful responses from students. If one student is louder than the others, ask this student to be silent for the next round of recitations. When you silence the loudest student, others will want that attention and the whole class becomes vibrant and attentive. It's a mystery of the classroom, but it works.

Chapter 7

Compound Direct Objects[A]

Perhaps you have heard the saying "less is more." If you shake too much salt on your french fries, then all you taste is the salt. Less salt means more french fry flavor. When creating or designing something, people often apply the idea of "less is more" so they can keep their creation from being too frilly or fancy. Authors apply "less is more" when writing well-crafted sentences. The idea is that using fewer well-chosen words is more effective than using too many words.

[A]Write the math equation - = + on the board. Discuss the concept of "less is more." Simplicity and clarity are more effective in design and in language than extravagance or overexplanation.

Authors often use compound subjects and compound verbs to minimize the number of words they use and thus maximize (make the most of) the effect of the words. In this chapter, you will learn about another way to do this: using **compound direct objects**. Using them allows you to combine short, choppy sentences into one longer, smoother sentence. Your fries could get cold by the time you say, "Please pass the ketchup. Please pass the salt." Try instead, "Please pass the ketchup and the salt."

Ideas to Understand[B]

[B]Write the poem "A Good Play," by Robert Louis Stevenson on the board. You can find it in its entirety in The Curious Child's Literary Appendix.

When a single transitive verb has more than one direct object connected with a conjunction, those direct objects are called a compound direct object. In the poem "A Good Play," the speaker uses this sentence structure as he remembers playing when he was a child with his friend Tom. Can you find the compound direct object?

We built a ship upon the stairs,
All made of back-bedroom chairs,
And filled it full of sofa pillows

From the Sidelines: While some publishers and style guides may prefer dropping the comma (often referred to as a series, serial, or Oxford comma) between the last two items in a series, many grammarians (including us) prefer the more logical rule of placing commas between all items in a series. Teach your students the following comma rule for compound direct objects: When a sentence includes three or more direct objects as a compound direct object, separate all of them with a comma, including the last two. For example: "We took a saw, several nails, and water." Discuss with the class how the poet chooses to repeat the conjunction *and* rather than use commas in order to preserve the rhythm of the poem and to emphasize the labor-intensive nature of the boys' shipbuilding.

To go a-sailing on the billows.
We took a saw and several nails,
And water in the nursery pails;
And Tom said, "Let us also take
An apple and a slice of cake";—
Which was enough for Tom and me
To go a-sailing on, till tea.[1]

tea: for the British, any meal eaten in the late afternoon or early evening

In the second stanza, Stevenson uses three nouns as a compound direct object: *saw*, *nails*, and *water*. All three complete the action of the same verb, *took*: "We took a saw and several nails and water in the nursery pails." He did not write, "We took a saw. We took several nails. We took water in the nursery pails." Why write three sentences to accomplish what he could do in one? Less is more.

Keep in mind that sometimes a sentence may contain two or more direct objects that are not a compound direct object. For instance, Stevenson's sentence, "We built a ship upon the stairs . . . and filled it full of sofa pillows," contains the two direct objects *ship* and *it*. However, they are not a compound because they complete the action of two separate verbs: *built* and *filled*. There is one subject, *we*; a compound verb, *built* and *filled*; and a separate direct object for each verb. *Built* what? A *ship*. *Filled* what? *It*. In that sentence the compound element is the two verbs, not the direct objects. In other words, the poet is really saying, "We built a ship. We filled it." Remember, compound direct objects always share the same verb, like this: We *built* a ship and a dock.

Unfortunately when using pronouns as compound direct objects, many people mistakenly choose subject pronouns instead of object pronouns. This is a problem. Notice in the two examples below how the mix-up can occur.

Incorrect: Mom called **Tom >and< I** for tea.

Correct: Mom called **Tom >and< me** for tea.

Incorrect: Did Dad want **Tom >or< I** to help?

Correct: Did Dad want **Tom >or< me** to help?

An easy way to check to see if you have the right pronoun when using a compound direct object is to drop the first pronoun, leaving the second

1. Robert Louis Stevenson, "A Good Play," from *Favorite Poems Old and New*, ed. Helen Ferris (New York: Doubleday & Company, Inc., 1957), pp. 101–102.

one to test it. Ask yourself if the remaining pronoun is an object pronoun. In other words, for the examples above, in your mind you would remove *Tom* to test the correctness of the pronoun *I*. You wouldn't say, "Mom called *I* for tea"; you would say, "Mom called *me*." The subject pronoun *I* is clearly the wrong choice, so "Mom called Tom and *me* for tea" is correct. "Did Dad want *I* to help?" No! He wanted *me* to help, so the object pronoun is the correct choice: "Did Dad want Tom or *me* to help?"

Do you have the object pronouns committed to memory? Here's a familiar chart to use for review.

Object Pronouns

	Singular	Plural
First Person	me	us
Second Person	you	you
Third Person	him, her, it	them

Terms to Remember[C]

Here you are at the last chapter of the book, and there are no new terms to memorize. Reviewing these four definitions will help you analyze and write sentences with compound direct objects, using fewer words to say more.

[C]Play the appropriate CD tracks/audio files and have students sing/chant along. Remind students to commit the songs to memory by listening to these tracks/files at other times as well.

Direct Object *(1–9)*

d-o, d-o
A direct object is an objective element
that tells what the subject is acting on.
d-o, d-o
It's a noun or pronoun after a transitive verb.
d-o, d-o
It answers the question *what* or *whom* after the verb
and is labeled *do*.

Four Classes of Verbs *(1–10)*

These are the four classes of verbs:
The four classes of verbs are transitive verbs, linking verbs, intransitive verbs, and helping verbs.
These are the four classes of verbs.
A transitive verb takes an objective element.
A linking verb joins a subject to a predicate.
An intransitive verb does not take an objective element or join a subject to a predicate.
A helping verb helps another verb express its meaning.
A helping verb helps another verb express its meaning.
These are the four classes of verbs.
These are the four classes of verbs.

Conjunction *(1–20)*

A conjunction is a part of speech.
It joins elements of the same rank or name.
When two or more words are joined this way, they're called compounds. *(Repeat.)*

Object Pronouns *(1–15)*

Object pronouns are in the objective case.
Me, you, him, her, it, us, you, them
Me, you, him, her, it, us, you, them.
Object pronouns are in the objective case.
Me, you, him, her, it, us, you, them
Me, you, him, her, it, us, you, them
Me, you, him, her, it, us, you, them.

Sentences to Analyze[D]

Before you begin, make sure that you mark the conjunctions with wings. The questions that have been added to your analysis script are there to help you analyze the sentence.

[D]Put the sentence on the board, and first mark conjunctions with angle brackets (> <) or "wings." After marking the wings, review the order of analysis chant. It should be reviewed every time you analyze a sentence. Model how to mark the sentence while the students chorally analyze the sentence, saying aloud the words in gray.

S PV
Tom took one (apple) and some (cake)
adj do adj do

a. (First, read the sentence aloud.) "Tom took one apple and some cake."

b. "Are there any conjunctions?" (Choral response: "Yes, sir.") (Since *and* is a conjunction, put wings before and after it.)

c. "The order of analysis is phrases, clauses, principal elements, modifiers."

d. "Are there any prepositional phrases?" (Choral response: "No, sir." Since there are none, you can answer *no*, and continue.)

e. "This is a sentence, and it is declarative."

f. "This sentence is about *Tom*. So, *Tom* is the subject because it is what the sentence is about." (Since *Tom* is the subject, underline it and place a capital letter *S* above it.)

g. "This sentence tells us that Tom *took*. So, *took* is the predicate because it is what the sentence tells us about *Tom*." (Since *took* tells something about Tom, double underline the predicate and a capital letter *P* above it.) "It is a predicate verb because it shows action. There is no linking verb because predicate verbs do not need linking verbs." (Since *took* shows action, place a capital letter *V* to the right of the letter *P* above the predicate.)

h. "*Apple* and *cake* tell us what Tom took." (Since *apple* and *cake* tell what Tom took, draw a circle around each of them.)

i. "So, *apple* and *cake* are objective elements because they complete the meaning of an action verb. They are direct objects because they tell *what* Tom took." (Write *do* in lowercase letters beneath each direct object.)

j. "*And* is the conjunction."

k. "*Some* tells us *how much* of the cake Tom took. So, *some* is an adjective element because it modifies a noun. It is an adjective." (Since *some* is an adjective, draw a straight line down from the adjective, then a horizontal line toward the word that it modifies, and then a straight line with an arrow pointing to the word it modifies. Write *adj* in lowercase letters in the elbow opposite the line with the arrow.)

l. "*One* tells us *how many* apples Tom took. So *one* is an adjective element because it modifies a noun. It is an adjective." (Since *one* is an adjective, draw a straight line down from the adjective, then a horizontal line toward the word that it modifies, and then a straight line with an arrow pointing to the word it modifies. Write *adj* in lowercase letters in the elbow opposite the line with the arrow.)

If you were really hungry when the server came to take your order at a restaurant, you would probably not waste words saying, "I would like a cheeseburger. I would like french fries. I would like applesauce." You would more likely apply the "less is more" principle to get your order placed more quickly: "I would like a cheeseburger, french fries, and applesauce." Now, that's an effective use of a compound direct object. But don't forget to add *please*!

Flip back to the illustration at the beginning of this chapter. Did you notice the bowl full of french fries? Is Fritz reaching for the salt or the ketchup? What do you like on your french fries? Why do you think the family is eating just french fries?

Notes

Well-Ordered Notes Introductory

Practice It

Play the game What Can You Do? Have the students stand beside their desks. Using one of the following transitive verbs, ask, "What can you ____________?" (e.g., What can you *color*?). The first student will respond by answering the question using a compound direct object. Next he turns to a fellow student and asks, "What can you ____________?" and so forth until every student answers the question. Write the following verbs on the board as options for the students to use; yet they are encouraged to think of their own.

Example:

Teacher: "What can you *color*?"
Student 1: "I can color a *map* or a *chart*."

color	wash	recount	pour	draw
crumble	nibble	list	shape	gobble
create	scrub	invent	climb	follow

Analyze It

As a class, analyze the following sentences (*S* = subject; *PV* = predicate verb; *hv* = helping verb; *adv* = adverb; *adj* = adjective; *do* = direct object; *p* = preposition; *op* = object of the preposition; *prep* = prepositional phrase). Write the sentences on the board. Have the students analyze the sentences, reciting the analysis aloud using the following script. While the students recite, you will mark the sentence on the board.

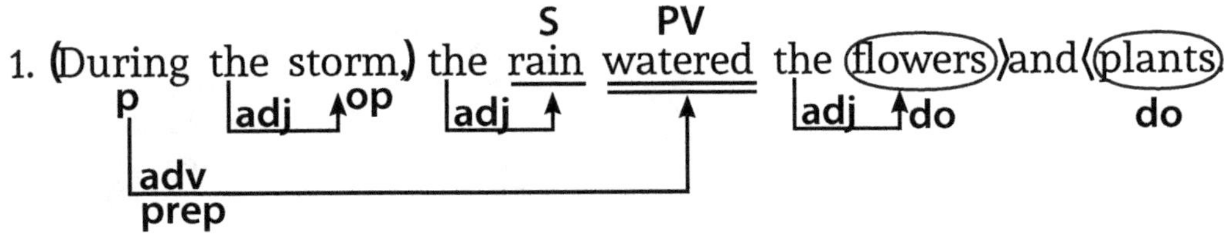

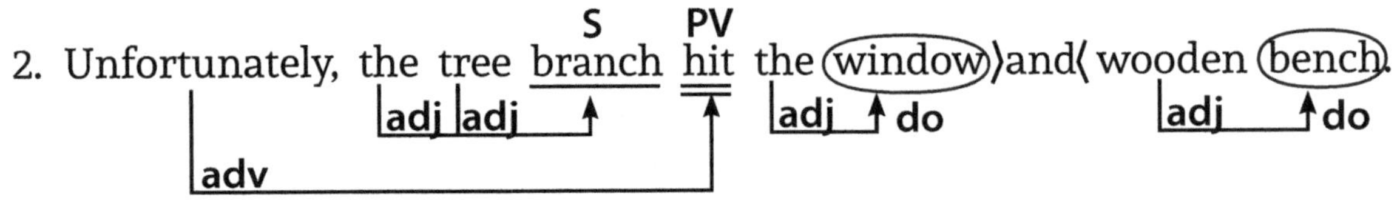

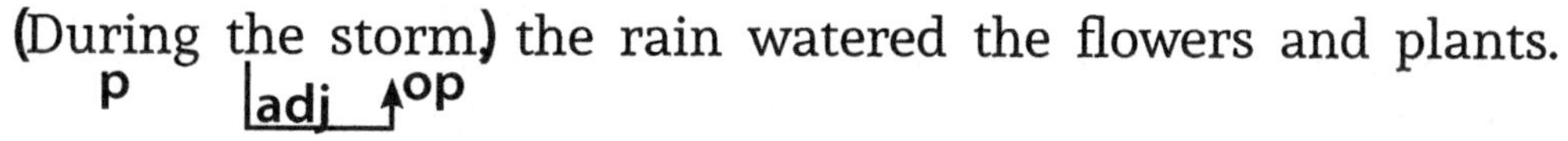

Part 1: Identify Phrases and Conjunctions

a. (First, read the sentence aloud.) "During the storm, the rain watered the flowers and plants."

b. "Are there any conjunctions?" (Choral response: "Yes, sir.") (Mark the conjunction *and* with two angle brackets.)

c. "The order of analysis is phrases, clauses, principal elements, modifiers."

d. "Are there any prepositional phrases?" (Choral response: "Yes, sir.") "*During the storm* is a prepositional phrase." (Place parentheses around the prepositional phrase.)

e. "*During* is the preposition." (Place a lowercase *p* underneath the preposition.)

f. "*Storm* is the object of the preposition." (Place a lowercase *op* underneath the object of the preposition.)

g. "*The* is an adjective."[1] (Draw a straight line down from the adjective, then a horizontal line toward the word that it modifies, and then a straight line with an arrow pointing to the word it modifies. Write *adj* in lowercase letters in the elbow opposite the line with the arrow.)

Part 2: Identify Principal Elements and Modifiers

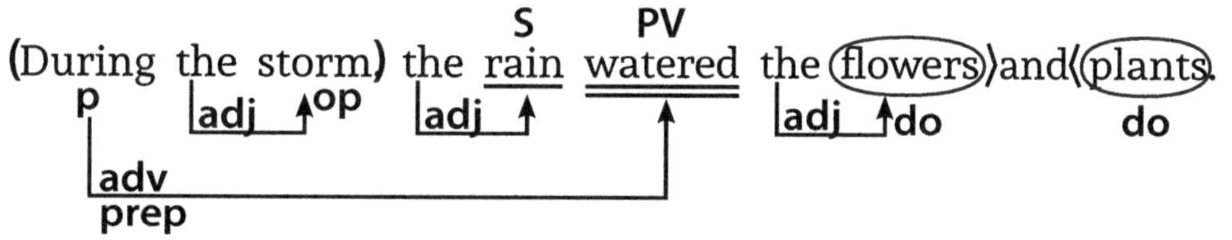

a. (Read the sentence aloud again.) "During the storm, the rain watered the flowers and plants."

b. "This is a sentence and it is declarative."

c. "This sentence is about *rain*." (Underline the subject.) "So, *rain* is the subject because it is what the sentence is about." (Place a capital letter *S* above each subject.)

d. "This sentence tells us that rain *watered*." (Double underline the predicate.) "So, *watered* is the predicate because it is what the sentence tells us about *rain*." (Place a capital letter *P* above the predicate.) "It is a predicate verb because it shows action." (Place a capital letter *V* to the right of the letter *P* above the predicate.) "There is no linking verb because predicate verbs do not need linking verbs."

e. "*Flowers* and *plants* tell us what the rain watered." (Draw a circle around each word.) "So, *flowers* and *plants* are objective elements because they complete the meaning of the action verb. They are direct objects because they tell *what* rain watered." (Write *do* in lowercase letters beneath the direct objects.)

1. The words *article adjective* can be substituted in place of the word *adjective*.

f. "*And* is the conjunction."

g. "*The* is an adjective."[2] (Draw a straight line down from the adjective, then a horizontal line toward the word that it modifies, and then a straight line with an arrow pointing to the word it modifies. Write *adj* in lowercase letters in the elbow opposite the line with the arrow.)

h. "*During the storm* tells us *when* the rain watered." (Draw a straight line down from the letter *p* that's under the preposition, then a horizontal line toward the word that it modifies, and then a straight line with an arrow pointing to the word it modifies.) "So, *during the storm* is an adverbial element because it modifies a verb. It is an adverbial prepositional phrase." (Write *adv* in lowercase letters in the elbow opposite the line with the arrow. Write *prep* in lowercase letters directly below the *adv*, underneath the modifier line.)

For the analysis of the second sentence, adjust the script accordingly.

2. The words *article adjective* can be substituted in place of the word *adjective*.

Notes

Introductory Lesson
Compound Direct Objects

The order of the lesson is: **Review It**, **Practice It**, **Learn It**, and **Analyze It**.

Review It: Sing/chant and review definitions as a class.

Review It

You now know that the more you recite, the more you remember. See if you can recite answers to the following questions:

What is a direct object? What are the four classes of verbs?

What is a transitive verb? What is an intransitive verb?

Practice It: For this warm-up, see Well-Ordered Notes Introductory on p. a of the teacher's pages for this chapter.

Learn It: Write the words on the board to do this part of the lesson orally, or ask the students to complete it in their books and then share with the class. (Answers may vary.)

Learn It

A sentence is a group of words that express a complete thought. The order of the words is important for the sentence to make sense. Construct sentences using the following strings of words.

Example: afternoon, somersaults, Heidi, during, did, long, the
During the long afternoon, Heidi did somersaults.

1. bone, table, Rex, steak, gobbled, under, the, the.

Rex gobbled the steak bone under the table.

2. shovel, neighbor, back, little, brought, yesterday, the, the.

The little neighbor brought back the shovel yesterday.

3. break, Dad, garage, spring, whole, organized, after, the, the

After the spring break, Dad organized the whole garage.

4. clay, potter, carefully, gray, old, shaped, the, the

The old potter carefully shaped the gray clay.

Analyze It

Analyze the following sentences (*S* = subject; *PV* = predicate verb; *hv* = helping verb; *adv* = adverb; *adj* = adjective; *do* = direct object; *p* = preposition; *op* = object of the preposition; *prep* = prepositional phrase).

> **Analyze It:** This is the essential part of the lesson. See p. a in Well-Ordered Notes Introductory.

S PV
1. (During the storm) the rain watered the (flowers) and (plants).
p adj op adj adj do do
adv prep

S PV
2. Unfortunately the tree branch hit the (window) and wooden (bench).
adj adj adj do adj do
adv

Introductory Practice
Compound Direct Objects

1. Analyze the following sentences (*S* = subject; *PV* = predicate verb; *hv* = helping verb; *adv* = adverb; *adj* = adjective; *do* = direct object; *p* = preposition; *op* = object of the preposition; *prep* = prepositional phrase).

a. (At the restaurant,) the waitress gave crayons and doodle sheets (to the kids.)

b. The three children nibbled saltines and breadsticks (at the table.)

c. Dad told riddles and jokes (during the long wait.)

d. Finally she brought the hamburgers and french fries (to them.)

2. On the lines provided, list the *compound direct objects* adverbs from the above sentences.

a. crayons

b. sheets

c. saltines

d. breadsticks

e. riddles

f. jokes

g. hamburgers

h. french fries

3. Construct a sentence using the following string of words: *sky, soars, bird, blue, the, the, in.*

   The blue bird soars in the sky.

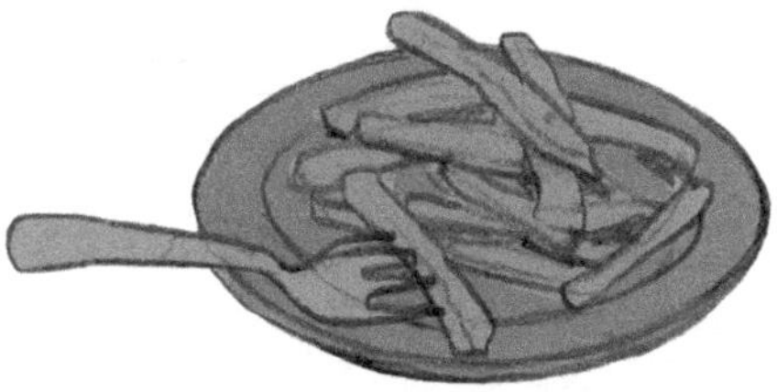

Well-Ordered Notes A

Practice It

Play the game Lightning, having students quickly recall proper nouns. Direct the students' attention to the Lessons to Learn A, Learn It section in their books, which defines common and proper nouns. Have each student stand beside her desk and be seated after she has provided a proper noun. To begin the game, state the category (e.g., cities: name a city in Ohio). The student has five seconds to give a proper noun. If she can, she may sit down; if not, she is to wait until you return to her. Connect the responses to the definition of a proper noun. Remember, this game is supposed to move quickly.

Example:

Teacher: "Cities—Name a city in Ohio."
Student: "Cincinnati is a city."
Teacher: "Cincinnati is a *proper noun* because it is the name of a particular city."

Mountain ranges	States	Months of the year	Names of family members
Restaurants	Football teams	Days of the week	Girls (or boys) in the class

Analyze It

As a class, analyze the following sentences (*S* = subject; *PV* = predicate verb; *hv* = helping verb; *adv* = adverb; *adj* = adjective; *do* = direct object; *p* = preposition; *op* = object of the preposition; *prep* = prepositional phrase). Write the sentences on the board. Have the students analyze the sentences, reciting the analysis aloud using the following script. While the students recite, you will mark the sentence on the board.

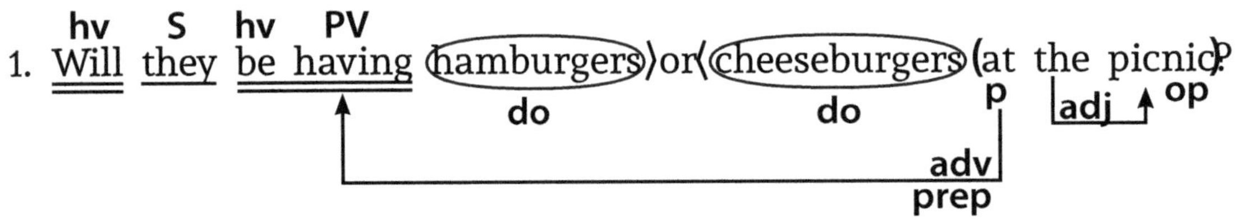

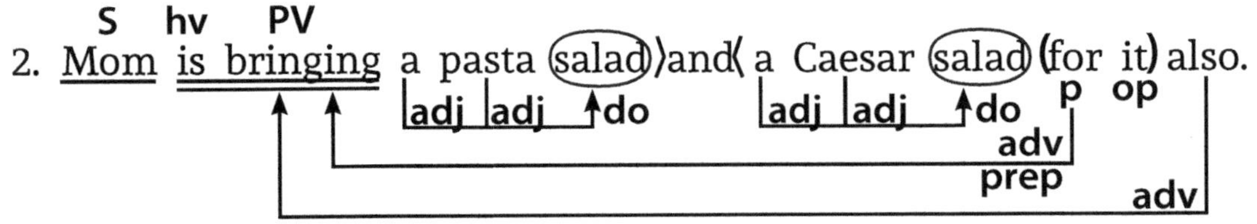

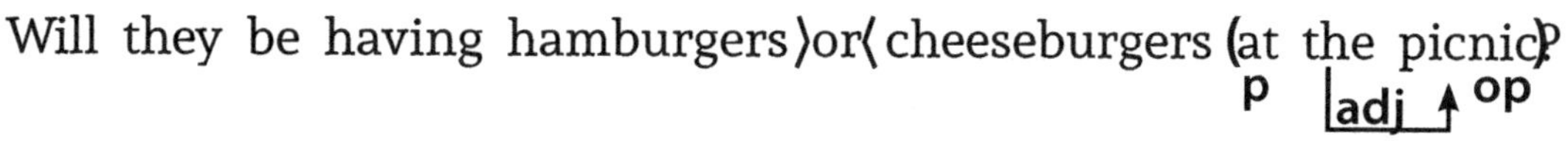

Part 1: Identify Phrases and Conjunctions

a. (First, read the sentence aloud.) "Will they be having hamburgers or cheeseburgers at the picnic?"

b. "Are there any conjunctions?"(Choral response: "Yes, sir.") (Mark the conjunction *or* with two angle brackets.)

c. "The order of analysis is phrases, clauses, principal elements, modifiers."

d. "Are there any prepositional phrases?" (Choral: "Yes, sir.") "*At the picnic* is a prepositional phrase." (Put parentheses around the prepositional phrase.)

e. "*At* is the preposition." (Place a lowercase *p* underneath the preposition.)

f. "*Picnic* is the object of the preposition." (Place a lowercase *op* underneath the object of the preposition.)

g. "*The* is an adjective."[1] (Draw a straight line down from the adjective, then a horizontal line toward the word that it modifies, and then a straight line with an arrow pointing to the word it modifies. Write *adj* in lowercase letters in the elbow opposite the line with the arrow.)

Part 2: Identify Principal Elements and Modifiers

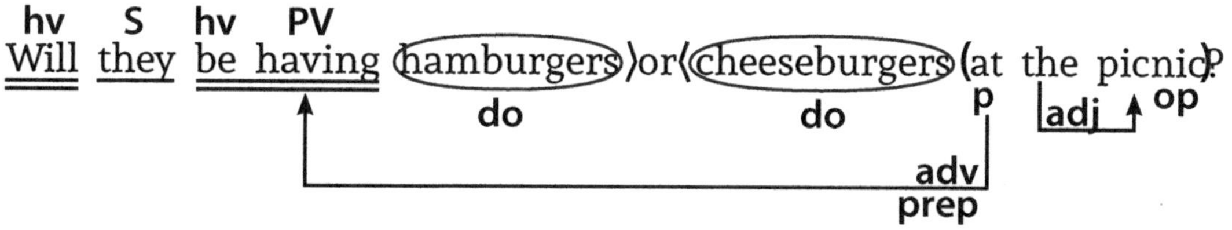

a. (Read the sentence aloud again.) "Will they be having hamburgers or cheeseburgers at the picnic?"

b. "This is a sentence and it is interrogative."

c. "This sentence is about *they*." (Underline the subject.) "So, *they* is the subject because it is what the sentence is about." (Place a capital letter *S* above the subject.)

d. "This sentence tells us that they *will be having*." (Double underline the helping verb and the predicate verb.) "So, *will be having* is the predicate because it is what the sentence tells us about *they*." (Place a capital letter *P* above the action verb.) "*Having* is a predicate verb because it shows action." (Place a capital letter *V* to the right of the letter *P*.) "There is no linking verb because predicate verbs do not need linking verbs. *Will* and *be* are helping verbs because they help the verb." (Place a lowercase *hv* above the helping verb.)

1. The words *article adjective* can be substituted in place of the word *adjective*.

e. "*Hamburgers* or *cheeseburgers* tell us what they will be having." (Draw a circle around each word.) "So, *hamburgers* or *cheeseburgers* are objective elements because they complete the meaning of the action verb. They are direct objects because they tell *what* they will be having." (Write *do* in lowercase letters beneath the direct objects.)

f. "*Or* is the conjunction."

g. "*At the picnic* tells us where they will be having hamburgers or cheeseburgers." (Draw a straight line down from the letter *p* that's under the preposition, then a horizontal line toward the word that it modifies, and then a straight line with an arrow pointing to the word it modifies.) "So, *at the picnic* is an adverbial element because it modifies a verb. It is an adverbial prepositional phrase." (Write *adv* in lowercase letters in the elbow opposite the line with the arrow. Write *prep* in lowercase letters directly below the *adv*, underneath the modifier line.)

For the analysis of the second sentence, adjust the script accordingly.

Notes

Lessons to Learn
Compound Direct Objects

A

The order of the lesson is: **Review It**, **Practice It**, **Learn It**, and **Analyze It**.

Review It: Sing/chant and review definitions as a class. Consider adding freshness by varying speed and volume or by asking individual students to paraphrase the meaning of a definition.

Review It

Give complete answers to the following statements and questions.

List the four classes of verbs.

What are the four classes of verbs?

Construct a sentence with a transitive verb.

What is a direct object?

Construct a sentence with a compound direct object.

What is the direct object in the sentence that you constructed?

Practice It: For this warm-up, see Well-Ordered Notes A.

To the Source:

■ **proper & common**

The Latin word for *common* is *communis*, meaning "public, shared by many, or general." The Latin word for *proper* is *proprius*, meaning "one's own, particular to itself."

Learn It

The two classes of nouns are proper■ and common■ nouns. Remember, a proper noun names a particular person, place, or thing and is always capitalized. Common nouns are all other nouns and may be preceded by an article adjective. Identify the class of nouns to which each of the following words belongs and, on the lines provided, write a complete sentence that tells how you know each noun is common or proper.

Example:

bulbs: **It is common because it names any bulbs.**
Aunt Gabby: **It is proper because it names a particular person.**

1. jump rope **It is common because it names any jump rope.** ______

2. Holland **It is proper because it names a particular place.** ______

From the Sidelines: When you work on common and proper nouns with the students, we suggest using a silly chant in a (fake) British accent: "A proper noun is capitalized. A proper noun is capitalized. A proper noun is capitalized." Use a gruff voice: "A common noun is not."

3. tulips **It is common because it names any tulip.**

4. Michigan **It is proper because it names a particular place.**

5. brothers **It is common because it names any brothers.**

6. fence **It is common because it names any fence.**

7. Fritz **It is proper because it names a particular person.**

Analyze It

Analyze the following sentences (*S* = subject; *PV* = predicate verb; *hv* = helping verb; *adv* = adverb; *adj* = adjective; *do* = direct object; *p* = preposition; *op* = object of the preposition; *prep* = prepositional phrase).

Analyze It: This is the essential part of the lesson. See Well-Ordered Notes A.

1. Will (hv) they (S) be (hv) having (PV) (hamburgers (do)) or (cheeseburgers (do)) (at (p) the (adj) picnic (op)) — adv prep

2. Mom (S) is (hv) bringing (PV) a (adj) pasta (adj) (salad (do)) and (a (adj) Caesar (adj) (salad (do)) (for (p) it (op)) — adv prep) also (adv).

Lessons to Practice A

Compound Direct Objects

1. Analyze the following sentences (*S* = subject; *PV* = predicate verb; *hv* = helping verb; *adv* = adverb; *adj* = adjective; *do* = direct object; *p* = preposition; *op* = object of the preposition; *prep* = prepositional phrase).

   a. The two kids lifted the thick branches and green leaves.
   S: kids; PV: lifted; adj adj (The, two → kids); adj adj do (the, thick → branches); adj do (green → leaves)

   b. (In the bushes) a secret nest had one blue egg and one white egg.
   S: nest; PV: had; p (In); adj op (the → bushes); adj adj (a, secret → nest); adj adj do (one, blue → egg); adj adj do (one, white → egg); adv prep (In the bushes → had)

   c. Theo noticed shells and feathers (on the ground).
   S: Theo; PV: noticed; do (shells); do (feathers); p (on); adj op (the → ground); adv prep (on the ground → noticed)

   d. (For science class) Peggy collected the eggshells and tiny feathers.
   S: Peggy; PV: collected; p (For); adj op (science → class); adj do (the → eggshells); adj do (tiny → feathers); adv prep (For science class → collected)

2. Identify the class of each of the following nouns by writing *proper* or *common* in the blank.

   a. Mrs. Smith ___**proper**___

   b. farmer ___**common**___

   c. sister ___**common**___

d. Theo **proper**

e. carrot **common**

f. sandbox **common**

g. Ohio **proper**

h. neighbor **common**

3. Construct a sentence using the following string of words: *deep, several, swim, sea, fish, the, in.*

   Several fish swim in the deep sea.

Well-Ordered Notes B

Practice It

Lead the class in the activity Construct It. Divide the class into teams of three or four students. Have each team complete the following sentences on their mini whiteboards by adding another direct object. Have each team share its sentence and identify the compound direct object.

Fewer than Five: Have each student work independently and then share with you and the others. Draw their attention to the variety in their answers and how the different compound direct objects create very different mental images.

Example: At the gym, the girls did stretches on the mat.
At the gym, the girls did stretches ___and flips___ on the mat.

1. The gymnast mastered the back handspring ___**and front flip**___.
2. Lucy was watching the older gymnasts ___**and the other girls**___.
3. She did not see Heidi ___**or the bench**___.
4. Suddenly Lucy bumped her ___**and the water bottles**___.
5. The other girls quickly brought towels ___**and rags**___.

Analyze It

As a class, analyze the following sentences (*S* = subject; *PV* = predicate verb; *hv* = helping verb; *adv* = adverb; *adj* = adjective; *do* = direct object; *p* = preposition; *op* = object of the preposition; *prep* = prepositional phrase). Write the sentences on the board. Have the students analyze the sentences, reciting the analysis aloud using the following script. While the students recite, you will mark the sentence on the board.

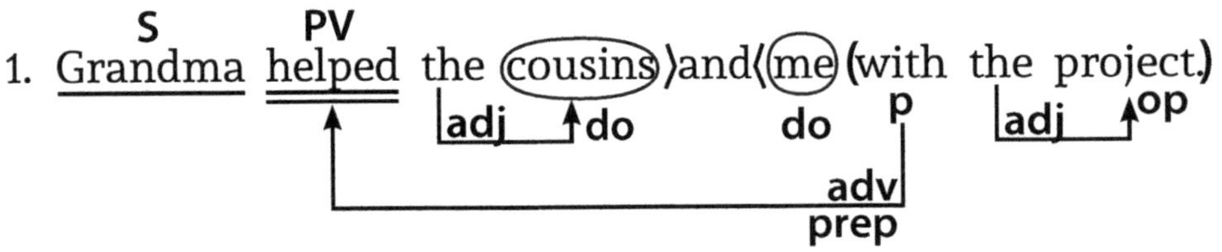

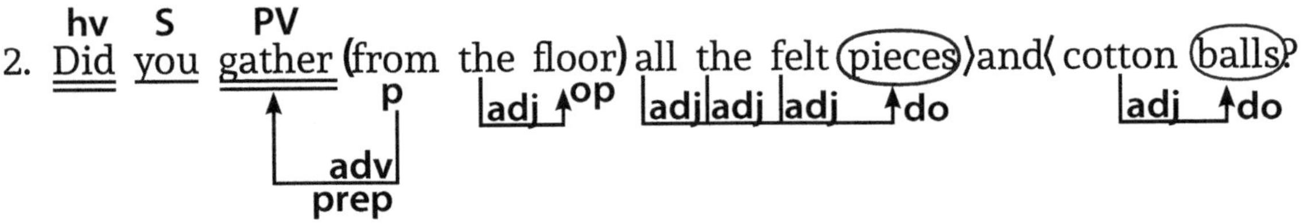

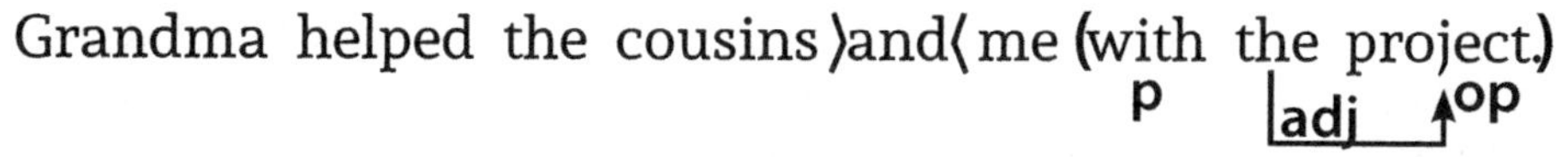

Part 1: Identify Phrases and Conjunctions

a. (First, read the sentence aloud.) "Grandma helped the cousins and me with the project."

a. "Are there any conjunctions?" (Choral response: "Yes, sir.") (Mark the conjunction *and* with two angle brackets.)

b. "The order of analysis is phrases, clauses, principal elements, modifiers."

c. "Are there any prepositional phrases?" (Choral answer: "Yes, sir.") "*With the project* is a prepositional phrase." (Place parentheses around the prepositional phrase.)

d. "*With* is the preposition." (Place a lowercase *p* underneath the preposition.)

e. "*Project* is the object of the preposition." (Place a lowercase *op* underneath the object of the preposition.)

f. "*The* is an adjective."[1] (Draw a straight line down from the adjective, then a horizontal line toward the word that it modifies, and then a straight line with an arrow pointing to the word it modifies. Write *adj* in lowercase letters in the elbow opposite the line with the arrow.)

Part 2: Identify Principal Elements and Modifiers

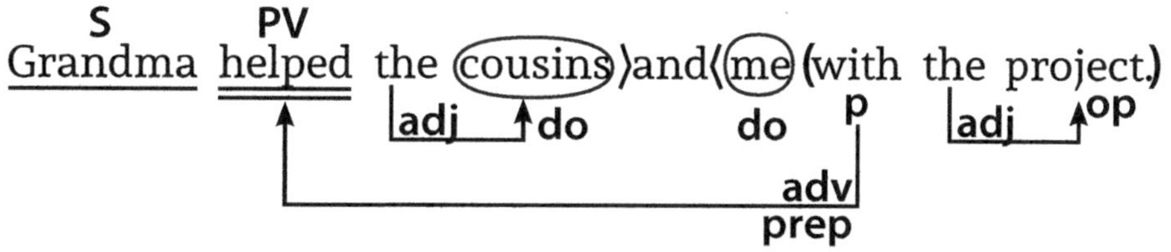

a. (Read the sentence aloud again.) "Grandma helped the cousins and me with the project."

b. "This is a sentence and it is declarative."

c. "This sentence is about *Grandma*." (Underline the subject.) "So, *Grandma* is the subject because it is what the sentence is about." (Place a capital letter *S* above the subject.)

d. "This sentence tells us that Grandma *helped*." (Double underline the predicate.) "So, *helped* is the predicate because it is what the sentence tells us about *Grandma*." (Place a capital letter *P* above the predicate.) "It is a predicate verb because it shows action." (Place a capital letter *V* to the right of the letter *P* above the predicate.) "There is no linking verb because predicate verbs do not need linking verbs."

e. "*Cousins* and *me* tell us whom Grandma helped." (Draw a circle around the words.) "So, *cousins* and *me* are objective elements because they complete the meaning of the action verb. They are direct objects because they tell *whom* Grandma helped." (Write ***do*** in lowercase letters beneath the direct objects.)

1. The words *article adjective* can be substituted in place of the word *adjective*.

f. "*And* is the conjunction."

g. "*With the project* tells us *how* Grandma helped the cousins and me." (Draw a straight line down from the letter *p* that's under the preposition, then a horizontal line toward the word that it modifies, and then a straight line with an arrow pointing to the word it modifies.) "So, *with the project* is an adverbial element because it modifies a verb. It is an adverbial prepositional phrase." (Write *adv* in lowercase letters in the elbow opposite the line with the arrow. Write *prep* in lowercase letters directly below the *adv*, underneath the modifier line.)

h. "*The* is an adjective."[2] (Draw a straight line down from the adjective, then a horizontal line toward the word that it modifies, and then a straight line with an arrow pointing to the word it modifies. Write *adj* in lowercase letters in the elbow opposite the line with the arrow.)

For the analysis of the second sentence, adjust the script accordingly.

2. The words *article adjective* can be substituted in place of the word *adjective*.

Notes

Lessons to Learn
Compound Direct Objects

B

The order of the lesson is: **Review It**, **Practice It**, **Learn It**, and **Analyze It**.

Review It: Sing/chant and review definitions as a class.

Review It

Think about object pronouns. Can you list all eight? See if you can create eight compound direct objects; each compound should include at least one of the object pronouns.

Example: *me*

Mom and ***me*****.**

Practice It: For this warm-up, see Well-Ordered Notes B.

Learn It: Write the sentences on the board if doing the lesson together as a class. Or have the students complete it in their books and share their answers orally. (Answers may vary.)

Learn It

Direct objects complete the meaning of the action verb. In the following sentences, fill in the missing part of the compound direct object.

Example: Dad watched Theo and ___the boys___ in his fields.

1. Theo played soccer and ___**kickball**___ near the new playground.

2. Four little cousins played tag and ___**four square**___ on the blacktop.

3. During the game, the kids shared nachos and ___**juice**___ with the other kids.

4. Afterward, Theo put away the equipment and ___**balls**___ into the gray crate near the wooden shed.

B Lessons to Learn
Compound Direct Objects

Analyze It

> **Analyze It:** This is the essential part of the lesson. See Well-Ordered Notes B.

Analyze the following sentences (*S* = subject; *PV* = predicate verb; *hv* = helping verb; *adv* = adverb; *adj* = adjective; *do* = direct object; *p* = preposition; *op* = object of the preposition; *prep* = prepositional phrase).

1. Grandma (S) helped (PV) the (adj) cousins (do) and me (do) (with (p) the (adj) project (op)) (adv prep).

2. Did (hv) you (S) gather (PV) (from (p) the (adj) floor (op)) (adv prep) all (adj) the (adj) felt (adj) pieces (do) and cotton (adj) balls?

Lessons to Practice B
Compound Direct Objects

1. Analyze the following sentences (*S* = subject; *PV* = predicate verb; *hv* = helping verb; *adv* = adverb; *adj* = adjective; *do* = direct object; *p* = preposition; *op* = object of the preposition; *prep* = prepositional phrase).

a. S PV
(During the rainy afternoon,) Mom quietly read (fables) and (fairytales) (to Fritz.)
p adj adj op adv do do p op
adv prep adv prep

b. hv S PV
Will Heidi now play (chess) or (checkers) (with Winston)?
adv do do p op
adv prep

c. S PV
(In the corner,) a gray spider slowly spun sticky (threads) and circular (webs) (for a trap.)
p adj op adj adj adv adj do adj do p adj op
adv prep adv prep

d. S PV
Stripes watched the sneaky (spider) and a clueless black (fly).
adj adj do adj adj adj do

2. Identify the class of each of the following nouns by writing *proper* or *common* in the blank.

   a. Missouri ___proper___

   b. firefighter ___common___

   c. swing set ___common___

   d. October ___proper___

   e. Stripes ___proper___

   f. Monday ___proper___

3. Construct a sentence using the following string of words: *enjoyment, read, books, children, for, those.*

   Those children read books for enjoyment.

Well-Ordered Notes C

Practice It

Play the game To the Board. Divide the students into two teams for this relay. Have one representative from each team stand at the board and write. Say one of the following compound direct objects (e.g., circles and squares) to the students, and then say, "Write." Each representative is to construct a sentence using the compound direct object. The winner receives a point for his team for being first to construct a sentence. Another point is rewarded for a neatly and correctly composed sentence (either or both teams can receive this point). Insist on legible writing, and reinforce the use of correct punctuation and capital letters. Just because it is a race doesn't mean that sloppy work is acceptable.

Fewer than Five: Adapt the relay by having each student write as many sentences as she can using the provided compound direct objects. You can participate too. Whoever constructs the most correct, neatly written sentences wins.

Example: circles and squares
Student 1: Fritz drew *circles and squares*.
Student 2: Coach Howard used *circles and squares*.

pollywogs and frogs	you and me	bread and butter	twigs and branches
celery and carrots	salt and pepper	hand and feet	Mom and her
moon and stars	bat and ball	Dad and me	hammer and nails

Analyze It

As a class, analyze the following sentences (*S* = subject; *PV* = predicate verb; *hv* = helping verb; *adv* = adverb; *adj* = adjective; *do* = direct object; *p* = preposition; *op* = object of the preposition; *prep* = prepositional phrase). Write the sentences on the board. Have the students analyze the sentences, reciting the analysis aloud using the following script. While the students recite, you will mark the sentence on the board.

1. (Under the bridge) the fishermen caught trout and walleye

S: fishermen; PV: caught; p: Under; adj: the; op: bridge; adj: the; do: trout; do: walleye; adv prep: (Under the bridge)

S PV
2. (On the shore,) the other fishermen built a fire pit⟩and⟨a small fire.
p adj op adj adj adj adj do adj adj do
adv
prep

(Under the bridge) the fishermen caught trout⟩and⟨walleye.
p adj op

Part 1: Identify Phrases and Conjunctions

a. (First, read the sentence aloud.) "Under the bridge, the fishermen caught trout and walleye."

b. "Are there any conjunctions?" (Choral response: "Yes, sir.") (Mark the conjunction with two angle brackets.)

c. "The order of analysis is phrases, clauses, principal elements, modifiers."

d. "Are there any prepositional phrases?" (Choral response: "Yes, sir.") "*Under the bridge* is a prepositional phrase." (Place parentheses around the prepositional phrase.)

e. "*Under* is the preposition." (Place a lowercase *p* underneath the preposition.)

f. "*Bridge* is the object of the preposition." (Place a lowercase *op* underneath the object of the preposition.)

g. "*The* is an adjective."[1] (Draw a straight line down from the adjective, then a horizontal line toward the word that it modifies, and then a straight line with an arrow pointing to the word it modifies. Write *adj* in lowercase letters in the elbow opposite the line with the arrow.)

Part 2: Identify Principal Elements and Modifiers

S PV
(Under the bridge) the fishermen caught trout⟩and⟨walleye.
p adj op adj do do
adv
prep

a. (Read the sentence aloud again.) "Under the bridge, the fishermen caught trout and walleye."

b. "This is a sentence and it is declarative."

c. "This sentence is about *fishermen*." (Underline the subject.) "So, *fishermen* is the subject because it is what the sentence is about." (Place a capital letter *S* above the subject.)

1. The words *article adjective* can be substituted in place of the word *adjective*.

d. "This sentence tells us that fishermen *caught*." (Double underline the predicate.) "So, *caught* is the predicate because it is what the sentence tells us about *fishermen*." (Place a capital letter *P* above the predicate.) "It is a predicate verb because it shows action." (Place a capital letter *V* to the right of the letter *P* above the predicate.) "There is no linking verb because predicate verbs do not need linking verbs."

e. "*Trout* and *walleye* tell us what the fishermen caught." (Draw a circle around the words.) "So, *trout* and *walleye* are objective elements because they complete the meaning of the action verb. They are direct objects because they tell *what* the fishermen caught." (Write *do* in lowercase letters beneath the direct objects.)

f. "*And* is the conjunction."

g. "*The* is an adjective."[2] (Draw a straight line down from the adjective, then a horizontal line toward the word that it modifies, and then a straight line with an arrow pointing to the word it modifies. Write *adj* in lowercase letters in the elbow opposite the line with the arrow.)

h. "*Under the bridge* tells us *how* the fishermen caught trout and walleye." (Draw a straight line down from the letter *p* that's under the preposition, then a horizontal line toward the word that it modifies, and then a straight line with an arrow pointing to the word it modifies.) "So, *under the bridge* is an adverbial element because it modifies a verb. It is an adverbial prepositional phrase." (Write *adv* in lowercase letters in the elbow opposite the line with the arrow. Write *prep* in lowercase letters directly below the *adv*, underneath the modifier line.)

For the analysis of the second sentence, adjust the script accordingly.

2. The words *article adjective* can be substituted in place of the word *adjective*.

Notes

Lessons to Learn
Compound Direct Objects

C

The order of the lesson is: **Review It**, **Practice It**, **Learn It**, and **Analyze It**.

Review It: Sing/chant and review definitions as a class. Consider adding freshness by varying speed and volume or by asking individual students to paraphrase the meaning of a definition.

Review It

Answer the following questions:

What are two classes of nouns?

What are the four classes of verbs?

What is a direct object?

What is a compound direct object?

What are object pronouns?

Name a plural, third-person object pronoun.

Practice It: For this warm-up, see Well-Ordered Notes C.

Learn It: This part of the lesson can be completed together orally, or it can be completed individually in the book. (Answers may vary.)

Learn It

Construct sentences with compound direct objects by adding another direct object and conjunction to each of the following sentences.

Example: In the room, he opened the closet ___and dresser drawers___.

1. Winston took from the shelf the tennis racket ___**and tennis balls**___
______________________________.

2. Next he swatted the pillows ___**and stuffed animals**___
______________________________.

3. Then he hit the old socks ___**and slippers**___
______________________________.

C Lessons to Learn
Compound Direct Objects

4. Did Winston just invent pillow tennis ____or sock tennis____

____?

Analyze It

> **Analyze It:** This is the essential part of the lesson. See Well-Ordered Notes C.

Analyze the following sentences (*S* = subject; *PV* = predicate verb; *hv* = helping verb; *adv* = adverb; *adj* = adjective; *do* = direct object; *p* = preposition; *op* = object of the preposition; *prep* = prepositional phrase).

1. (Under the bridge,) the fishermen caught trout and walleye.

   - Under: p; the: adj; bridge: op; (Under the bridge): adv prep → caught
   - the: adj → fishermen
   - fishermen: S
   - caught: PV
   - trout: do; walleye: do

2. (On the shore,) the other fishermen built a fire pit and a small fire.

   - On: p; the: adj; shore: op; (On the shore): adv prep → built
   - the: adj; other: adj → fishermen
   - fishermen: S
   - built: PV
   - a: adj; fire: adj; pit: do
   - a: adj; small: adj; fire: do

Lessons to Practice

Compound Direct Objects

C

1. Analyze the following sentences (*S* = subject; *PV* = predicate verb; *hv* = helping verb; *adv* = adverb; *adj* = adjective; *do* = direct object; *p* = preposition; *op* = object of the preposition; *prep* = prepositional phrase).

   a. (On Saturday) the family carried the brownies and cookies (to the school fair.)

   S: family; PV: carried; On (p), Saturday (op) — adv prep; the (adj); the (adj), brownies (do); cookies (do); to (p), the (adj), school (adj), fair (op) — adv prep

   b. Winston threw the spongy ball and the softball (at the target.)

   S: Winston; PV: threw; the (adj), spongy (adj), ball (do); the (adj), softball (do); at (p), the (adj), target (op) — adv prep

   c. May I have caramel corn or an orange slushy?

   hv: May; S: I; PV: have; caramel (adj), corn (do); an (adj), orange (adj), slushy (do)

   d. (At the end,) Mr. Wilson awarded the first-place poem and best sketch.

   S: Mr. Wilson; PV: awarded; At (p), the (adj), end (op) — adv prep; the (adj), first-place (adj), poem (do); best (adj), sketch (do)

2. Identify the class of each of the following nouns by writing *proper* or *common* in the blank.

   a. hands ______common______

   b. Coach Stevens ______proper______

   c. Big Dipper ______proper______

   d. daffodils ______common______

e. wave **common**

f. cloud **common**

3. Construct a sentence using the following string of words: *work, make, hands, light, many, the.*

Many hands make the work light.

Review It: Sing/chant and review definitions as a class.

Review It

Answer the following questions.

What are the four classes of verbs?

What is a direct object?

What is a transitive verb?

What are object pronouns?

Name a plural, first-person object pronoun.

Name a singular, second-person object pronoun.

Learn It: Prepare a noun jar, filling it with various nouns written on cards. Have the students select one card each or choose one from the list supplied here. Then, each student should think of a complementary noun and construct a sentence using both nouns as a compound direct object.

Learn It

Construct a sentence with a compound direct object. Choose one noun from the list below or from the class "noun jar." Add a noun of your own to form the compound direct object. Then, construct the rest of the sentence. See how many sentences you can make.

Example: ***hammer***
Uncle Ulysses uses the *hammer* and *nails*.

cups	cupcake	spade	pepper	sprinkler
blanket	ducklings	crocus	ketchup	Fritz
shoes	pickle	bread	cheese	pencils
table	skates	story	books	milk
sandwich	fork	baseball	peanuts	hands

On the lines provided, write your favorite newly constructed sentence.

In my lunchbox, I have a sandwich and a cupcake.

Lessons to Practice—Review

Compound Direct Objects

1. Analyze the following sentences: (*S* = subject; *PV* = predicate verb; *hv* = helping verb; *adv* = adverb; *adj* = adjective; *do* = direct object; *p* = preposition; *op* = object of the preposition; *prep* = prepositional phrase).

   a. (After school) the scouts followed the van and buses (to the nature center.)

   S: scouts; PV: followed; p: After; op: school; adj: the; adj: the; do: van; do: buses; p: to; adj: the; adj: nature; op: center; adv prep; adv prep

   b. Unfortunately Theo left the water bottles and snack bags (on the bus.)

   S: Theo; PV: left; adv: Unfortunately; adj: the; adj: water; do: bottles; adj: snack; do: bags; p: on; adj: the; op: bus; adv prep

   c. Fourteen hungry boys rode horses and ponies (through the grassy fields.)

   S: boys; PV: rode; adj: Fourteen; adj: hungry; do: horses; do: ponies; p: through; adj: the; adj: grassy; op: fields; adv prep

   d. The scouts later saw field hawks and black ravens (in the meadow.)

   S: scouts; PV: saw; adj: The; adv: later; adj: field; do: hawks; adj: black; do: ravens; p: in; adj: the; op: meadow; adv prep

2. Identify the class of each of the following nouns by writing *proper* or *common* in the blank.

   a. Texas ____proper____

   b. cherries ____common____

   c. patriot ____common____

d. Thursday **proper**

e. thumb **common**

f. Peggy **proper**

3. Construct a sentence using the following string of words: *alone, the, the, tree, apple, boy, climbed, young.*

The young boy climbed the apple tree alone.

Notes

Christopher Morley was an American poet who loved to write. In the poem "Animal Crackers," the narrator describes his favorite indulgence (special treat) using clever words and delicious images. Do you have a favorite after-school treat or dessert? Make a class list of favorites.

Animal Crackers

by Christopher Morley (1890–1957)

Animal crackers, and cocoa to drink,
That is the finest of suppers, I think;
When I'm grown up and can have what I please
I think I shall always insist upon these.

What do you choose when you're offered a treat?
When Mother says, "What would you like best to eat?"
Is it waffles and syrup, or cinnamon toast?
It's cocoa and animals that *I* love the most!

The kitchen's the coziest place that I know:
The kettle is singing, the stove is aglow,
And there in the twilight, how jolly to see
The cocoa and animals waiting for me.

Daddy and Mother dine later in state,
With Mary to cook for them, Susan to wait,
But they don't have nearly as much fun as I
Who eat in the kitchen with Nurse standing by;
And Daddy once said, he would like to be me
Having cocoa and animals once more for tea![1]

in state: formally

nurse: a nanny or woman who is hired to help take care of little children

1. Christopher Morley, "Animal Crackers," in *Favorite Poems Old and New*, ed. Helen Ferris (New York: Doubleday & Company, Inc., 1957), p. 43.

Questions to Ponder

1. What is the speaker's favorite supper?
2. What is the coziest place for the speaker to enjoy a treat? Why?
3. What does "the kettle is singing, the stove is aglow" mean?
4. Is the person speaking in the poem a grown man or a child?

From the Sideline: For possible answers to these discussion questions, see p. a of the teacher's pages. For even more suggestions for discussion and for enrichment activities related to the poem, see p. b.

Extras: Please note that the teacher's pages for this chapter include more material for extra practice, a quiz, and another Lessons to Enjoy section with discussion questions and activities. All this material, in reproducible form, is also included in the PDF that accompanies the textbook.

Lessons to Enjoy—Poem

Questions to Ponder

1. What is the speaker's favorite supper?

   The speaker's favorite supper is animal crackers to eat and cocoa to drink. Your students will surely react to such a meal! Have them answer the questions the poet asks in the second stanza.

2. What is the coziest place for the speaker to enjoy a treat? Why?

   The kitchen is the coziest place. It is warm and glowing and jolly in the evening. In contrast to the dining room where the parents eat "in state," the kitchen is informal and snug. There is comfort and security in the orderliness of the household, with the parents, the servants, and the children in their place, fulfilling their roles in a predictable routine.

3. What does "the kettle is singing, the stove is aglow" mean?

   The boiling water in the tea kettle is causing it to whistle, or sing. A coal-burning stove might glow if hot enough, or the glow from the embers might show through the spaces in the stovetop or door. These are images that capture the coziness of the kitchen for the poet. He associates the whistling kettle and the hot stove with the treats of his childhood.

4. Is the person speaking in the poem a grown man or a child?

   The speaker is a grown man, but the "I" and the "me" in the poem is a child. He says, "When I'm grown up," and he contrasts himself with his father who "would like to be me." Explain to the students that the speaker is playing a role perhaps to share a happy childhood memory or perhaps to create a little story that is not from his own childhood at all. (After all, Morley was an American, but the family in the poem seems British.)

Well-Ordered Notes—Poem

Read

- Give the students animal crackers and cocoa to enjoy while you read the poem aloud. Explain what may seem unfamiliar about the family in the poem, such as calling a meal "tea" and having servants.
- Have the students memorize the poem.

Retell

- Discuss the poem using the provided questions.
- Write on the board the following three sentences excerpted, and slightly adapted, from the poem. Ask the students to name the compound elements and identify a compound subject, a compound verb, and a compound direct object.
  - Daddy and Mother dine later in state. (compound subject)
  - I'm (or I am) grown up and can have what I please. (compound verb *am* and *can have*)
  - I love cocoa and animals for a treat. (compound direct object)

From the Sidelines: While "Animal Crackers" contains compound elements as objects, none of the lines include a compound direct object. Nonetheless, if you use these slightly altered excerpts, the poem provides a nice review for all the compound elements studied so far.

Record

- Have the students write skits about the short narrative in the poem. Have them act it out with props, and perhaps save the animal crackers and cocoa for this part of the lesson rather than when you first read the poem.

Practice Sheet
Compound Direct Objects
ANSWERS

Analyze the following sentences (*S* = subject; *PV* = predicate verb; *hv* = helping verb; *adv* = adverb; *adj* = adjective; *do* = direct object; *p* = preposition; *op* = object of the preposition; *prep* = prepositional phrase).

S PV
1. (On Monday afternoon) Winston painted posters and banners.
p adj op do do
adv prep

hv S PV
2. Would you get the paintbrushes or the rollers (for him)?
adj do adj do p op
adv prep

S PV
3. (On stage) the director called the young actors and actresses.
p op adj adj adj do do
adv prep

S S PV
4. Later Winston and Heidi stacked the crates and boxes (off the stage.)
adv adj do do p adj op
adv prep

hv S PV
5. Did they bring (from the truck) the wooden table and chairs?
p adj op adj adj do do
adv prep

S PV
6. The stagehand quietly collected the costumes and props.
adj adv adj do do

Practice Sheet
ANSWERS
Compound Direct Objects

S PV
7. (Behind the curtain) several actors nibbled (celery) and (carrots).
p adj op adj do do
adv prep

hv S PV
8. Is she collecting the (money) or the (tickets) (for the play)?
adj do adj do p adj op
adv prep

S PV
9. Aunt Gabby brought (Peggy) and (Lucy) (with her).
do do p op
adv prep

hv S PV
10. Will the cousins sign the autograph (books) or the (programs) later?
adj adj adj do adj do
adv

Quiz

Compound Direct Objects — ANSWERS

1. Analyze the following sentences (*S* = subject; *PV* = predicate verb; *hv* = helping verb; *adv* = adverb; *adj* = adjective; *do* = direct object; *p* = preposition; *op* = object of the preposition; *prep* = prepositional phrase).

a. (At piano lessons) Mrs. Smith greeted the (children) and (parents).
S: Mrs. Smith; PV: greeted
p adj op — adv prep (modifies greeted)
adj do; do

b. Peggy played (on the piano) a fast (song) and a slow (song).
S: Peggy; PV: played
p adj op — adv prep (modifies played)
adj adj do; adj adj do

c. (During the lesson) Theo missed a high (note) and some low (notes).
S: Theo; PV: missed
p adj op — adv prep (modifies missed)
adj adj do; adj adj do

d. (On the floor) Lucy sorted (buttons) and colorful (beads).
S: Lucy; PV: sorted
p adj op — adv prep (modifies sorted)
do; adj do

2. Identify the class of each of the following nouns by writing *proper* or *common* in the blank.

a. deer ____common____

b. Africa ____proper____

c. Wisconsin ____proper____

d. wrench ____common____

e. spider ____common____

f. Uncle Ulysses ____proper____

3. Construct a sentence using the following string of words: *early, east, sun, rises, the, the, in.*

The sun rises early in the east.

Lessons to Enjoy—Fable

Compound Direct Objects

Have you ever tripped over your feet only to have someone laugh at you? Have you ever then watched while the scoffer (a person who mocks someone) slips and falls down too? This next fable tells of a hare and a partridge both running for their lives. You may be surprised how the fable ends.

The Hare and the Partridge[1]

by Jean de La Fontaine

A Hare and a Partridge lived side by side in a big field. They were good neighbors and got along well enough. One day, a pack of Hunting Dogs came tearing across their field, barking and snapping and attacking everything that moved. The Hare was forced to run for cover through the trees. She found a place to hide under a pile of sticks and crouched there, shivering and quaking. Sadly, her overheated body gave off a smell that drew the Dogs' noses. In a jiffy, the Dogs found the poor Hare and scattered her pile of sticks. Then they finished her off.

scoffed: mocked

Later, after the Dogs had left, the Partridge stepped out of hiding. She stuck her beak in the air and scoffed to the dead Hare, "You always said you were so swift. So now what has become of your feet? I'd much rather be a Partridge than a Hare any day."

talons: the claws of a bird of prey

At that moment, out of the clear, blue sky, a Hawk struck the Partridge with her sharp talons and carried her off to her nest.

Moral: Never laugh at another person's misfortunes.

1. Jean de la Fontaine, "The Hare and the Partridge," taken from *Writing & Rhetoric Book 1: Fable* by Paul Kortepeter (Camp Hill, PA: Classical Academic Press, 2013), p. 33.

Questions to Ponder

1. How does the fable begin before the Hunting Dogs arrive?
2. What happens to the poor Hare?
3. What does "stuck her beak in the air and scoffed" mean?
4. What lesson can be learned from the Partridge?

Lessons to Enjoy—Fable

Questions to Ponder

1. How does the fable begin before the Hunting Dogs arrive?

   The Hare and the Partridge live peacefully as neighbors.

2. What happens to the poor Hare?

   She gets chased and eaten by the dogs. Unlike the Partridge, she is a sympathetic character in the tale: she does nothing wrong; she is terrified; and she can't help that the Dogs smell her scent.

3. What does "stuck her beak in the air and scoffed" mean?

   Sticking one's beak or one's nose in the air is a classic symbol of self-importance, of being "stuck up." The Partridge's mockery of the poor Hare is shocking. And she pays the price. If she had acted more humbly and had shown more sympathy toward the Hare, she may have seen the Hawk in time to escape.

4. What lesson can be learned from the Partridge?

   Laughing in mockery at the Hare made the Partridge blind to her own danger. Ask the students to think of real-life examples of the moral, such as one sibling laughing at another sibling for tripping on shoelaces only to fall himself, or fans taunting a baseball player on the opposing team for "striking out" only to see a player on their own team do the same thing.

Well-Ordered Notes—Fable

Read

- Encourage the students to enjoy the fable as you read it aloud. Bring in some still life pictures of hares and partridges (such as *Dead Hare with Partridges with Instruments of the Chase* by Jan Weenix, 1704) and show them to the students.
- Have students sing/chant the definition of a fable (Fable, 1–14).

Retell

- Discuss the tale using the provided questions.
- Have the students act out the fable using sock puppets. You can make a set in advance or have students make the different characters. See instructions below.

Record

- Have the students rewrite the fable in their copybooks using other animals (i.e., a hawk, snake, and mouse).
- Have students adorn their rewrite of the fable by adding a colorful border using different shapes, such as animal prints.

Sock Puppets

1. Put an old sock on your hand so that your fingers are in the toe part of the sock and your thumb is in the heel part.
2. Open and close your hand, and determine where the eyes of the puppet will be.
3. Draw two large dots with markers where the eyes should be or use a needle and thread and sew on buttons on the dots.
4. Cut yarn or fabric strips for hair and cut felt for ears or nose.
5. Glue on the hair, ears, and nose.

Fable Sentences
Compound Direct Objects
ANSWERS

Analyze the following sentences (*S* = subject; *PV* = predicate verb; *hv* = helping verb; *adv* = adverb; *adj* = adjective; *do* = direct object; *p* = preposition; *op* = object of the preposition; *prep* = prepositional phrase).

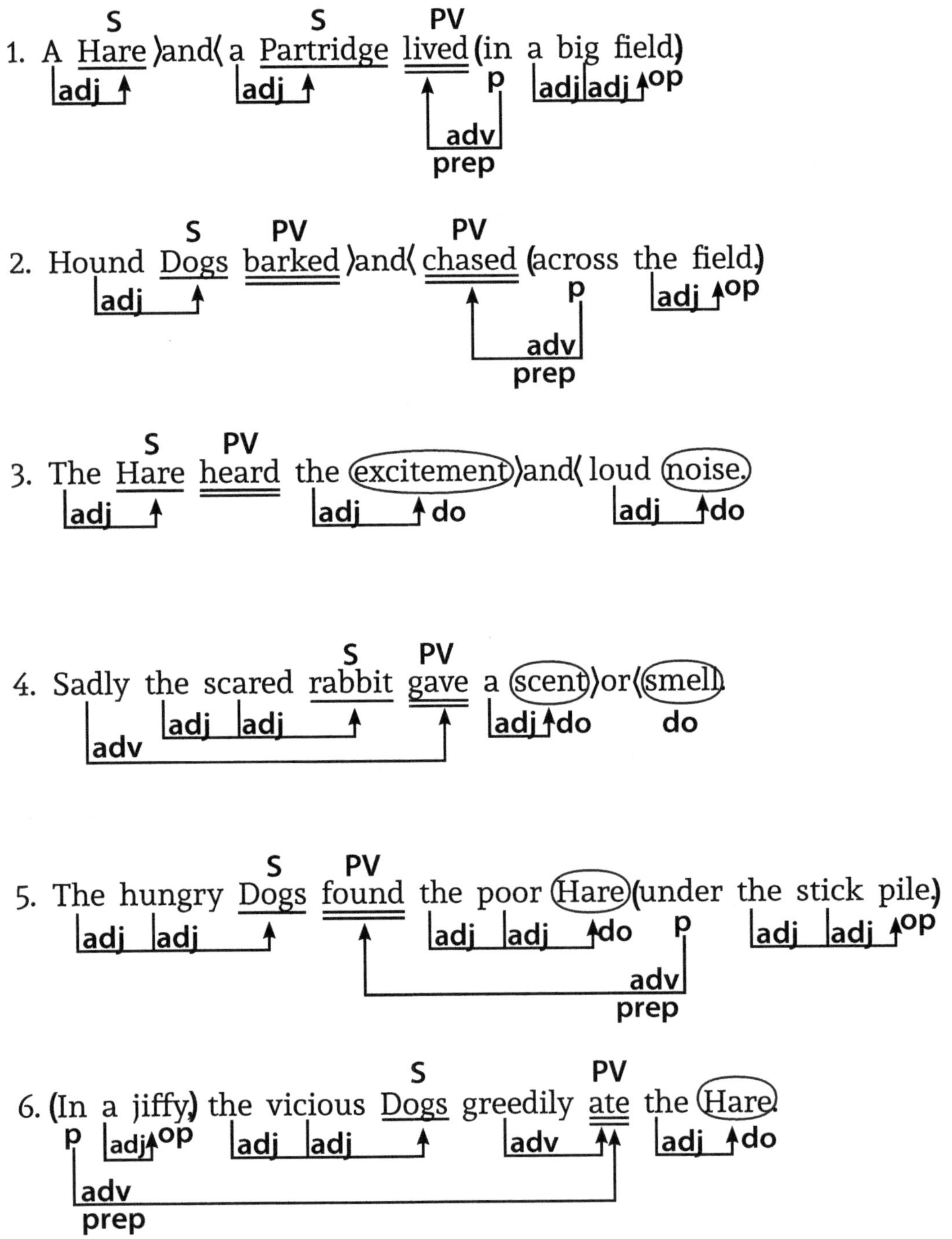

Fable Sentences

Compound Direct Objects

7. Later the selfish Partridge saw the pile and the lost Hare.
   (S: Partridge; PV: saw; adv: Later; adj: the, selfish; adj: the → do: pile; adj: the, lost → do: Hare)

8. The heartless Partridge sneered and scoffed (at the tragedy).
   (S: Partridge; PV: sneered; PV: scoffed; adj: The, heartless; p: at; adj: the → op: tragedy; adv prep)

9. Does misfortune follow Partridges or Hares?
   (hv: Does; S: misfortune; PV: follow; do: Partridges; do: Hares)

10. Suddenly a Hawk attacked the Partridge (with sharp talons).
    (S: Hawk; PV: attacked; adv: Suddenly; adj: a; adj: the → do: Partridge; p: with; adj: sharp → op: talons; adv prep)

The Curious Child's Literary Appendix

In each chapter, we have used a classic poem or excerpt from a classic book to illustrate the grammatical principles taught in that chapter. Reading just a few lines from a fine piece of literature is like getting a small sample of something savory (delicious) at the grocery store. That is called "whetting your appetite." If you want more, you beg to be allowed to buy what you only tasted.

Have you been tantalized by any of the literary samples? If so, you can find the fuller feast here in this appendix. All the poems are presented in their entirety. All the excerpts from fiction are presented in more detail to whet (sharpen) your appetite for the whole book from which they are taken.

Of course, you can really treat yourself to a banquet at the library, where you can check out and read the novels or entire collections of poetry. *Bon appetit!* (Enjoy!)

Chapter 1

Charlotte's Web

From chapter 6, "Summer Days"

by E.B. White (1899–1985)

"Look," he began in his sharp voice, "you say you have seven goslings. There were eight eggs. What happened to the other egg? Why didn't it hatch?"

goslings: baby geese

"It's a dud, I guess," said the goose.

"What are you going to do with it?" continued Templeton, his little round beady eyes fixed on the goose.

beady: small, round, and shiny
fixed: stared

"You can have it," replied the goose. "Roll it away and add it to that nasty collection of yours." (Templeton had a habit of picking up unusual objects around the farm and storing them in his home. He saved everything.)

"Certainly-ertainly-ertainly," said the gander. "You may have the egg. But I'll tell you one thing, Templeton, if I ever catch you poking-oking-oking your ugly nose around our goslings, I'll give you the worst pounding a rat ever took." And the gander opened his strong wings and beat the air with them to show his power. He was strong and brave, but the truth is, both the goose and the gander were worried about Templeton. And with good reason. The rat had no morals, no conscience, no scruples, no consideration, no decency, no milk of rodent kindness, no compunctions, no higher feeling, no friendliness, no anything. He would kill a gosling if he could get away with it—the goose knew that.

gander: male goose
pounding: beating
morals: standards or acceptable ways to behave or believe
conscience: an inner, guiding feeling about right or wrong
scruples: restraint from doing wrong

Everybody knew it.[1]

consideration: careful thought over a period of time
decency: behavior that is acceptable and proper
milk of rodent kindness: compassion or goodness (a play on the phrase "milk of human kindness")
compunctions: uneasiness about the rightness of an action
higher feeling: sentiment or warm wishes

1. E.B. White, "Summer Days," *Charlotte's Web* (New York: HarperTrophy, 1980), pp. 45–46.

Chapter 2

From the Sideline: Throughout the literary appendix, you'll note that, where appropriate, we have retained the British single quotation marks for dialogue.

Just So Stories

From chapter 7, "The Beginning of the Armadillos"

by Rudyard Kipling (1865–1936)

'But I *am* Tortoise,' said Slow-and-Solid. 'Your mother was quite right. She said that you were to scoop me out of my shell with your paw. Begin.'

'You didn't say she said that a minute ago,' said Painted Jaguar, sucking the prickles out of his paddy-paw. 'You said she said something quite different.'

prickles: small, sharp points like thorns

'Well, suppose you say that I said that she said something quite different, I don't see that it makes any difference; because if she said what you said I said she said, it's just the same as if I said what she said she said. On the other hand, if you think she said that you were to uncoil me with a scoop, instead of pawing me into drops with a shell, I can't help that, can I?'

'But you said you wanted to be scooped out of your shell with my paw,' said Painted Jaguar.

'If you'll think again you'll find that I didn't say anything of the kind. I said that your mother said that you were to scoop me out of my shell,' said Slow-and-Solid.

'What will happen if I do?' said the Jaguar most sniffily and most cautious.

sniffily: showing contempt (lack of respect) or haughtiness (pridefulness)

'I don't know, because I've never been scooped out of my shell before; but I tell you truly, if you want to see me swim away you've only got to drop me into the water.'

'I don't believe it,' said Painted Jaguar.[1]

1. Rudyard Kipling, "The Beginning of the Armadillos," *Just So Stories* (New York: Doubleday, 1952), p. 39.

Chapter 3

Moon Folly

by Fannie Stearns Davis (1884–1966)

I will go up the mountain after the Moon:
She is caught in a dead fir-tree.
Like a great pale apple of silver and pearl,
Like a great pale apple is she.

I will leap and will clasp her with quick cold hands
And carry her home in my sack.
I will set her down safe on the oaken bench
That stands at the chimney-back.

And then I will sit by the fire all night,
And sit by the fire all day.
I will gnaw at the Moon to my heart's delight,
Till I gnaw her slowly away.

And while I grow mad with the Moon's cold taste,
The World may beat on my door,
Crying "Come out!" and crying "Make haste!
And give us the Moon once more!"

But I shall not answer them ever at all;
I will laugh, as I count and hide
The great black beautiful seeds of the Moon
In a flower-pot deep and wide.

Then I will lie down and go fast asleep,
Drunken with flame and aswoon.
But the seeds will sprout, and the seeds will leap:
The subtle swift seeds of the Moon.

aswoon: dazed or light headed

subtle: delicate or obscure

And some day, all of the world that beats
And cries at my door, shall see
A thousand moon-leaves spring from my thatch
On a marvelous white Moon-tree!

Then each shall have Moons to his heart's desire:
Apples of silver and pearl:
Apples of orange and copper fire,
Setting his five wits aswirl.

aswirl: swirling

And then they will thank me, who mock me now,
"Wanting the Moon is he!"
Oh, I'm off to the mountain after the Moon,
Ere she falls from the dead fir-tree![1]

1. Fannie Stearns Davis, "Moon Folly" from In Poetry, Vol. I, ed. Harriet Monroe (New York: A.M.S. Reprint CO, Vol. 1, No. 6, March 1912–1913), pp. 183–184. Available at: https://books.google.com/books?id=9MARAAAAYAAJ.

Chapter 4

The Wind in the Willows

From chapter 3, "The Wild Wood"

by Kenneth Grahame (1859–1932)

In the winter time the Rat slept a great deal, retiring early and rising late. During his short day he sometimes scribbled poetry or did other small domestic jobs about the house; and, of course, there were always animals dropping in for a chat, and consequently there was a good deal of story-telling and comparing notes on the past summer and all its doings.

domestic: household

Such a rich chapter it had been, when one came to look back on it all! With illustrations so numerous and so very highly coloured! The pageant of the river bank had marched steadily along, unfolding itself in scene-pictures that succeeded each other in stately procession. Purple loosestrife arrived early, shaking luxuriant tangled locks along the edge of the mirror whence its own face laughed back at it. Willow-herb, tender and wistful, like a pink sunset cloud, was not slow to follow. Comfrey, the purple hand-in-hand with the white, crept forth to take its place in the line; and at last one morning the diffident and delaying dog-rose stepped delicately on the stage, and one knew, as if string-music had announced it in stately chords that strayed into a gavotte, that June at last was here.[1]

coloured: colored
pageant: a parade or procession
stately: grand manner; dignified
loosestrife: a purple wildflower
luxuriant: lush
whence: from which
willow-herb: a wildflower
wistful: quiet, silent, regretful
comfrey: wildflower
diffident: bashful
dog-rose: a pink or white wildflower
gavotte: a French dance

1. Kenneth Grahame, "The Wild Wood," *The Wind in the Willows* (New York: The New American Library, Inc., 1969), pp. 56–57.

Chapter 5

The Walrus and the Carpenter

by Lewis Carroll (1832–1898)

The sun was shining on the sea,
   Shining with all his might:
He did his very best to make
   The billows smooth and bright—
And this was odd, because it was
   The middle of the night.

billows: waves

The moon was shining sulkily,
   Because she thought the sun
Had got no business to be there
   After the day was done—
'It's very rude of him,' she said,
   'To come and spoil the fun.'

sulkily: unhappily

The sea was wet as wet could be,
   The sands were dry as dry.
You could not see a cloud, because
   No cloud was in the sky:
No birds were flying overhead—
   There were no birds to fly.

The Walrus and the Carpenter
   Were walking close at hand:
They wept like anything to see
   Such quantities of sand:
'If this were only cleared away,'
   They said, 'it would be grand!'

'If seven maids with seven mops
   Swept it for half a year,
Do you suppose,' the Walrus said,
   'That they could get it clear?'

'I doubt it,' said the Carpenter,
  And shed a bitter tear.

'O Oysters, come and walk with us!'
  The Walrus did beseech.
'A pleasant walk, a pleasant talk,
  Along the briny beach:
We cannot do with more than four,
  To give a hand to each.'

beseech: beg

briny: salty water

The eldest Oyster looked at him,
  But never a word he said:
The eldest Oyster winked his eye,
  And shook his heavy head—
Meaning to say he did not choose
  To leave the oyster-bed.

But four young Oysters hurried up,
  All eager for the treat:
Their coats were brushed, their faces washed,
  Their shoes were clean and neat—
And this was odd, because, you know,
  They hadn't any feet.

Four other Oysters followed them,
  And yet another four;
And thick and fast they came at last,
  And more, and more, and more—
All hopping through the frothy waves,
  And scrambling to the shore.

frothy: foamy, bubbly
scrambling: struggle clumsily

The Walrus and the Carpenter
  Walked on a mile or so,
And then they rested on a rock
  Conveniently low:
And all the little Oysters stood
  And waited in a row.

'The time has come,' the Walrus said,
  'To talk of many things:

Of shoes—and ships—and sealing wax—
  Of cabbages—and kings—
And why the sea is boiling hot—
  And whether pigs have wings.'

'But wait a bit,' the Oysters cried,
  'Before we have our chat;
For some of us are out of breath,
  And all of us are fat!'
'No hurry!' said the Carpenter.
  They thanked him much for that.

'A loaf of bread,' the Walrus said,
  'Is what we chiefly need:
Pepper and vinegar besides
  Are very good indeed—
Now if you're ready, Oysters dear,
  We can begin to feed.'

'But not on us!' the Oysters cried,
  Turning a little blue.
'After such kindness, that would be
  A dismal thing to do!'
'The night is fine,' the Walrus said.
  'Do you admire the view?'

dismal: terrible, dark

'It was so kind of you to come!
  And you are very nice!'
The Carpenter said nothing but
  'Cut us another slice--
I wish you were not quite so deaf—
  I've had to ask you twice!'

'It seems a shame,' the Walrus said,
  'To play them such a trick,
After we've brought them out so far,
  And made them trot so quick!'
The Carpenter said nothing but
  'The butter's spread too thick!'

trot: run at a slow, steady pace

'I weep for you,' the Walrus said:
   'I deeply sympathize.'
With sobs and tears he sorted out
   Those of the largest size,
Holding his pocket-handkerchief
   Before his streaming eyes.

'O Oysters,' said the Carpenter,
   'You've had a pleasant run!
Shall we be trotting home again?'
   But answer came there none—
And this was scarcely odd, because
   They'd eaten every one.[1]

sympathize: express pity or compassion

1. Lewis Carroll, "The Walrus and the Carpenter," *Through the Looking-Glass* (New York: Random House, 1916), pp. 56–61.

Chapter 6

Just So Stories

From "How the Whale Got His Throat"

by Rudyard Kipling (1865–1936)

'Noble and generous Cetacean, have you ever tasted Man?'

'No,' said the Whale. 'What is it like?'

'Nice,' said the small 'Stute Fish. 'Nice but nubbly.'

'Then fetch me some,' said the Whale, and he made the sea froth up with his tail.

'One at a time is enough,' said the 'Stute Fish. 'If you swim to latitude Fifty North, longitude Forty West (that is magic), you will find, sitting *on* a raft, *in* the middle of the sea, with nothing on but a pair of blue canvas breeches, a pair of suspenders (you must *not* forget the suspenders, Best Beloved), and a jack-knife, one shipwrecked Mariner, who, it is only fair to tell you, is a man of infinite-resource-and-sagacity.'

So the Whale swam and swam to latitude Fifty North, longitude Forty West, as fast as he could swim, and *on* a raft *in* the middle of the sea, *with* nothing to wear except a pair of blue canvas breeches, a pair of suspenders (you must particularly remember the suspenders, Best Beloved), *and* a jack-knife, he found one single, solitary shipwrecked Mariner, trailing his toes in the water. (He had his mummy's leave to paddle, or else he would never have done it, because he was a man of infinite-resource-and-sagacity.)

Then the Whale opened his mouth back and back and back till it nearly touched his tail, and he swallowed the shipwrecked Mariner, and the raft he was sitting on, and his blue canvas breeches, and the suspenders (which you *must*

Cetacean: whale

nubbly: rough or irregular, textured

froth: small bubbles, foam

latitude: the distance north or south of the equator measured in degrees
longitude: distance measured by degrees or time east or west between the North and South Poles
breeches: short pants that are fastened just below the knee
suspenders: a pair of straps that pass over the shoulders and fasten to the waist of pants or a skirt
Mariner: sailor
infinite: unlimited, never ending
sagacity: quality of being wise or having good judgment

not forget), *and* the jack-knife—He swallowed them all down into his warm, dark, inside cupboards, and then he smacked his lips—so, and turned round three times on his tail.[1]

1. Rudyard Kipling, "How the Whale Got His Throat," *Just So Stories* (New York: Doubleday, CO, 1952), p. 9.

Chapter 7

"A Good Play"

by Robert Louis Stevenson (1850–1894)

We built a ship upon the stairs,
All made of back-bedroom chairs,
And filled it full of sofa pillows
To go a-sailing on the billows.

billows: a great swell or surge of water

We took a saw and several nails,
And water in the nursery pails;
And Tom said, "Let us also take
An apple and a slice of cake";—
Which was enough for Tom and me
To go a-sailing on, till tea.

tea: for the British, any meal eaten in the late afternoon or early evening

We sailed along for days and days,
And had the very best of plays;
But Tom fell out and hurt his knee,
So there was no one left but me.[1]

1. Robert Louis Stevenson, "A Good Play," in *Favorite Poems Old and New*, ed. Helen Ferris (New York: Doubleday & Company, Inc., 1957), pp. 101–102.

Biographies
Meet the Authors

Aesop *(c. 620–564 BC)*[1]

Everything we know about the ancient Greek fable teller Aesop is speculation. His life story itself may be a fable. That makes Aesop legendary. According to tradition, he lived in the sixth century BC and told his animal stories orally. The story goes that Aesop was a slave who was extremely ugly, even misshapen, but he was also extraordinarily clever. He was able to win his freedom through his wit, revealing to his master surprising truths beneath the surface of everyday life. In the end, he became an advisor to kings. Aesop's fables were passed down through generations of storytellers until finally, about 300 years after he told them, the fables were written down in a collection. The fables, such as "The Tortoise and the Hare," feature tales of animals who behave like humans and demonstrate moral lessons through their folly. (See chapters 1, 2, 3, and 6.)

Carroll, Lewis *(1832–1898)*[2]

Charles Lutwidge Dodgson, born in England in 1832, was a successful mathematician, university professor, and deacon who used the pen name Lewis Carroll when he published nonsense literature, a kind of writing that combines things that make sense with things that do not. Carroll's poems "The Walrus and the Carpenter" and "Jabberwocky" are considered superb examples of literary nonsense. While on a picnic one day in 1862, he made up a complex nonsensical tale to entertain his young friend, Alice Liddel, and her sisters. The result is his world famous *Alice's Adventures in Wonderland*. Carroll stammered when he talked and, playing with the sound of his last name, Dodgson, referred to himself as the Dodo, who appears in the book. Carroll died of pneumonia in 1898, better known for his children's books than for his mathematics. (See chapter 5 and the literary appendix.)

Davis, Fannie Stearns *(1884–1966)*[3]

Fannie Stearns Davis was an English teacher and poet who graduated from Smith College in 1904 during a time when many women did not have access to college educations. Editor of the classic history book, *A Day in Old Athens*, which was authored by her well-known brother William, Fannie Stearns Davis should not be forgotten for her own writing. She published two volumes of poetry, *Myself and I* in 1913 and *Crack O' Dawn* in 1915, which have appealed to many modern readers. For example, folk singer Jan Luby recently set Davis's poem "Moon Folly" to music. Davis was born in Cleveland, Ohio, in 1884 and died in 1966. (See chapter 3 and the literary appendix.)

Field, Eugene *(1850–1895)*[4]

More than thirty schools in the United States are named Eugene Field Elementary School after the writer who has been called "The Poet of Childhood." However, Eugene Field was not a very serious student himself. He dropped out of three different colleges and never graduated from any of them. He was more of a practical joker than a student. That sense of humor served him well as he made a living from writing satirical columns for newspapers to support his wife and eight children. Field may have been a journalist in the adult world, but for children he wrote poem after charming poem, including "The Gingham Dog and the Calico Cat" and "The Sugar-Plum Tree." He was often caught making funny faces at children in public when he thought no one else was watching. Field advised reading in bed because, as he wrote, "no book can be appreciated until it has been slept with and dreamed over."[5] He was born in St. Louis, Missouri, in 1850 and died in 1895 at the age of forty-five in Chicago. (See chapter 5.)

Grahame, Kenneth *(1859–1932)*[6]

When Kenneth Grahame was little, he lived near the River Thames in England, where he learned how to row a boat. Exploring the river and the nearby woods inspired him years later to tell his son Alistair stories about the animals encountered there. In his stories the animals act and dress like humans, and one of them—Toad—is as strong-willed as it is said Alistair himself was. Later, the tales would become Grahame's most enduring book, *The Wind in the Willows*. Grahame was born in Scotland in 1859 and did not even start going to school until he was nine years old. By the time he graduated, though, he had won a number of academic and athletic awards. Unable to afford to go to Oxford University as he wished, he worked as a banker for years, all along continuing to write stories and essays. By the time of his death in 1932, Grahame was an acclaimed author. (See chapter 4 and the literary appendix.)

Kipling, Rudyard *(1865–1936)*[7]

Even though he spent most of his life in England and America, Rudyard Kipling always considered his home to be India, where he was born in 1865. As a youth, he explored the busy markets of Bombay, learned the native language, and came to appreciate the people and culture of India. One collection of his stories for children, *The Jungle Book*, is set in India and includes stories about a boy named Mowgli who is raised by wolves. Like many children's authors, Kipling first told his stories aloud to his own family. His daughter Josephine used to ask him to tell his tales "just so" or exactly as he told them before. That's how his series of *Just So Stories* got its title. Kipling published many poems, stories, essays, and books for adults too. He was awarded the Nobel Prize in Literature in 1907 partly because he was so accomplished in narration. He died in 1936 in London. (See chapters 2 and 6 and the literary appendix.)

Lear, Edward *(1812–1888)*[8]

Edward Lear, who had twenty siblings, was raised by his oldest sister after his impoverished family had to split up. He became a serious artist, traveling widely from his English birthplace. He illustrated books about plants and animals, and he painted landscapes of the places he visited. Remembered today mostly for writing nonsense, as in his collection of poetry called *The Book of Nonsense*, Lear often created silly animal characters and illustrated his poems with his own pen-and-ink drawings. Wanderers like Lear himself, his characters are often on journeys, such as "The Owl and the Pussycat" going "off to sea in a beautiful pea green boat."[9] Lear had a special talent for writing limericks (a humorous form of poetry he made popular) and for making up neologisms (new words that sound real but are actually nonsense), such as the owl and pussy-cat's *runcible* spoon. Although he had many close friends, he died alone in 1888 at his villa on the Mediterranean coast. (See chapter 2.)

Morley, Christopher *(1890–1957)*[10]

An American "man of letters" (a person dedicated to reading and writing), Christopher Morley was a poet, novelist, essayist, playwright, journalist, and editor. He was immersed in the world of writers and publishers for his entire career, and he was admired both for his wit and his kindness. He was born in Pennsylvania in 1890 to English parents who valued education highly. His father was a professor; his musician mother taught him to love literature; two of his brothers, like himself, were awarded prestigious Rhodes Scholarships, which allowed them to study at Oxford University in England. Morley's favorite place to write was in a cabin he called the Knothole. He built it himself on the property where he lived with his wife and four children. In 1951, he suffered a series of strokes which kept him from writing as much as he wanted in the last years of his life. He died in 1957. (See chapter 7.)

Morris, George Pope *(1802–1864)*[11]

Born in Philadelphia in 1802, George Pope Morris was a successful and respected journalist and editor in New York in the early nineteenth century. He founded several magazines, one of which is still published under the title *Town & Country*, but he was most revered as a poet and songwriter. His work was so popular even after his death in 1864 that Union soldiers sang his patriotic lyrics during the Civil War in their encampments. "Woodman, Spare That Tree," perhaps his most famous poem-song, is sometimes quoted or its title paraphrased by environmentalists today. It was set to music shortly after it was first published. Back then, CDs and electronic devices didn't exist, so instead people bought sheet music so they could play a song at home on an instrument and sing along. Morris published many such poems as songs with beautifully illustrated title pages. (See chapter 1.)

Rossetti, Christina *(1830–1894)*[12]

Considered one of the most important English poets of her time, Christina Rossetti wrote in a broad range of styles and about many different topics: both children's and adult literature; both fantastic and religious works; both lighthearted, humorous poems and dark, brooding ones. Born in 1830, she grew into a beautiful young woman and was a model for her brother, Dante Gabriel Rossetti, who was a famous painter, poet, illustrator, and translator. She was high spirited and passionate and worked hard her whole life to control her temper. Relying on a deep faith in God, she considered spiritual beauty, rather than physical beauty, most important, so she devoted herself to writing and to the people she loved. She died in London in 1894. In the midst of all her accomplishments, one of her children's books stands out as particularly musical and witty. *Sing-Song: A Nursery Rhyme Book* includes some poems that teach children virtues such as patience, some that help children remember a lesson such as the order of the months, and some with playful rhymes and rhythms that are just plain fun for children. (See chapter 6.)

Shakespeare, William *(1564–1616)*

Perhaps the most esteemed English writer of all time, William Shakespeare is a bit of a mystery. We don't know much for sure about his life, except for bits of information found in public records. He was born on April 23, 1564—we think—and he died on his birthday in 1616. He was raised in Stratford-upon-Avon, and that is where his wife and children lived when he was writing, performing, and producing plays in London. He was acclaimed during his own lifetime for his comedies, such as *A Midsummer Night's Dream*, and for his tragedies, such as *Romeo and Juliet*. In all, he wrote more than thirty-five plays, which, more than those of any other single playwright, have been produced throughout the years in many languages around the world. From his plays, we feel we do know a lot about Shakespeare: his love of a good story, his profound spirituality, his deep understanding of human emotions, and his clear awareness of the way people behave—sometimes foolishly, sometimes tragically, sometimes heroically. (See chapter 4.)

Stevenson, Robert Lewis *(1850–1894)*[13]

Best known for his adventure books *Treasure Island* and *Kidnapped* and for his horror story *The Strange Case of Dr. Jekyll and Mr. Hyde*, Robert Lewis Stevenson also wrote poetry, essays, short stories, other novels, and travelogues (a written work about someone's experiences while traveling). He was born in Scotland in 1850, and was often so sick as a child that he couldn't go to school regularly. He was a voracious reader and started writing stories when he was very young. At various times during his life, he wrote as he recuperated from serious illness. Even so, Stevenson traveled much in Europe and across the United States. He was quite tall and thin, and he liked to dress outlandishly and wear his hair long. One of his favorite themes to write about was the difference between being truly good and only appearing good. He died in 1894. (See chapter 7 and the literary appendix.)

White, E.B. *(1899–1985)*[14]

Named Elwyn Brooks White when he was born in New York in 1899, the author of *Charlotte's Web* never liked that name. When he grew up, he used his initials for his published writing and he let his friends call him Andy. He wrote many essays, poems, and books for adults, but perhaps his best-loved works are for children. He loved animals. The idea for *Charlotte's Web* came to him one day when he was watching a spider spin an egg sac. He also wrote *Stuart Little* about a little mouse who gets adopted by a human family, not as a pet but as a son, and *The Trumpet of the Swan* about a trumpeter swan born without a voice. White has influenced many other writers, especially with a famous book called *The Elements of Style*. Even as a successful and influential writer, he always said that writing is difficult. He died at his farm in 1985 when he was eighty-six years old. (See chapter 1 and the literary appendix.) (Image courtesy of White Literary LLC, CC BY-SA 3.0, https://commons.wikimedia.org/w/index.php?curid=14518529.)

Wylie, Elinor *(1885–1928)*[15]

No one could call Elinor Wylie a dabbler. She worked very hard as a writer, publishing four volumes of poetry and four novels in just seven years during the 1920s. Born in New Jersey in 1885 and raised in Pennsylvania, Wylie grew up privileged as part of a socially prominent family: Her grandfather had been the governor of Pennsylvania; her father served as solicitor general of the United States; her aunt was a published poet. Wylie was considered to be very beautiful, elegant, and witty. Independent and strong-willed, she made some personal decisions that brought many difficulties in her life. Through those trials, she immersed herself in books and in writing. Wylie died suddenly in 1928 from a stroke when she was only forty-three. (See chapter 3.)

Works Referenced

1. *Encyclopedia Britannica*, s.v. "Aesop: Legendary Greek Fabulist," accessed October 14, 2015, http://www.britannica.com/biography/Aesop.
   Encyclopedia of World Biography, vol. 24, s.v. "Aesop."
2. "Lewis Carroll in the Museum," *LearningMore*, Oxford University Museum of Natural History, March 29, 2006, accessed October 14, 2015, http://www.oum.ox.ac.uk/learning/pdfs/dodgson.pdf.
   Encyclopedia of World Biography, vol. 24, s.v. "Lewis Carroll."
3. *PoemHunter.com*, s.v. "Fannie Stearns Davis," accessed October 14, 2015, http://www.poemhunter.com/fannie-stearns-davis/biography/.
4. *The Poetry Foundation*, s.v. "Eugene Field," accessed October 14, 2015, http://www.poetryfoundation.org/bio/eugene-field.
5. Eugene Field, "The Luxury of Reading in Bed," *Love Affairs of a Bibliomaniac* (Whitefish, MT: Kessinger Publishing, 2005), p. 31.
   Dictionary of American Biography, s.v. "Eugene Field" (New York: Charles Scribner's Sons, 1936).
6. "Biography," *Kenneth Graham Society*, accessed October 14, 2015, http://www.kennethgrahamesociety.net/biography.htm.
   Encyclopedia of World Biography, vol. 28, s.v. "Kenneth Grahame."
7. *Biography.com*, s.v. "Rudyard Kipling," accessed October 14, 2015, http://www.biography.com/people/rudyard-kipling-9365581.
   Encyclopedia Britannica, s.v. "Rudyard Kipling," accessed October 14, 2015, http://www.britannica.com/biography/Rudyard-Kipling.
   Encyclopedia of World Biography, s.v. "Joseph Rudyard Kipling."
8. Edward Lear, *The Owl and the Pussycat*, illustrated by Jan Brett (New York: Putnam, 1991), n.p.
   Authors and Artists for Young Adults, vol. 48, s.v. "Edward Lear," *Biography in Context*. Detroit: Gale, 2003.
   The Poetry Foundation, s.v. "Edward Lear, 1812–1888," accessed October 14, 2015, http://www.poetryfoundation.org/bio/edward-lear.
9. Lear, Edward. *The Owl and the Pussycat*. Illustrated by Jan Brett. New York: Putnam, 1991.
10. C.D. Merriman, "Christopher Morley," *The Literature Network*, accessed October 14, 2105, http://www.online-literature.com/morley.
11. *Dictionary of American Biography*, s.v. "George Pope Morris" (New York: Charles Scribner's Sons, 1936).
12. *Encyclopedia Britannica*, s.v. "Christina Rossetti," accessed October 14, 2015, http://www.britannica.com/biography/Christina-Rossetti.
    Major Authors and Illustrators for Children and Young Adults, s.v. "Christina (Georgina) Rossetti" (Detroit: Gale, 2002).
13. *Encyclopedia Britannica*, s.v. "Robert Louis Stevenson," accessed October 14, 2015, http://www.britannica.com/biography/Robert-Louis-Stevenson.
    Encyclopedia of World Biography, vol. 28, s.v. "Robert Louis Stevenson."
14. *Biography.com*, s.v. "E.B. White," accessed October 14, 2015, http://www.biography.com/people/eb-white-9529308.
    Encyclopedia of World Biography, vol. 28, s.v. "E. B. White."
15. *Dictionary of American Biography*, s.v. "Elinor Morton Hoyt Wylie" (New York: Charles Scribner's Sons, 1936).
    Encyclopedia Britannica, s.v. "Elinor Wylie," accessed October 14, 2015, http://www.britannica.com/biography/Elinor-Wylie.

Bibliography
Seek the Sources

Aesop. "The Ant and the Grasshopper." In *Writing & Rhetoric Book 1: Fable.* Written by Paul Kortepeter. Camp Hill, PA: Classical Academic Press, 2013.

———. "The Dog and Her Reflection." In *Writing & Rhetoric Book 1: Fable.* Written by Paul Kortepeter. Camp Hill, PA: Classical Academic Press, 2013.

———. "The Mice in Council." In *Writing & Rhetoric Book 1: Fable.* Written by Paul Kortepeter. Camp Hill, PA: Classical Academic Press, 2013.

———. "The Shepherd Boy and the Wolf." In *Writing and Rhetoric Book 1: Fable.* Written by Paul Kortepeter. Camp Hill, PA: Classical Academic Press, 2013.

Anonymous. "The Tale of the Chinese Farmer." In *Writing & Rhetoric Book 1: Fable.* Written by Paul Kortepeter. Camp Hill, PA: Classical Academic Press, 2013.

Anonymous. "The Trees Choose a King." In *Writing & Rhetoric Book 1: Fable.* Written by Paul Kortepeter. Camp Hill, PA: Classical Academic Press, 2013.

Carroll, Lewis. "The Walrus and the Carpenter." *Through the Looking-Glass.* New York: Random House, 1916.

Davis, Fannie Stearns. "Moon Folly." From *In Poetry*, vol. I. Edited by Harriet Monroe. New York: A.M.S. Reprint CO, vol. 1, no. 6, March 1912–1913. Available at: https://books.google.com/books?id=9MARAAAAYAAJ.

Field, Eugene. "Wynken, Blynken, and Nod." In *Favorite Poems Old and New.* Edited by Helen Ferris. New York: Doubleday, 1957.

Grahame, Kenneth. "The Wild Wood." *The Wind in the Willows.* New York: The New American Library, Inc., 1969.

Kipling, Rudyard. "How the Whale Got His Throat." *Just So Stories.* New York: Doubleday, 1952.

———. "The Beginning of the Armadillos." *Just So Stories.* New York: Doubleday, 1952.

La Fontaine, Jean de. "The Hare and the Partridge." In *Writing & Rhetoric Book 1: Fable.* Written by Paul Kortepeter. Camp Hill, PA: Classical Academic Press, 2013.

Lear, Edward. "Calico Pie." *The Golden Treasury of Poetry.* Edited by Louis Untermeyer. New York: Golden Books Publishing, 1998.

Morley, Christopher. "Animal Crackers." In *Favorite Poems Old and New*. Edited by Helen Ferris. New York: Doubleday, 1957.

Morris, George Pope. "Woodman, Spare That Tree." *Favorite Poems Old and New*. Edited by Helen Ferris. New York: Doubleday, 1957.

Rossetti, Christina. "I Dug and Dug Amongst the Snow." In *Illustrated Poems and Songs for Young People*. Edited by Mrs. Lucy Sale Barker. London: George Routledge and Sons, 1885. Available at: https://books.google.com/books?id=c4ubK21PVw4C.

Shakespeare, William. "A Wood near Athens." Act II , Scene 1. *A Midsummer Night's Dream*. In *World Scope Family Library: Works of William Shakespeare*. Edited by W.G. Clark and W.A. Wright. New York: The Universal Guide, Inc., 1950.

Stevenson, Robert Louis. "A Good Play." In *Favorite Poems Old and New*. Edited by Helen Ferris. New York: Doubleday, 1957.

White, E.B. "Summer Days." *Charlotte's Web*. New York: HarperTrophy, 1980.

Wylie, Elinor. "Velvet Shoes." In *Favorite Poems Old and New*. Edited by Helen Ferris. New York: Doubleday, 1957.

Glossary of Terms

	Book & Level	Chapter
A		
Adjective: An adjective is a part of speech. It is used to describe or define the meaning of a noun or pronoun (*see also* noun, pronoun). It answers the questions *how many, whose, which one*, or *what kind*. It modifies a noun or pronoun.	**1A**	**5**
Adjective Element: A word (or a group of words) that modifies nouns or pronouns.	**1A**	**5**
Adjectival Prepositional Phrase: A group of words that includes a preposition followed by a noun or pronoun (*see* object of the preposition), and any words that modify the object of the preposition. The entire phrase is an adjective and modifies nouns or pronouns, answering the questions *how many, whose, which one*, or *what kind*. (This concept is covered in *WOL Level 2*.)	**1B**	**3**
Adverb: An adverb is a part of speech. It modifies a verb, an adjective, (or) adverb. It answers the questions *how, when*, or *where*. An adverb is a part of speech.	**1A**	**4**
Adverbial Element: A word (or a group of words) that modifies verbs, adjectives, and adverbs.	**1A**	**4**
Adverbial Prepositional Phrase: A group of words that includes a preposition followed by a noun or pronoun (*see* object of the preposition), and any words that modify the object of the preposition. The entire phrase is an adverb usually modifying a verb, answering the questions *when, where*, or *how*.	**1B**	**3**

	Book & Level	Chapter
Antecedent: The antecedent is a noun, clause, or phrase to which a pronoun refers. If the antecedent is singular, then the pronoun is singular too. But if the noun, clause, or phrase is plural, then the pronoun must be plural too. The antecedent determines which pronoun is used.	1A	7
Antonym: An antonyms is a word that has the opposite meaning of another word. For example, *night* and *day* are antonyms.	1B	6
Auxiliary Verb: *See* helping verb.	1A	3

C

Clause: A clause is a group of words containing a subject and a predicate.	1A	4
Common Noun: A noun that names any person, place, thing or idea. *See also* noun; proper noun.	1B	3
Compound Direct Object: Two or more direct objects that are joined with a conjunction and that together function as a single direct object for a transitive verb.	1B	7
Compound Subject: Two or more subjects that are joined with a conjunction and that together function as a single subject in the sentence.	1B	5
Compound Verb: Two or more verbs that are joined with a conjunction and that together function as a single verb for a single subject.	1B	6
Conjunction: A part of speech that joins words, phrases, or clauses. Conjunctions indicate the relationship between the elements that they join.	1A	1
Consonant: A letter of the alphabet that represents a constricted speech sound. The indefinite article "a" is used before words beginning with consonants (*b*, *c*, *d*, *f*, *g*, *h*, *j*, *k*, *l*, *m*, *n*, *p*, *q*, *r*, *s*, *t*, *v*, *w*, *x*, *y*, and z).	1A	5

	Book & Level	Chapter
Contraction: A shortened form of two words that uses an apostrophe in place of the letters and spaces left out. *WOL Level 1* focuses on contractions with subject pronouns and verbs, such as *I'm* for *I am* or *they've* for *they have*, and on contractions with verbs and the adverb *not*, such as *didn't* for *did not*.	1A	8

D

Declarative Sentence: One of the four kinds of sentences. It makes a statement and ends with a period.	1A	1
Definite Article: The adjective *the*. It identifies a particular noun and is placed before nouns or adjectives.	1A	5
Direct Object: A direct object is an objective element that tells what the subject is acting on. It is a noun or pronoun after a transitive verb. It answers the question *what* or *whom* after the verb and is labeled *do*.	1A	6

E

Eight Parts of Speech: The eight parts of speech are classes of words with the same kind of meaning and use. They are nouns, verbs, adjectives, adverbs, prepositions, pronouns, conjunctions, and interjections.	1A	1
Exclamatory Sentence: One of the four kinds of sentences. It expresses strong feeling and ends with an exclamation point.	1A	1

F

First Person: A grammatical category of pronouns used by the speaker to refer to himself or herself (i.e., the subject pronouns *I* or *we* and the object pronouns *me* or *us*). *See also* person.	1A	7
Fragment: A group of words that is not a complete sentence because it lacks a subject, a predicate, or both.	1B	4

	Book & Level	Chapter
G		
Gender: A grammatical category or classification into which nouns and pronouns can be sorted—namely *male, female,* or *neuter.* For example: a *king* is masculine (*he* is a male); a *queen* is feminine (*she* is a female); and a *throne* is neuter (*it* is neither masculine nor feminine). *See also* neuter.	1B	2
H		
Helping Verb: Helps another verb express its meaning. It is placed alongside a transitive, linking, or intransitive verb to form a verb phrase. Both words work together as one action. The helping verbs are *am, is, are, was, were, be, being, been, have, has, had, do, did, does, may, might, must, should, would, could, shall, will, can.*	1A	3
Homonym: A homonyms is a word that sounds the same but has a different meaning and sometimes spelling. For example, *bark* meaning the sound a dog makes and *bark* meaning the outer covering of a tree are homonyms.	1B	6
I		
Imperative Sentence: One of the four kinds of sentences. It gives a command and ends with a period or exclamation point.	1A	1
Implied Subject: A subject that does not appear in the sentence but is indirectly expressed or suggested. *See also* subject.	1A	1
Indefinite Article: The adjective *a* or *an*. It is placed before non-specific nouns and identifies them as being singular; *a* is used before nouns or adjectives beginning with a consonant, and *an* is used before nouns or adjectives beginning with a vowel sound.	1A	5
Interjection: A part of speech that is a word or short phrase that expresses strong emotion. It is inserted into a sentence or stands alone.	1A	1
Interrogative Sentence: One of the four kinds of sentences. It asks a question and ends with a question mark.	1A	1

	Book & Level	Chapter
Intransitive Verb: A verb that does not take an objective element or join the subject to the predicate.	1A	6
Introductory Prepositional Phrase: An adverbial prepositional phrase that is located at the beginning of a sentence and modifies the verb.	1B	4

L

Linking Verb: A verb that joins the subject to the predicate. In other words, it is the glue that joins the subject either to a noun that renames the subject or to an adjective that describes the subject. Linking verbs express a state of being.	1A	3

M

Modifier: A word (or a group of words) that modifies or changes the meaning of word. Adjectives modify nouns and pronouns; adverbs usually modify verbs, but adverbs also can modify adjectives and other adverbs.	1A	4

N

Neuter: The gender of a pronoun that is neither male nor female. The pronoun *it* is neuter, and sometimes the pronouns *they* and *them* can be neuter.	1B	2
Nominative Case: The grammatical term indicating that a noun or pronoun is the subject in a sentence or a clause rather than its object. Also known as the *subjective case.*	1A	7
Noun: A noun is a part of speech. It names a person, place, or thing. A noun names a quality or an idea. A noun may be singular or plural.	1A	2
Number: A property of a noun or pronoun that tells how many. Singular in number means only one, and plural in number means more than one.	1A	3

	Book & Level	Chapter
O		
Object of the Preposition: The noun or pronoun after the preposition. It is joined by the preposition to another word in the sentence in a modifying relationship.	1B	1
Object Pronoun: A personal pronoun that is used as a direct object or the object of the preposition (i.e., *me, us, you, him, her, it, them*).	1A	7
Objective Element: A word or group of words that completes the meaning of the action verb. *See also* direct object. An objective element can also include indirect objects or the objects of prepositions.	1A	6
Order of Analysis: The order in which sentences are analyzed: phrases, clauses, principal elements, and modifiers.	1B	3
Ordinal Adjective: A word that denotes what place an object is in an order, such as *first, second, third,* or *fourth.*	1A	5
P		
Person: A property of a noun or pronoun that distinguishes among speaker, addressee, and others. There are three persons: first person (the one speaking), second person (the one being spoken to); and third person (the one being spoken about).	1A	7
Personal Pronoun: A pronoun that primarily takes the place of names of persons, hence *person*al pronoun. However, it can replace things too. *See also* pronoun, object pronoun, subject pronoun.	1A	7
Phrase: A group of words behaving like one part of speech. A phrase does not contain a subject and a predicate.	1A	3
Plural: A grammatical category for nouns, pronouns, and verbs that refer to more than one thing.	1A	3
Predicate: One of the principal elements in a sentence. It tells something about the subject like what it is doing or being.	1A	2
Predicate Verb: An action verb showing what the subject does.	1A	3

	Book & Level	Chapter
Preposition: A preposition is a part of speech used to show the relationship between certain words in a sentence. It is a word that joins its object, which is the noun or pronoun that follows it, to another word in a sentence, which can be a noun, pronoun, verb, adverb, or adjective. *WOL Level 1* focuses on prepositions that connect a noun or pronoun to a verb, showing a relationship of location (*where*), time (*when*), or manner (*how*). Some of the most common prepositions are *aboard, about, above, across, after, against, along, among, around, before, behind, below, beneath, beside, between, beyond, at, by, down, during, except, for, from, inside, in, into, near, of, off, on, out, outside, over, past, since, through, throughout, to, toward, under, up, until, upon, with, within, without, underneath.*	1B	3
Prepositional Phrase: A group of words including a preposition, an object of the preposition, and any words that modify that object. All these words together behave as a single part of speech, either an adverb or an adjective.	1B	3
Principal Clause: A group of words containing a subject and a predicate and able to stand independently as a sentence.	1A	4
Principal Elements: Principal elements are the parts of the sentence that are needed for the sentence to be completed. Subject and predicate are those parts.	1A	2
Pronoun: A pronoun is a part of speech used in place of a noun or of more than one noun. A pronoun is a part of speech.	1A	7
Proper noun: A noun that refers to a particular person, place, thing, or idea. It begins with a capital letter. *See also* common noun; noun.	1B	3

S

Second Person: A grammatical category for pronouns used by the speaker to refer to the person being spoken *to* (i.e., *you* as either a singular or plural subject pronoun or a singular or plural object pronoun). *See also* person.	1A	7

	Book & Level	Chapter
Sentence: A sentence is a group of words expressing a complete thought. There are four kinds of them: Declarative Sentence – Makes a statement. Interrogative Sentence – Asks a question. Imperative Sentence – Gives a command. Exclamatory Sentence – Expresses strong feeling.	1A	1
Simple Predicate: The verb or verb phrase in a sentence.	1A	3
Singular: A grammatical category for nouns, pronouns, and verbs that refer to only one thing.	1A	3
Stanza: A group of lines in a poem.	1A	3
Subject: One of the principal elements in a sentence. It is a noun or pronoun and is what the sentence is about.	1A	1
Subject Pronoun: A personal pronoun that is used as the subject in a sentence (i.e., *I, we, you, he, she, it, they*).	1A	7
Subject-Verb Agreement: A correct sentence structure in which the subject and verb agree in person (first, second, or third person) and number (singular or plural).	1B	2
Subordinate element: A word (or a group of words) that change or limit the meaning of the principal elements. Also known as a modifier.	1A	4
Synonym: A synonyms is a word that means almost the same thing as another word. For example, *happy* and *glad* are synonyms.	1B	6
Syntax: Word order. It is the way in which words are combined to form phrases, clauses, or sentences.	1A	2

T

Tense: A form of a verb that is used to show time or when an action occurs, as in past, present, and future.	1A	3
Third Person: A grammatical category for pronouns used by the speaker to refer to anyone or anything being spoken about that is not the speaker or the one addressed (i.e., the subject pronouns *he, she, it*, or *they* and the object pronouns *him, her*, or *them*). *See also* person.	1A	7

	Book & Level	Chapter
Transitive Verb: A verb that takes an objective element (i.e., a direct object). It transitions from the subject to the direct object.	1A	6

V

Verb: A part of speech that shows action or a state of being.	1A	3
Verb Phrase: A helping verb together with either an action verb or a linking verb.	1A	3
Vowel: A letter of the alphabet that represents a voiced speech sound. The indefinite article "an" is used before words beginning with vowels: *a, e, i, o, u*.	1A	5

Song Lyrics

Eight Parts of Speech *(1–1)*

The eight parts of speech are classes of words
with the same kind of meaning and use.
They are: nouns, verbs, adjectives, adverbs,
prepositions, pronouns, conjunctions, interjections.
These are the eight parts of speech,
classes of words with the same kind of meaning and use. *(Repeat.)*

Sentence *(1–2)*

A sentence is a group of words expressing a complete thought.
There are four kinds of sentences:
Declarative sentence—makes a statement.
Interrogative sentence—asks a question.
Imperative sentence—gives a command.
Exclamatory sentence—expresses strong feelings.
A sentence is a group of words expressing a complete thought.
There are four kinds of sentences. *(Repeat.)*

Principal Elements *(1–3)*

Principal elements are the parts of the sentence
that are needed for the sentence to be completed.
Subject and predicate are those two parts.

Subject and Predicate *(1–4)*

A subject, a subject is a noun or a pronoun
and is what the sentence is about (*clap, clap*).
A predicate, a predicate tells us something about the subject
like what it is doing or being *(clap, clap)*.

From the Sideline: We recommend that you familiarize yourself with the songs and chants in the book before teaching them to your students.

When you see *(Repeat.)* at the end of a song, it means that all of the song lyrics are sung through once and then repeated. If *(repeat)* appears at the end of one or more lines in the song it means that those specific lines are repeated. For songs that have the notation *(echo)*, at the end of a line, you may want to split your class into two groups and have one group echo the other group as they sing the song.

Noun *(1–5)*

A noun is a part of speech.
It names a person, place, or thing.
A noun names a quality or an idea.
A noun is a part of speech.
It names a person, place, or thing.
A noun may be singular *(clap)* or plural *(clap clap clap). (Repeat.)*

Verb and Helping Verb *(1–6)*

A verb is a part of speech. *(echo)*
A verb shows action or a state of being. *(echo)*
A verb is a part of speech. *(echo)*
A verb shows action or a state of being. *(echo)*
A helping verb helps another verb to express its meaning.
A helping verb stands near the verb.
It is called an auxiliary.
Am, is, are, was, were, be, being, been, has, have, had, do, does,
did, may, might, must, should, could, would, shall, will, *and* can.
A helping verb stands near the verb and is called an auxiliary.
A helping verb stands near the verb. It is called an auxiliary.

Adverb *(1–7)*

An adverb is a part of speech.
It modifies a verb or another adverb.
It can also modify an adjective
and answers three questions: *how? when*? or *where*?
It answers three questions: *how? when*? or *where*?

Adjective *(1–8)*

An adjective is a part of speech
used to describe or define
the meaning of a noun or pronoun.
It answers the questions:
How many? (echo)
Whose? (echo)
Which one? (echo)

or *What kind? (echo)*
It modifies a noun or pronoun.
It modifies a noun or pronoun.

Direct Object *(1–9)*

d-o, d-o
A direct object is an objective element
that tells what the subject is acting on.
d-o, d-o
It's a noun or pronoun after a transitive verb.
d-o, d-o
It answers the question *what* or *whom* after the verb
and is labeled *do.*

Four Classes of Verbs *(1–10)*

These are the four classes of verbs:
The four classes of verbs are transitive verbs, linking verbs,
intransitive verbs, and helping verbs.
These are the four classes of verbs.
A transitive verb takes an objective element.
A linking verb joins a subject to a predicate.
An intransitive verb does not take an objective element
or join a subject to a predicate.
A helping verb helps another verb express its meaning.
A helping verb helps another verb express its meaning.
These are the four classes of verbs.
These are the four classes of verbs.

Pronoun *(1–11)*

A pronoun is a part of speech
used in place of a noun or nouns.
A pronoun is a part of speech
used in place of a noun or nouns.
A pronoun is a part of speech.

Subject Pronouns *(1–12)*

Subject pronouns are in the nominative case:
  I, you, he, she, it, we, you, they *(repeat).*
Subject pronouns are in the nominative case:
  I, you, he, she, it, we, you, they *(repeat).*

Antecedent *(1–13)*

The antecedent is a noun, clause, or phrase
  to which a pronoun refers.
If the antecedent is singular,
  then the pronoun is singular too.
But if the noun, clause, or phrase is plural,
  then the pronoun must be plural too.
The antecedent determines which pronoun is used.

Fable *(1–14)*

A fable (echo)
  is a moral tale.
A fable (echo)
  is not a fairy tale.
A fable is short, direct, and clear.
Animals are characters sneaky or sincere.
Teaching lessons not to be deceived,
  fables warn us not to be naive.

Object Pronouns *(1–15)*

Object pronouns are in the objective case.
  Me, you, him, her, it, us, you, them
  Me, you, him, her, it, us, you, them.
Object pronouns are in the objective case.
  Me, you, him, her, it, us, you, them
  Me, you, him, her, it, us, you, them
  Me, you, him, her, it, us, you, them.

Preposition *(1–16)*

A preposition *(a preposition)*
is a part of speech *(is a part of speech)*
used to show the relationship
between certain words in a sentence *(in a sentence). (Repeat.)*

List of Prepositions *(1–17)*

Aboard, about, above, across, after, against, along, among, around
Preposition Words
Before, behind, below, beneath, beside, between, beyond, at, by
Preposition Words
Down, during, except, for, from, inside, in, into, near
Preposition Words
Of, off, on, out, outside, over, past, since, through
Preposition Words
Throughout, to, toward,
Under, up, until,
Upon, with, within,
Without, underneath
Preposition Words
Preposition Words
Preposition Words!

Phrase *(1–18)*

A phrase is a group of words
behaving like one part of speech
not containing a subject or a predicate. *(Repeat.)*

Object of the Preposition *(1–19)*

The object of the preposition
The object of the preposition
is the noun or pronoun
after the preposition. *(Repeat.)*

Conjunction *(1–20)*

A conjunction is a part of speech.
It joins elements of the same rank or name.
When two or more words are joined this way,
they're called compounds. *(Repeat.)*

Synonyms, Antonyms, and Homonyms *(1–21)*

Synonyms, antonyms, and homonyms
Synonyms are words that mean almost the same thing.
Antonyms are words that have the opposite meaning.
Homonyms are words that sound the same, but have different meaning and sometimes spelling—words that sound the same, but do not mean the same thing.
Synonyms, antonyms, and homonyms
Synonyms: little and small
Antonyms: short and tall
Homonyms: threw the ball, walk through the mall
Synonyms, antonyms, and homonyms
Synonyms, antonyms, and homonyms.

About the Title

The title of this series was inspired by a passage in a small book by Josef Pieper titled *Abuse of Language—Abuse of Power*. In the book, Pieper writes,

> [T]he well-ordered human existence, including especially its social dimension, is essentially based on the well-ordered language employed. A well-ordered language here does not primarily mean its formal perfection, even though I agree . . . that every correctly placed comma is decisive. No, a language is well ordered when its words express reality with as little omission as possible.[1]

Language is the means by which we make sense of reality. It is the medium by which we perceive truth. Therefore, a well-ordered language—one that best represents reality with as little distortion as possible—would provide the best access to truth. Language education, then, should be focused on developing as complete and accurate an understanding of language as possible.

While the pursuit of truth through language involves careful thinking (logic) and eloquent expression (rhetoric), the youngest students must first acquire a solid foundation in the structure and function of the language itself (grammar). Mirroring the well-ordered nature of language, effective educators employ an approach to language instruction that is itself well-ordered, structured, and disciplined. Critics of a well-organized and disciplined approach often confuse its form with the disposition of those who employ it. The disciplined approach to language study can be employed through intimidation and aggression, but it can just as easily be administered with love and compassion. The disciplined approach—often mischaracterized as "drill-and-kill"—actually respects the humanity of the student because it acknowledges that children learn differently than mature adults do.

For children to feast upon the rich cuisine of that which is good, true, and beautiful, they should first be shown how to taste, savor, and digest what they encounter. Without proper instruction that will cultivate their taste, students may turn from the "feast" in disgust, reject further sustenance, and perhaps never return. By acquiring a well-ordered language, students will also acquire that taste for language that will lead them to the great feast that awaits. To impart this taste is to avoid one of the greatest errors of modern educational theory, which is the assumption that children can learn without first acquiring those tools of learning that we call the language arts.

---

1. Josef Pieper, *Abuse of Language—Abuse of Power* (San Francisco: Ignatius Press, 1992), p. 36.

A CREATIVE APPROACH TO THE CLASSICAL PROGYMNASMATA
Writing & Rhetoric
BOOK 5: DESCRIPTION & IMPERSONATION
PAUL KORTEPETER

TEACHER'S EDITION
A CREATIVE APPROACH TO THE CLASSICAL PROGYMNASMATA
Writing & Rhetoric
BOOK 1: FABLE
PAUL KORTEPETER